New Highlight 2

2

two

3

three

Als Hörtext oder Song auf der Audio-CD vorhanden; die Track-Angaben beziehen sich auf die Vollfassung (Bestellnummer 344509):
1 ⊙ 2 = CD 1, Track 2.

W ◉   Zusätzliche Aufgaben auf der CD-ROM im Workbook

Kann dem Portfolio-Ordner hinzugefügt werden

Aufgaben:

○ leicht   ◐ mittel   ● schwierig

Begleitend zum Schülerbuch finden sich unter www.new-highlight.de interaktive Online-Übungen, die am Ende jeder Unit bearbeitet werden können.

* Fakultativ (wahlfreie Bestandteile des Lehrwerks)

Welcome

HOW WERE THE SCHOOL HOLIDAYS?

Nice! I went to London.

Good! But I had lots of work on the farm.

OK! I was at home. The weather was great.

Great! I went to Spain.

AND YOU? Talk to a partner.

How were your school holidays?

How was the weather?

Great!

Nice!

Terrible!   OK!

SONG: In the holidays

1 2 **a) Listen to verses 1–5. Who's singing?**

→ Tom • Sarah • Emma • Jamie • Everybody

b) Sing the song in your class.

back!

MY HOLIDAYS

A

I went to the sea.

B

I went to Spain.

C

I went camping.

D
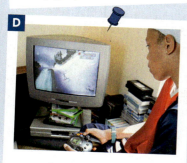
I was at home.

E

I went to the swimming pool.

F

I went to the park.

G

I saw my grandma.

H

I saw lots of friends.

I

I had lots of work at home.

AND YOU? Talk to a partner.

I was …

I went …

I had …

I saw …

►W 1, 1–2

WHAT CAN YOU SEE?

►W 2, 3–4

Back at school

One, two, three, four, ...

1 **Our school song**

1◉3 **Look at the pictures A–D and listen to the song. Put the pictures in the right order.**

2 **You and a partner: Ask and answer questions about the pictures.**

YOU	YOUR PARTNER
Can you see a school?	– Yes, I can.
In which picture?	– Picture C.
Can you see a white uniform?	– No, I can't.
Can you ...?	– ...

3 **Classroom game**
Look at this picture. Close your book.
What's in the classroom?

4 **And in your classroom?**
Work in groups. Make labels
for things in your classroom.

chair

Thursday 12th
board
teacher
poster
dictionary
homework diary
uniform
table
pencil
ruler
rubber
pencil case
exercise book
pen
cupboard
bag
chair
pupils
door
picture
book
window
shelf
computer

5 **Work in groups. Pick one pupil in your group. He or she has to do what you say.**
Use the words in the pictures.

Sit on the teacher's chair, please.

Tipp:
An das Ende einer
Aufforderung gehört
immer ein „please". Sonst
klingt sie unhöflich.

→
- Open the ..., please.
- Find a ..., please.
- Write on the ..., please.
- Go to the ..., please.
- Stand at the ..., please.
- Close the ..., please.
- ..., please.

▶ W 3, 1

6 **Collect classroom words and make lists in your exercise book.**

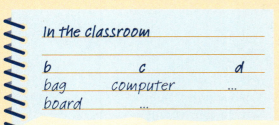

In the classroom

b   c   d
bag   computer   ...
board   ...

Tipp:
Mithilfe von Wortlisten
kannst du dir Wörter
besser merken.

▶ Wordbank 1, p. 125

THE FIRST DAY BACK AT SCHOOL

Tipp:
Du musst nicht jedes Wort verstehen. Überfliege den Text und suche die Namen heraus.

1 **Look at the pictures:**
Who's back at school? Find out.

1⊙5

It's Monday, September 4th.
The holidays are over.
It's the first day back at school.

It's five to nine now.
The pupils are arriving at Drake School.
Tom, Jamie, Emma and Sarah are there too. Emma is talking about the summer. Sarah, Tom and Jamie are laughing.

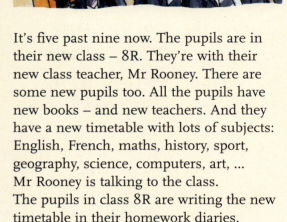

It's five past nine now. The pupils are in their new class – 8R. They're with their new class teacher, Mr Rooney. There are some new pupils too. All the pupils have new books – and new teachers. And they have a new timetable with lots of subjects: English, French, maths, history, sport, geography, science, computers, art, …
Mr Rooney is talking to the class.
The pupils in class 8R are writing the new timetable in their homework diaries.

2 **You and a partner: Ask and answer questions about the text.**
The pictures can help you.

YOU		YOUR PARTNER
Who's	arriving at school?	– Emma.
	talking about the summer?	– The Drake School pupils.
	laughing?	– The pupils in class 8R.
	talking to class 8R?	– Sarah, Tom and Jamie.
	writing?	– Mr Rooney.

3 **AND YOU? Answer questions about your school.**

1 What class are you in now?
2 Do you have new books/ teachers/subjects?

3 Who's your new class teacher?
4 What are your subjects?
5 What's your favourite subject?

▶ Wordbank 2, p. 125

4 The timetable

1⊙6

	Monday	Tuesday
9.00–9.30	CLASS TIME	CLASS TIME
9.30–10.15	▮▮▮▮▮	art
10.15–11.00	French	▮▮▮
11.00–11.15	BREAK	BREAK
11.15–12.00	▮▮▮▮▮▮	maths
12.00–12.45	science	▮▮▮▮▮▮▮
12.45–1.30	LUNCH	LUNCH
1.30–2.10	sport	English
2.10–2.50	sport	▮▮▮▮▮
2.50–3.30	▮▮▮▮▮▮▮▮	geography

a) **First write this timetable in your exercise book.**

b) **Then listen to Mr Rooney and finish the timetable for Monday and Tuesday.**

c) **Now write *your* timetable in English.**

▸ Wordbank 2, p. 125

▸ W 3, 2

5 Finish the box with a partner. Then write it in your exercise book.

HERE AND THERE

• In England pupils have uniforms.
  In Germany we …
• At Drake School pupils have … lessons
  every day. We have …
• In class 8R pupils have French, …
  We have …

PROJECT – A brochure for new pupils

The pupils in class 8R are helping new pupils at Drake School.
They're making a brochure about the school.

A brochure for new pupils

SCHOOL NAME:	Drake School
PUPILS:	648
TEACHERS:	34
SUBJECTS:	French, English, maths, history, computers, geography, art, sport, science, …
SPORTS:	Football, hockey, badminton, basketball, rugby
SCHOOL CLUBS:	Art club, school band, judo club, computer club

SCHOOL TIMES:
SCHOOL OPENS AT:	9.00
LESSON TIMES:	9.30–13.30
BREAK:	11.00–11.15
LUNCH:	12.45–11.30

THESE PEOPLE CAN HELP YOU:	
	– Your class teacher
	– Your buddy

6 Work in groups and make a brochure like this about your school.

Tipp:
Nur die Sprachen
(*English, French*) werden
großgeschrieben – alle
anderen Schulfächer klein.

7 Give your brochure to the new classes.

Tipp:
Auf den Seiten 106 und
107 erfährst du mehr
über *buddies*.

▸ W 3, 3

1 Look at the pictures.
1 Where does the story happen?
2 Who isn't very happy?

2 Now read the text.
1 Who are the six people in the story?
2 Where's the new boy from?
3 Where do the friends want to go on Saturday?

Old friends and new friends

1◉ 7

It's Monday, the first day back at school.
It's quarter past ten. Class 8R is in the
French room. Tom is sitting next to Jamie.
Emma is sitting next to Sarah.

5 "The first day back at school is OK,"
Jamie says.
"You see all your old friends again."

It's eleven o'clock – time for the break.
The pupils are in the playground.
10 Jamie, Tom, Sarah and Emma are talking
and laughing. A boy is reading a football
magazine. He isn't talking to the other
pupils. He's alone. He's a new pupil at
Drake School. He's in class 8R too.

It's quarter past eleven and the break is over. 15
The pupils are going to the classrooms.
"Are you an Exeter City fan?" Tom asks the
new boy.
"Yes, I am. My dad plays for Exeter City.
He's new in the team," he answers. 20
"Oh! What's his name?" Tom asks.
"Mohamed Hassan," the boy answers.
"Oh yes! He's good," Tom says.
"We moved here from Somalia in August,"
the boy says. 25
"Welcome to Exeter. Do you like it here?"
Tom asks.
"Yes, I do. But I don't know many people."
"Well, I'm Tom and I'm an Exeter City fan."
"Hi, Tom. I'm Tariq." 30

It's Friday now, quarter to four.
The first week at school is over and everybody is happy.
But Jamie isn't very happy.

35 "Where's Tom?" he asks Sarah.
"He's with his new friend, Tariq," she answers.
"They're making plans for the weekend."
"So Tom has no time for his old friends now,"
Jamie says.

40 It's seven o'clock in the evening.
Jamie is at home. He's watching TV.
"Jamie!" Mrs Fraser shouts. "Tom is on the phone."
"Hi," Jamie says.
"Jamie, I have a surprise. Tariq has tickets

45 for the football match tomorrow," Tom says.
"Oh! Is Exeter City playing?" Jamie asks.
"Yes, Exeter City and Manchester United!
It's here in Exeter. Emma and Sarah are coming.
Do you want to come too?" Tom asks.

50 "Great! Thanks, Tom," Jamie says.
"That's OK. We're old friends!" Tom answers.

15

fifteen

3 Read the story again.
Are the sentences right or wrong?

1 Jamie and Tom aren't in class 8R.
2 Jamie is sitting next to Emma.
3 Tariq is alone in the playground.
4 Tariq is from Germany.
5 He doesn't know many people in Exeter.
6 Tom is going to Manchester on Saturday.
7 Jamie is going to a football match with
   Tom and Tariq at the weekend.
8 Emma and Sarah are going too.

4 Finish Emma's e-mail to her dad. Use words from the story.

Hi Dad,
It's Friday and the first week back at … is over.
I'm in class …. I'm with my old … – Sarah,
Jamie and Tom. There's a new … in our class.
His name is …. He's from …. He's a football ….
His dad … for Exeter City. We're … plans for
tomorrow. We have … for a football match –
Exeter City and Manchester United!
Bye, Emma

5 Write a text for an e-mail from Tariq to his friend Jamila. Here are some ideas:

Hi …,
We have seven lessons …
I have lots of subjects: French, …
I'm in class …
I'm at Drake …
Our uniform is …
Bye, …
Exeter is OK, but …
Dad plays for …
I have a new friend, …
Tomorrow we're going to …
Our class teacher is …

Tipp:
Wenn du fertig bist,
tausche deine E-Mail mit
der deiner Partnerin/deines
Partners. Welche Mail
findest du besser?

▶ W 4, 4–5

1 Words in the story

a) Match the words.

All the words are on pages 14–15.

1	old	a	plans
2	quarter	b	the phone
3	on	c	Somalia
4	football	d	friends
5	from	e	magazine
6	making	f	past ten

b) Finish the sentences.

Use the words in a).

1 Jamie and Tom are ...
2 It's time for French – it's ...
3 Tom is ... at home. He's talking to Jamie.
4 *TEAM* is my favourite ...
5 Tariq moved to England ...
6 Tariq and Tom are ...

2 Nonsense words

These words are in the story too.

a) BOP is wrong. But what's right?

1 The pupils are **BOP** the playground.
2 Tariq is **BOP** class 8R.
3 He moved here **BOP** August.
4 Tariq's dad is new **BOP** the team.
5 The football match is **BOP** Exeter.

b) What's BIP?

1 Tom is sitting next **BIP** Jamie.
2 Tariq isn't talking **BIP** the other pupils.
3 The pupils are going **BIP** the classroom.
4 Welcome **BIP** Exeter.
5 It's quarter **BIP** four.

3 Find the missing word.

a) These are easy.

1 read – reading
  talk – ...
2 laugh – laughing
  watch – ...

b) But these aren't easy.

1 mak**e** – mak**ing**
  writ**e** – ...
2 hav**e** – hav**ing**
  com**e** – ...

No e with *-ing*.

c) And these aren't easy.

1 ge**t** – ge**tt**ing
  si**t** – ...
2 sto**p** – sto**pp**ing
  pu**t** – ...

4 Find ten school words

in the box. These words are in Unit 1.

X	Y	B	H	I	S	T	O	R	Y	R	S
B	Z	R	E	P	X	I	B	C	U	S	P
C	P	E	D	Q	N	M	M	B	X	T	O
C	L	A	S	S	T	E	A	C	H	E	R
Z	A	K	V	X	X	T	A	D	Y	F	T
W	Y	T	S	C	L	A	S	S	Z	E	G
P	G	Q	R	S	U	B	J	E	C	T	L
P	R	O	E	N	G	L	I	S	H	J	K
T	O	L	M	N	K	E	W	I	U	H	A
P	U	P	I	L	J	F	G	V	E	F	Y
R	N	P	O	M	I	H	Z	D	B	G	W
S	D	Q	N	L	K	Y	H	I	J	C	V

5 AND YOU? Write about your school.

I'm in class ...
My class teacher is ...
My favourite teacher is ...
There are ... pupils in my class.
I usually sit next to ...
We have ... subjects.
Our subjects are ...
My favourite subject is ...
In the breaks we can ...

Tipp:
Versuche deinen Text frei vorzutragen.

▶ W 5, 6–8 ▶ W ○

Dictionary work

1 Read the text about Drake School. Is it like your school or is it different?

Drake School plan

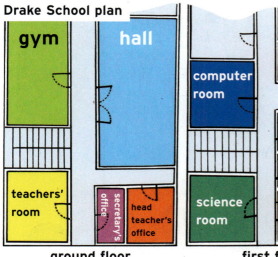

ground floor   first floor

On the ground floor you can see the teachers' room, the head teacher's office and the secretary's office. The gym and the hall are on the ground floor too.

On the first floor you can see lots of classrooms, the computer room, the science room, the art room and the French room.

The library, the boys' toilets and the girls' toilets are on the first floor too.

2 The right word

a) What's *plan* in German? Can you guess?

Look at the picture in exercise 1.

In the dictionary there are four German words for *plan*. Which German words are right here?

> **plan** [plæn] **1** planen, vorhaben; **2** Plan; Grundriss

b) Find *floor* in the text. Which German words are right here?

> **floor** [flɔː] **1** Fußboden; **2** Stockwerk; **on the first floor** im ersten Stock(werk) **ground floor** Erdgeschoss, Parterre

c) Find the English words in the text for these words.

... [hedˈtiːtʃə] Schulleiter, Schulleiterin

... [ˈɒfɪs] Büro

... [dʒɪm] Turnhalle

... [ˈsekrətri] Sekretär, Sekretärin

... [ˈlaɪbrəri] Bücherei

... [hɔːl] **1** Aula; **2** Flur

... [ˈtɔɪlət] Toilette

Tipp: Manchmal findest du im Wörterbuch mehr als eine Bedeutung für ein Wort. Dann musst du dir den Text anschauen um herauszufinden, welche Bedeutung hier passt.

 3 And your school?

Draw a plan of your school and write a text. Work with a partner.

Exercise 1 can help you.

▶ Wordbank 3, p. 125
▶ W 6, 9–10 ▶ W

IN THE CLASSROOM

LISTENING

 1 **Listen to the dialogues 1–4 and match them with the pictures A–D.**

1 Dialogue 1 – *Picture D*
2 Dialogue 2 – ...
3 Dialogue 3 – ...
4 Dialogue 4 – ...

 2 **Listen again.**
Match the sentences and make the four dialogues.

1 Hurry up! We're late for French.
2 Don't eat in the classroom, please.
3 Let's go to my house after school.
4 Close your books and don't talk, please.

A Sorry, I can't. I'm meeting Tariq in Exeter.
B OK, OK! I'm coming!
C Oh no! We're doing an English test!
D I'm not eating, Ms Brown.

 3 **PRONUNCIATION:**
a) **Listen and repeat.**
b) **Practise the dialogues in exercise 2 with a partner.**

4 **Make sentences for the pictures.** Exercise 2 can help you.

Don't ...   Hurry ...!

Don't ...

Close ...

Let's ...
your house.

► W 7, 11

SPEAKING

5 **No school things**

1⊚ 10 **a)** **Who has no pen or book? Find out.**

b) **Practise the dialogue with a partner.**

JAMIE	Tom, can I borrow your pen, please?
TOM	Sorry, I'm using it. Ask Sarah.
JAMIE	Sarah, can I borrow your pen, please?
SARAH	Oh, OK. Here you are. I have two.
JAMIE	Thanks. Can I look at your English book?
SARAH	OK. But where are your school things?
JAMIE	In the bus!

6 **Emma's questions**

a) **Finish the dialogue.**   Exercise 5 can help you.

EMMA	Jamie, can I ... your ruler, please?
JAMIE	Sorry, I'm ... it. Ask Tom.
EMMA	Tom, ... I borrow your ruler, please?
TOM	Oh, OK. Here ... are.
EMMA	Thanks. Can I ... at your maths book?
TOM	OK. But where ... your school things?
EMMA	At home!

 b) **Listen and check.**

1⊚ 11

c) **Now act the dialogue in groups.**

7 **ROLE PLAY**

Partner A: Ask Partner B.

Can I borrow your ..., please?

Partner B: Pick a boy or girl. Then look at page 122 and answer the questions.

Daniel   Sophie   Emily   Thomas

▶ W 7, 12

8 **Dialogues: First write the dialogues with a partner. Then act the dialogues.**

The sentences on pages 18–19 can help you.

1 PARTNER A Bitte deine Partnerin/deinen Partner, dir ihren/seinen Bleistift zu leihen.
PARTNER B Sage OK und überreiche ihn ihr/ihm.
PARTNER A Bedanke dich.

2 PARTNER A Schlage vor, dass ihr nach der Schule zu dir geht.
PARTNER B Sage, dass es dir leidtut, aber dass du nicht kannst. Du triffst dich mit deinen Freunden/Freundinnen.

3 PARTNER A Sage deiner Partnerin/deinem Partner, dass sie/er sich beeilen soll.
PARTNER B Sage, dass du kommst.

▶ W 7, 13 ▶ W

IN THE PLAYGROUND

20

twenty

1 **Match these answers (1–6) with the people (A–F) in the Drake School playground.**

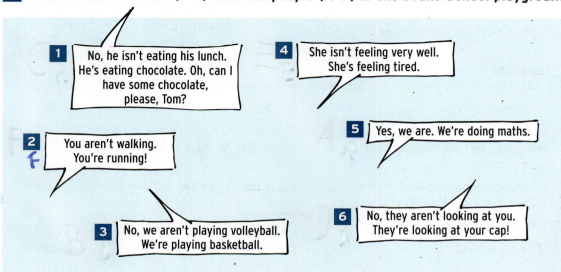

1 No, he isn't eating his lunch. He's eating chocolate. Oh, can I have some chocolate, please, Tom?

2 You aren't walking. You're running!

3 No, we aren't playing volleyball. We're playing basketball.

4 She isn't feeling very well. She's feeling tired.

5 Yes, we are. We're doing maths.

6 No, they aren't looking at you. They're looking at your cap!

2 WORD SEARCH

a) Find the missing words on pages 12–19.

1 Emma is ... about the summer. (p. 12)
2 A boy is ... a football magazine. (p. 14)
3 He isn't ... to the other pupils. (p. 14)
4 They're ... plans for the weekend. (p. 15)
5 He's ... TV. (p. 15)

6 Is Exeter City ...? (p. 15)
7 I'm not ..., Ms Brown. (p. 18)
8 We're ... an English test! (p. 18)
9 Tom, can I borrow your pen, please?
   – Sorry, I'm ... it. (p. 19)

b) Find these missing words on page 20.

1 Am I ... too fast?
2 Is Tom ... his lunch?
3 Is Sarah ... OK?
4 Are we ... volleyball now?
5 Are you ... your homework now?
6 Are they ... at me?

c) Now find these missing words on page 20.

1 You aren't ... You're running!
2 No, he isn't ... his lunch.
3 She isn't ... very well.
4 No, we aren't ... volleyball.
5 No, they aren't ... at you.

3 OVER TO YOU! Look at exercise 2 again and finish the checkpoint.

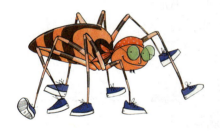

CHECKPOINT

Present progressive

Wenn du sagst, was gerade geschieht – oder nicht geschieht –, enden die Verben (z. B. *talk*, *read*) auf: ...

▶ Eine Übersicht über diese Regeln findest du auf der Summary-Seite 85.
▶ Extra practice, pp. 82 ff.
▶ W 8–9

NACH DIESER UNIT KANN ICH ...

Dinge im Klassenzimmer benennen.	▶ *bag, board, book, chair, door, exercise book, homework diary, ruler, shelf, table, window*
meine Schulfächer benennen.	▶ *art, computers, English, French, geography, German, history, maths, science, sport*
sagen, was gerade im Klassenzimmer geschieht oder nicht geschieht.	▶ *Some pupils are writing. / Tom isn't listening.*
etwas über meine Schule oder meine Klasse sagen.	▶ *I'm at Pestalozzi School. I'm in class 6b.*
sagen, dass jemand etwas tun oder nicht tun soll.	▶ *Hurry up! / Don't eat in the classroom.*
Vorschläge machen.	▶ *Let's go to my house after school.*
um etwas bitten.	▶ *Can I borrow your pen? / Can I look at your book?*

From Germany to England

1 Lots of people go to England every year. How do they go? Talk to your partner.

They go by ship. They go by ...

There's a tunnel to England.
Trains go through the tunnel.
There are trains for cars too.
The tunnel is the fastest way to
England for cars.

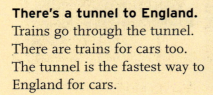

 2 Listen to the three people.
1 ⊙ 12 **Which pictures are right, A or B?**

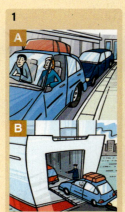

3 AND YOU? Ask a partner.

YOU	Do you usually go on holiday?
YOUR PARTNER	Yes, we do./ No, we don't.
YOU	How do you go?
YOUR PARTNER	By car.
	...
	...

▶ W 11, 1–2

Lots of things are different in England.

4 **Time: Talk to a partner.**

When it's two o'clock in England,
it's three o'clock in Germany.

When it's ... in England, what time is it in Germany?
– It's ...
When it's ... in Germany, what time is it in England?
– It's ...

5 **Roads: Look at the pictures.** The *List of numbers* on page 167 can help you.

A
Drive on the Left
Tenez la Gauche
Links Fahren

In England you drive
on the ...

B
NATIONAL
SPEED LIMIT
60 = 95
mph   km/h
70 = 110
mph   km/h

What's 60 miles
in kilometres?

C
A 2
London 70 miles

How many kilometres
to London?

6 **Work with a partner. Finish the *Here and there* box.
Then write it in your exercise book.**

HERE AND THERE

England and Germany: What's right?

- You can go to England by ship or through the ...
- England and Germany have/don't have different time.
- In England people use miles/kilometres. In Germany ...
- In England people drive on the left/on the right. In Germany ...
- People can drive faster in Germany/England than in
  England/Germany.

▶ W 11, 3

23

twenty-three

FROM KREFELD TO EXETER

 1 **Look at the pictures. Is the text about a trip by train? Find out.**

1◉ 13

Tom's mum is German. Her youngest brother, Klaus, lives in Krefeld. Tom's cousin Jutta has English at school. So her parents thought a trip to Exeter was a good idea.

On Saturday morning Jutta and her father went to Düsseldorf Airport, the nearest airport to their home. The plane was fast and it wasn't more expensive than the train. In fact, the plane ticket was cheaper!

Tom and his mother went by car to London Heathrow, the most important airport in England. Exeter Airport is much nearer to Exeter than Heathrow. But it's only a small airport and planes from Germany don't go there. The trip to Heathrow by car was long – four hours.

2 **Find five things about Tom's cousin in the text.**

1 Tom's cousin's name is …
2 She lives in …
3 She has … at school.
4 Her father is Mrs Price's …
5 Her father's name is …

3 **Find the missing words in the text.**

1 Düsseldorf is the … airport to Krefeld.
2 The plane ticket was … than the train ticket.
3 London Heathrow is the … airport in England.
4 Exeter Airport is much … to Exeter than London Heathrow.

 4 **At Heathrow Airport. Look at the picture. Is Mrs Price happy? Now listen and check.**

1◉ 14

5 **Listen again. Who says what?**

1◉ 14

1 Where's Jutta?
2 Where's your mobile?
3 It's in my bag.
4 It's terrible.
5 I can look at all the shops here!

► W 12, 4–5

POEM

1 🔊 15

I left the house

1 I left the house at ten to three,
   And waited for a ship.
   But all the ships were on the sea,
   And so I had no trip.

2 I left the house at ten to five,
   And waited for a bus.
   We waited there a long, long time,
   No bus arrived for us.

3 I left the house at ten to nine,
   And waited for a train.
   "No trains this week" was on a sign,
   So I went home again.

4 I left the house at ten to one,
   And sat in my old car.
   And sat and sat and sat and sat,
   Then said, "It's goodbye, car!"

5 I left my dreams at ten to eight,
   I'm in my room again.
   And mum is shouting, "Jill, you're late!
   You have to get your plane!"

🔊 **6** **Match the pictures (A–E) with the verses (1–5).**

7 **Learn the poem by heart.**

Tipp:
Bildet Gruppen. Jede/Jeder trägt eine Strophe vor. Ihr könnt auch eine Aufnahme machen.

8 **Exciting Exeter – The Underground Passages**
a) **Read the text.**

Exeter's Underground Passages are one of the most exciting places for young people in Exeter. You can walk through the old water passages with a guide. In some passages you can't walk, you can only crawl! But are they too exciting for you???

b) **What do you think?**
Talk to a partner.

I think the Underground Passages are exciting.
I don't think they're exciting. I don't want to crawl.

▶ W 12, 6

25

twenty-five

STORY

1 Who isn't in the story?

Tom   Mrs Price   Mr Price   Jutta   the guide

Tipp:
Sieh dir die Bilder auf S. 26 und 27 an. Überfliege den Text und achte nur auf die Namen. Wer kommt nicht vor?

2 Was Exeter exciting for Jutta? Find out.

1⊙ 16

Exciting Exeter?

Tom, Jutta and Mrs Price were at the River Exe.
"This is a very small river," Jutta said. "The Rhine is much bigger than the Exe."

5 "Yes, it is," said Mrs Price. "The Rhine is the longest river in Germany. Let's have a nice cup of tea now. Look, there's a cafe."
"Ugh! Tea!" said Jutta. "Tea is the worst drink in the world! Let's look at CDs."

10 They went to Sidwell Street.
"We have much better shops in Krefeld," Jutta said. "And CDs are cheaper in Germany too." Tom said nothing. Jutta was right!

15 "What can we do now?" said Mrs Price.
"I know. Let's go to the sea at Exmouth."
"Nein, danke," said Jutta. " You can't go swimming in October. I want to do something different, something more
20 exciting."
"Exciting?" said Mrs Price. "I'm going to that cafe. I'd like a cup of tea now. Are you coming?"

"OK, Jutta. I know something exciting," said Tom. "Let's go! See you later, Mum!" 25
Soon they were at Exeter's Underground Passages and in a tunnel. Jutta thought it was great.
Then the guide said, "This is our smallest tunnel. You can't stand in it. You can only 30
crawl. Who wants to go in?"
"That's exciting!" Jutta said. "Let's crawl in, Tom."

So Tom went with her, but he wasn't very
35 happy. In fact, he was frightened. Then
Jutta stopped. "Are you OK?" Tom asked.
"I'm frightened!" Jutta said. "Help me!"
"Think of a big field," Tom said. Jutta
thought of the big fields at home near the
40 Rhine.
"How are you feeling now?"
"Better, thank you."
"OK, let's go!"
Soon they were back in the bigger tunnel.
45 "Thanks, Tom," said Jutta. "Let's go to a
cafe now. That was exciting, too exciting!"

3 **Match the pictures with the sentences.**

a) She's thinking of big fields.

b) They're talking about tea.

c) She's going to a cafe.

d) They're waiting for their guide.

4 **Finish the sentences with the right words.**

1 Tom, Jutta and Mrs Price were at the River Exe/Rhine.
2 Jutta doesn't like tea/cola.
3 They went to the park/shops.
4 Jutta wanted to do something exciting/boring.
5 Tom and Jutta were happy/frightened in the very small tunnel.
6 Jutta said, "That was/wasn't too exciting!"

5 **Is Jutta nice? What do you think?**

– Yes, I think she's nice. She's cool.
– No, she isn't nice to Mrs Price and Tom.

6 **A postcard from Exeter**
You're Jutta. Finish the postcard to your English teacher in Krefeld.

Dear Mr Morschel,

I'm on holiday in ... . I'm visiting my ... .
His name is Tom. Exeter has some nice
shops, but CDs are ... than in Germany.
We went to the ... Passages. We went in a
very ... tunnel too. Then I was ... in the
small tunnel. But ... was with me, so it
was OK. Exeter isn't boring. It's very ...!
See you soon,
Jutta Link

▶ W 13, 7–8

27

twenty-seven

1 ODD WORD OUT

You can check your answers in exercise 2.

1 day, month, week, ~~October~~
2 ~~boring~~, exciting, good, great
3 guides, ~~cousins~~, bus drivers, teachers
4 went, stopped, ~~frightened~~, waited
5 great, good, cool, ~~expensive~~
6 ~~airport~~, ship, plane, car

2 Finish the sentences.

Look at exercise 1 again.

1 November comes after ....
2 *Tagesthemen* is often ..... for children.
3 Your dad's brother's children are your ....
4 This tunnel is very small! I'm ....
5 English CDs aren't cheap. They're ....
6 Exeter has a small ....

3 Match the words.

→ big • great • worst • exciting • cheap • something • come • left

↔

→ right • go • expensive • terrible • nothing • small • best • boring

1 big – small   2 great – ....   3 worst – ....

4 What are they saying?

1 a cafe / Let's / go to
2 the tunnel / Let's / go in
3 Let's / a nice cup of tea / have
4 town / go to / Let's
5 walk / Let's / in the park
6 go swimming / in the sea / Let's

5 Tickets from Exeter

Find the right words in the box.

→ August • tea • field • River • sea • tunnel

1 TRIP TO THE  sea AT EXMOUTH.

From: Exeter Bus Station
To: Exmouth

2 UNDERGROUND PASSAGES

One child
Saturday, 10th ....

3 QUINN'S QUADS ONE TEENAGER

Ticket and
a cup of ....

4 SADDLES AND PADDLES

One hour on the
.... Exe, Exeter

5 BROWN'S FARM

Summer car park
Ticket for one car in our big
....
near the River Exe.

6 EUROSTAR

Fast train to London
Ticket for school group
From Lille to London through the
....

► W 14, 9–10 ► W

Interpreting

Jutta often helps people in Krefeld.

> I'd like the chicken, please.

JUTTA   Sie möchte das Hähnchen.

Tipp:
Du gibst wieder, was die andere Person sagen will. Zum Beispiel wird aus „I" nicht „ich", sondern „er" oder „sie".

> Can you help me, please? I can't find my car. I don't know where it is.

JUTTA   Er kann sein Auto nicht finden.

Tipp:
Du brauchst nicht Wort für Wort zu übersetzen. Es kommt auf den Sinn an.

Help these people.

1

> Do you know a bike shop near here?

YOU   Sie fragt …

2

> I can't find the bike track to Krefeld.

YOU   Er …

3

> I'd like a cup of tea, please.

YOU   …

4

> This is the worst room in the world. Do you have a better room, please?

YOU   Er möchte …

5

> I'd like two tickets for the film, please. Is it in English?

YOU   …

6

> This is terrible. It isn't easy with my left hand. I'm very sorry.

YOU   …

▶ W 15, 11–12   ▶ W ◯

AT SCHOOL AND AT HOME WITH A VISITOR

LISTENING

 1 **Nice to meet you, Jutta.**

1◉17
a) Look at the picture. Is it Sunday?
b) Listen to the CD and check.
c) Listen again. Put the sentences in the right order.

A MS BROWN Nice to meet you, Jutta.

B JUTTA I don't have school in the afternoon, you see.

C JUTTA Well, it's OK, but I think my school in Germany is better.

E MS BROWN I think that's a very interesting idea!   **D** TOM This is Jutta, Ms Brown.

F MS BROWN And what do you think of school in England?

d) Listen again and check your answers to c).

 2 **Now Jutta is talking to Tom's friends. Listen.**

1◉18
a) Finish the sentences.

1	Jeans and a T-shirt	a)	is the worst singer in the world.
2	German TV	b)	are the coolest band in the world.
3	Max Miller	c)	is more expensive here than in Germany.
4	*The Gang Girls*	d)	are nicer than a school uniform.
5	The new CD	e)	is better than English TV.

 b) Listen again and check your answers to a).   c) PRONUNCIATION: Listen and repeat.

1◉18   1◉19

3 **AND YOU? Make a dialogue with a partner.**

Borussia Dortmund		best	football team	
Peter Maffay		worst	singer	
GZSZ	is the	most interesting	programme	in Germany.
Kaufstadt		most boring	shop	

– No, he/she/it isn't!
– You're right.

▶ W 16, 13–14

SPEAKING

4 Jutta is having breakfast.

1⦿ 20 **a) How's Jutta feeling? Find out.**

MR PRICE Is the breakfast OK, Jutta?

JUTTA Yes, thank you. I like English food. There's only one thing.

MR PRICE What is it?

JUTTA Can I have a glass of milk instead of tea, please?

MR PRICE Yes, of course.

JUTTA Thank you.

MR PRICE Do you like it here?

JUTTA Yes, I do. Everybody is very nice.

MR PRICE How are you feeling?

JUTTA Well, not bad, thank you. But I miss my dog.

b) Practise the dialogue with a partner.

5 Now Jutta is having lunch.

a) Finish the dialogue.   Look at exercise 4 again.

MRS PRICE ..., Jutta?

JUTTA Yes, thank you. I like English ... . There's ....

MRS PRICE What is it?

JUTTA Can I have ... water ... tea, please?

MRS PRICE ...

JUTTA ...

MRS PRICE ... here?

JUTTA Yes, I do. Everybody ...

MRS PRICE How are ...?

JUTTA ..., thank you. But I ... my family.

1⦿ 21 **b) Listen and check.**

c) Act the dialogue with a partner.

6 AND YOU? Tell a partner.

– I like/I don't like ... for breakfast.
– I have/I don't have ... for lunch.
– I think ... is/are nicer than ...

▶ Wordbank 4, p. 126

7 The ABC game

Animals are better than ...
... books. Books are better than ...
... cars. Cars are better than ...
... are better than ...

The *Dictionary* on pages 147–157 can help you.

▶ W 17, 15–16 ▶ W ⦿

LOOK AT LANGUAGE

A QUIZ ABOUT EXETER AND ENGLAND

1 **What do you know? Is it right or wrong?**

Look at Unit 2 again.

2 English school uniforms are the coolest clothes in the world.

1 The Exe is smaller than the Rhine.

3 CDs are more expensive in England than in Germany.

4 Heathrow is the most important airport in England.

5 People can drive faster in England than in Germany.
6 The Underground Passages are the most boring place in Exeter.
7 Exeter Airport is the nearest airport to Exeter.
8 Exeter isn't the biggest town in England.
9 Homework is bad in Germany. But it's worse in England – it's in the evening!
10 Kilometres are longer than miles.

Answers:

1 right, 2 wrong, 3 right, 4 right, 5 wrong, 6 wrong, 7 right, 8 right, 9 right, 10 wrong

8–10: You're the best.
5–7: OK.
0–4: Not very good!

2 **Write the list in your exercise book and put in the missing words. They're all in the quiz.**

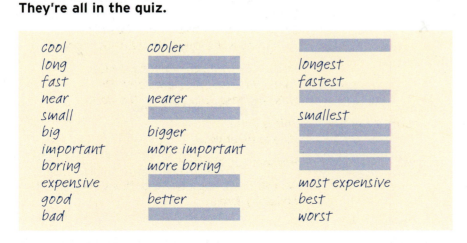

cool	cooler	
long		longest
fast		fastest
near	nearer	
small		smallest
big	bigger	
important	more important	
boring	more boring	
expensive		most expensive
good	better	best
bad		worst

3 WORD SEARCH

a) Find the missing words in the unit.

1 The tunnel is the … way to England for cars. (p. 22)
2 In fact, the plane ticket was …! (p. 24)
3 Exeter Airport is much … to Exeter than Heathrow. (p. 24)
4 The Rhine is the … river in Germany. (p. 26)
5 Exeter isn't the … town in England. (p. 32)

b) Find these words.

1 The plane was fast and it wasn't … than the train. (p. 24)
2 I want to do something different, something … (p. 26)
3 Heathrow is the … airport in England. (p. 32)
4 The Underground Passages are the … place in Exeter. (p. 32)

4 OVER TO YOU! Look at exercise 3 again and finish the checkpoint.

CHECKPOINT

Vergleiche
Bei kurzen Adjektiven (z. B. *fast, cheap*) endet die Vergleichsform auf -… oder -…

Bei längeren Adjektiven (z. B. *expensive, exciting*) bildest du die Vergleichsform mit … oder …

Einige Adjektive sind unregelmäßig und haben besondere Formen:
good – better – …
bad – … – …

▸ Eine Übersicht über diese Regeln findest du auf der Summary-Seite 89.

▸ Extra practice, pp. 86 ff.

▸ W 18–19

33

thirty-three

NACH DIESER UNIT KANN ICH …

einige Informationen über England geben.	▸ *In England people use miles.* *In England people drive on the left.*
Vergleiche machen.	▸ *You can drive faster in Germany than in England.* *Exeter Airport is nearer than Heathrow.* *The Rhine is the longest river in Germany.*
meine Meinung äußern.	▸ *Well, I think my own clothes are nicer.* *That's the worst programme on TV.* *He's the most boring boy in the world.*
jemanden vorstellen und begrüßen.	▸ *This is Jutta.* *Nice to meet you.*
fragen, wie es jemandem geht.	▸ *How are you feeling?*
sagen, wie es mir geht.	▸ *I'm OK, thank you. / Not bad, thank you.* *I miss my family.*

People and places

1 What are the jobs in the pictures?

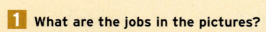

- baggage handler
- bus driver
- cook
- farmer
- gardener
- hairdresser
- police officer
- security guard
- shop assistant
- teacher

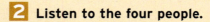

2 Listen to the four people.

1 ⊙ 22

a) **Where do they work?**

b) **What are their jobs?**

▶ W 23, 1–2

3 AND YOU? Talk about your family and friends.

My mum works
in a factory.

My cousin works
in a hospital.

My brother works
in a restaurant.

My sister is a police
officer.

My dad doesn't have
a job.

My friend's mum
works in a bank.

My mum works ...

My cousin is a ...

 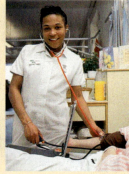 

→ in a shop • in a park • in a cafe • in a bookshop • in a supermarket • in a youth
club • in a museum • at an airport • at a school • at a sports centre • on a farm

► Wordbank 5, p. 126

4 Jobs network: What are the jobs? Where do people work?

a) Finish the network in your exercise book.

All the words are on pages 34 and 35.

► Wordbank 5, p. 126

b) Make sentences with a partner.

A cook works in a restaurant.
A baggage handler works at ...
A teacher ...

Tipp:
Nimm dir viel Platz in deinem Heft
für das *jobs network*. Schmücke es
mit Farben und Zeichnungen aus.
So wirst du dich besser an die
Wörter erinnern.

► W 23, 3

DREAM JOBS?

1 Who are these two people?
What are their jobs?
Read or listen and find out.

1⊙ 23

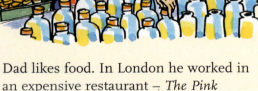

A

B

SARAH

We moved to Exeter last year, but mum and dad had no jobs. After a month mum got a job in a shop. But she wasn't happy. Then she got a job in a factory. But the work was too hard. And last week she got a new job. Now she's a motorbike courier. It's her dream job. Mum is a motorbike fan.

Dad likes food. In London he worked in an expensive restaurant – *The Pink Panther*. He was a cook there.
In Exeter he looked for a job in a good restaurant. He went to lots of places. But there were no jobs.
Then he got a job in a fast food restaurant – *Supermacs*.
The food is terrible – and not very healthy! It isn't his dream job.

2 Sarah's parents.
All the words are in the text.

The Johnsons moved to ... last year. But Sarah's mum and dad had no .... After a month her mum got a job in a .... Then she got a job in a .... Now she's a motorbike .... It's her ... job.
Sarah's dad worked in a ... in London. He was a ... in *The Pink Panther*. In Exeter he got a job in a fast ... restaurant. But it isn't his dream ...

▶ W 24, 4–5

3 Favourite food: Pupils in Sarah's class often eat these things.
AND YOU? Talk to a partner.

I like …

I love …

I don't like …

I often eat …

My favourite food is …

I eat … but I don't eat …

… is/are healthy.

… isn't/aren't very healthy.

chips

hamburgers

vegetables

salad

crisps

chicken

ice cream

pizza

fruit

► Wordbank 6, p. 127

► W 24, 6

---

4 The food song

1 ⊚ 24

a) Listen. What food words are in the song?

b) Write your own food song.

I love …
And I love chips.
I love …
On my lips.
And grandma says,
That's OK,
If you eat your …
Every day!

I love …
Banana ice cream.
When I think of …
It's a dream!
And grandad says,
That's OK,
If you eat …
Every day!

5 Finish the *Here and there* box
with a partner. Then make a fast food
network in your exercise book.

HERE AND THERE

- In England some people eat lots of
  fast food, like hamburgers and fish
  and chips.
- In Germany some people eat lots
  of fast food too, like …

► Wordbank 6, p. 127

1 **Before you read: Answer these questions in your group.**

1 How many fast food restaurants do you know?
2 How many people in your group eat fast food every week?
3 How many people don't eat fast food?
4 What fast food do people in your group like?

2 **Now find out:**

1 What's the story about –
a new car? / a new house? / a new restaurant?
2 Who wants a new job –
Mr Johnson? / Mrs Johnson? / Jake Johnson?
3 What's the name of the new project –
Supermacs? / *The Sun?* / *The Old Shop?*

Tipp:
Schau dir zuerst die Bilder der Geschichte an. Sie geben dir viele Informationen. Lies dann die Geschichte und achte zunächst nur auf die Beantwortung der Fragen.

A NEW PROJECT

1⊙ 26   It was Friday evening. Sarah, her mum, her sister and her brother were at home. At six o'clock the door opened and Sarah's dad came in. He said nothing. He wasn't happy.
5   "Are you OK?" Mrs Johnson asked.
"I hate my job at *Supermacs,*" Mr Johnson said. "I can't go back."
"Dad, then you have to leave *Supermacs.* You have to open your own restaurant," Sarah said.
10   Everybody laughed.
"That isn't a bad idea," Mr Johnson said.
"But first we have to find out some things ..."

Early on Saturday Sarah and her dad went to Exeter.
15   They looked at lots of restaurants and cafes. There was lots of different food. But it wasn't cheap. And it wasn't all healthy.
20   "OK, Sarah, Exeter needs a cheap, healthy fast food restaurant. That's our new project," Mr Johnson said.

Pizza Hawaii   £ 8.99
Chicken and chips   £ 5.50
Hamburger   £ 6.95
Fish and chips   £ 5.75

In November Mr Johnson rented an old shop in Alphington. It wasn't very expensive. He
25 went to the bank and borrowed some money. He bought lots of things – tables, chairs, cupboards and things for the kitchen. The family helped at the weekend. It was lots of work. After four weeks the new restaurant was
30 ready. The name was *The Sun*.

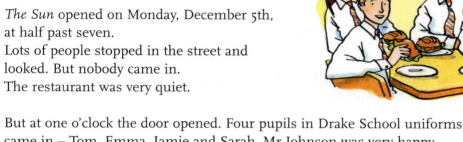

The Sun opened on Monday, December 5th, at half past seven.
Lots of people stopped in the street and looked. But nobody came in.
35 The restaurant was very quiet.

But at one o'clock the door opened. Four pupils in Drake School uniforms came in – Tom, Emma, Jamie and Sarah. Mr Johnson was very happy. He made salad rolls for everybody. Then the door opened again and more young people came in.
40 "Dad, I think our new project is going to be OK," Sarah said.
"Let's wait and see," Mr Johnson laughed.

3 The blue words are wrong.
What are the right words?

1 "I hate my house," Mr Johnson said.
2 "You have to open your own shop."
3 Sarah and her dad went to London.
4 The friends helped at the weekend.
5 Lots of pupils stopped in the street.
6 Four boys in Drake School uniforms came in.

4 Pick the right red words.

Mr Johnson's job at *Supermacs* was great/terrible. Sarah's idea was good/bad. The other restaurants in Exeter were expensive/cheap. And the fast food wasn't different/healthy.
Mr Johnson opened/closed his restaurant at half past seven. On Monday afternoon Mr Johnson was frightened/happy.
– I think this story is interesting/easy/OK.

5 INTERPRETING: You're in a restaurant in London with your small brother, Sven. Say what he can have, in German.

The Hungry Horse Restaurant

Fish and chips	£ 4.95
Fish, chips and vegetables	£ 5.95
Hamburger, salad and chips	£ 7.25
Chicken salad	£ 4.40
Chicken roll	£ 2.75
Pizza Big	£ 6.95
Small	£ 3.95
Fruit salad and ice cream	£ 2.95
Cup of tea or coffee	£ 1.25
Apple or orange juice	£ 1.50

SVEN   Ich habe Hunger und Durst. Was kann ich bestellen? Aber bloß keinen Salat und kein Gemüse!

YOU   Schauen wir mal. Du kannst …

▶ W 25, 7–8

1 Find the right words in the story. All the words are on pages 38–39.

1 The door ...

2 Sarah's dad ... in.

3 Mr Johnson ... nothing.

4 Everybody ...

5 Mr Johnson ... to the bank.

6 He ... some money.

2 Finish these sentences.

All the words are on pages 38–39.
1 We went to town and we ... at the shops.
2 Mum ... a new car on Monday.
3 Dad ... great salad rolls for my last birthday party.
4 The traffic lights were red and the cars ...
5 On Friday I ... my friend with her homework.
6 Last July we ... a house near the sea for a week.

Tipp:
Löse das Rätsel in deinem Heft.

3 ODD WORD OUT

1 gardener, cook, shop assistant, year
2 month, factory, hospital, restaurant
3 got, week, came, said
4 early, healthy, ready, courier
5 December, January, Saturday, June
6 November, Tuesday, Friday, Sunday
7 salad, vegetables, weekend, fruit
8 London, Alphington, Exeter, Monday

4 Time words: Finish the sentences.

Use the words in exercise 3.
1 The Johnsons moved to Exeter last ...
2 After a ... Sarah's mum got a job in a shop.
3 Last ... she got a new job.
4 Now she's a motorbike ...
5 On ... Sarah and her dad went to Exeter.
6 In ... Mr Johnson rented an old shop.
7 Everybody helped at the ...
8 *The Sun* opened on ...

5 Collect words in this unit. Make lists or networks in your exercise book.

Time words
last year
...

Jobs
teacher
...

Places
factory
...

Food
salad
...

▶ Wordbank 5, p. 126
▶ Wordbank 6, p. 127
▶ W 5, 9–11 ▶ W ⚪

Writing a story

Use these ideas – or your own ideas – and write a story in your exercise book.

A **When was it?**

It was | Monday morning.
Tuesday afternoon.
Wednesday evening.
last week.
last month.
...

B **Where were you?**

I was in a | cafe.
restaurant.
fast food restaurant.
...

C **Who was with you?**

I was | alone.
with my friends.
with my family.
with my mum.
...

J **Finish your story.**

They were happy and said, | "Thanks."
"That's great!"
"Here's some money."
"..."

D **What happened?**

Some | girls
boys
people
children
... | came in.

I **What happened then?**

I followed the | girls
boys
people
children
... | into the street.
to a shop.
to the station.
to the park.
...

E **What happened then?**

They had some | food.
drinks.
fish and chips.
salad rolls.
hamburgers.
...

H **Where was it?**

It was | on a chair.
next to a table.
next to the door.
...

F **And then?**

After | some time
a long time
... | they left the | restaurant.
cafe.
...

G **And then?**

Then I saw | a mobile.
a bag.
some money.
...

▶ W 27, 12 ▶ W ○

ON THE PHONE
LISTENING

 1 **Listen. Which two pictures are right?**

1⊙ 27

A · **B** · **C** · **D**

 2 **Listen again. What does Sarah say?**

1⊙ 27

SARAH	... (1)
MRS BAKER	Oh hello, Sarah. Emma! The phone!
EMMA	Hi, Sarah. What's up?
SARAH	... (2)
EMMA	Fine. I visited dad yesterday. It was his birthday. What about you?
SARAH	... (3)
EMMA	Poor you! See you tomorrow. And thanks for calling.
SARAH	... (4)

A Hi. Oh, nothing. How was your weekend?

B That's OK. See you tomorrow. Bye.

C Hello, Mrs Baker. Can I speak to Emma, please?

D Oh, I helped dad in the restaurant.

3 **AND YOU? Make a dialogue with a partner about your weekend.**

A How was your weekend?
B OK. / Fine. / Terrible. / ...
  I visited ... / helped ... / went to ... / ...
A Great! / Poor you!
B How was your weekend?
A OK. / Fine. / Terrible. / ...
  I ...
B Great! / Poor you!

?

 4 **PRONUNCIATION:**

1⊙ 28 **a)** **Listen and repeat.**

1	worked	2	moved	3	visited
	laughed		opened		rented
	looked		borrowed		waited

b) **Now listen to these words. Are they the same or different?**

1 helped – walked
2 stayed – crawled
3 stopped – wanted
4 answered – shouted
5 missed – liked
6 learned – closed

Tipp:
Achte auf die Aussprache am Ende der Wörter. Es gibt drei Möglichkeiten...
1 worked [... t]
2 moved [... d]
3 visited [... ɪd]

 ▶ W 28, 13–15

SPEAKING

 5 **Jamie's accident**

1 ⊙ 29 **a) What happened? Find out.**

SARAH Hi, Jamie. It's Sarah.
JAMIE Oh hi, Sarah.
SARAH You weren't at school today.
JAMIE I had an accident yesterday.
SARAH Oh! What happened?
JAMIE I fell off my quad and I hurt my hand.
SARAH Are you OK?
JAMIE Yes, I'm fine now, thanks. I can go to school tomorrow.
SARAH OK. See you tomorrow.
JAMIE OK. Bye. And thanks for calling.

b) Practise the dialogue with a partner.

6 **AND YOU?**

a) Make a dialogue on the phone with a partner.

A Hi, … . It's …
B Oh hi, …
A You weren't at …
B I had an …
A Oh! What …?
B I fell off my … and I hurt my …
A Are you …?
B Yes, I'm …
A OK. See you …
B OK. Bye. And thanks …

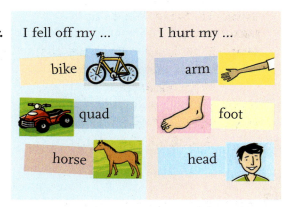

I fell off my …   I hurt my …

bike   quad   horse   arm   foot   head

b) Act the dialogue with a partner.

7 **ROLE PLAY**

Partner A: Talk to Partner B on the phone.

Hi, Kylie / Alex / Lynn / Justin. It's …
…
How was your weekend?
…
You weren't at school yesterday.
…
Oh! What happened?
…
Are you OK?
…
OK. See you tomorrow.
…
OK. Bye. And thanks for calling.

Partner B: Pick a boy or girl. Then look at page 123 and answer Partner A's questions – on the phone.

 Kylie   **Alex**   **Lynn**   **Justin**

▶ W 29, 16–17 ▶ W ⊙

43

forty-three

DO YOU REMEMBER ...?

1 ⊙ 30

It was the lunch break at Drake School.

EMMA I can't wait for the summer.

TOM Oh, yes! Do you remember our trip to Exmouth last summer?

EMMA July 1st – it was my birthday. We all went to the beach.

JAMIE The sea came in and our things were in the water.

SARAH Yes, that was terrible. But dad bought new T-shirts. And everybody had a big ice cream.

EMMA That was great. Do you remember your first day at our school, Tariq?

TARIQ Oh, yes – September 4th. I knew nobody. But then I met Tom in the playground.

TOM I saw your football magazine.

TARIQ And we talked about Exeter City.

JAMIE And do you remember September 9th?

SARAH September 9th?

JAMIE Yes, on September 9th Manchester United came to Exeter.

TARIQ I remember September 9th. That was a great day. Exeter City: 2 – Manchester United: 1!

SARAH Do you remember your trip to the Underground Passages last month, Tom?

TOM Shut up, Sarah. That isn't funny!

1 Match the dates with the pictures A–C.

→ July 1st • September 4th • September 9th

2 Verbs, verbs, verbs: Find the simple past forms in the dialogue.

went
came in
bought
...

> **Tipp:**
> Verben im *simple past* geben an, was jemand getan hat oder was geschehen ist.

3 WORD SEARCH

a) Find the simple past forms of these verbs. **b) Now find the simple past forms of these verbs.**

1 move (p. 36)	8 borrow (p. 39)
2 work (p. 36)	9 help (p. 39)
3 look (p. 36)	10 stop (p. 39)
4 open (p. 38)	11 happen (p. 41)
5 ask (p. 38)	12 follow (p. 41)
6 laugh (p. 38)	13 visit (p. 42)
7 rent (p. 39)	14 talk (p. 44)

1 have (p. 36)	8 leave (p. 41)
2 get (p. 36)	9 see (p. 41)
3 go (p. 36)	10 fall (p. 43)
4 come (p. 38)	11 hurt (p. 43)
5 say (p. 38)	12 know (p. 44)
6 buy (p. 39)	13 meet (p. 44)
7 make (p. 39)	

4 OVER TO YOU!

Finish the checkpoint. Can you find more examples?

CHECKPOINT

Simple past

Mit dem *simple past* sagst du, was in der Vergangenheit geschah. Damit kannst du Geschichten erzählen.
Regelmäßige Verben enden auf *-ed*.
Beispiele: *look – looked; ...*

Unregelmäßige Verben haben besondere Vergangenheitsformen. Beispiele: *get – got; ...*

▶ Eine Übersicht über diese Regeln findest du auf der Summary-Seite 93.

▶ Extra practice, pp. 90 ff.

▶ Liste der unregelmäßigen Verben, p. 169

▶ W 30–31

NACH DIESER UNIT KANN ICH ...

Berufe benennen.	▶ *baggage handler, bus driver, cook, gardener, farmer, hairdresser, police officer, shop assistant, security guard, teacher*
sagen, was jemand von Beruf ist.	▶ *My dad is a cook.*
sagen, wo jemand arbeitet.	▶ *My mum works at a bank.*
Speisen benennen.	▶ *chips, crisps, chicken, fruit, hamburgers, ice cream, salad, vegetables*
sagen, was mein Lieblingsessen ist.	▶ *My favourite food is pizza. I love hamburgers and salad.*
sagen, was ich am Wochenende gemacht habe.	▶ *On Saturday I went to the cinema. On Sunday I watched TV.*
erzählen, was geschehen ist.	▶ *I had an accident yesterday. I fell off my bike. I hurt my arm.*
sagen, woran ich mich erinnere.	▶ *I remember my first day at school.*

Weitere Übungen: www.new-highlight.de

▶ W 32, Test yourself ▶ W ⚪

▶ Extra reading, pp. 110–111

A weekend in Exeter

1 This is High Street in Exeter on a Sunday afternoon.

a) What can you see? Tell a partner.

b) What's different from Germany? Tell a partner. Don't forget – it's Sunday!

2 Signs in Exeter

a) Look at the signs.

2

DEBENHAMS DEPARTMENT STORE

SUNDAY	11:00 AM – 5:00 PM
MONDAY	9:00 AM – 5:30 PM
TUESDAY	9:00 AM – 5:30 PM
WEDNESDAY	9:00 AM – 5:30 PM
THURSDAY	9:00 AM – 5:30 PM
FRIDAY	9:00 AM – 6:00 PM
SATURDAY	9:00 AM – 6:00 PM

b) Make the sentences.

The *List of numbers* on page 167 can help you.

1 This big *Tesco* supermarket ...
2 The department store is open ...
3 The bank ...
4 The post office is open on Saturdays but ...

A on Sundays.

B it's closed on Sundays.

C is open 24 hours a day.

D isn't open on Sundays and Mondays.

3 Opening Hours

Monday	Closed
Tuesday	10.30 – 20.00
Wednesday	10.30 – 20.00
Thursday	10.30 – 20.00
Friday	09.00 – 18.00
Saturday	09.00 – 13.00
Sunday	Closed

HOUSEHOLD BANK

4 POST OFFICE

Monday	8:30 – 17:30
Tuesday	8:30 – 17:30
Wednesday	8:30 – 17:30
Thursday	8:30 – 17:30
Friday	8:30 – 17:30
Saturday	8:30 – 12.30

3 Listen. Where do the people want to go?

1 ◉ 31   The places are in exercise 2.

1 The boy wants to go to ...
2 The man and woman want to go to ...
3 The woman wants to ...
4 The girls want to ...

▶ W 33, 1

Sunday in Exeter. What do people do?

They go shopping.

They hire bikes or canoes.

They buy ice cream.

They go to the Underground Passages.

They go to the river or to the parks.

They go to cafes and have a cup of tea.

4 AND YOU? Tell your partner what you'd like to do in Exeter.

I'd like to go shopping.

I wouldn't like to go to the park.

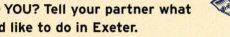

I'd like to ...

I wouldn't like to ...

5 Make lists or networks.

What can you buy in shops? – Clothes, ...
Where can you go? – To parks, ...
What can you have at a cafe? – Tea, ...
What can you hire? – Quads, ...

▶ Wordbank 7, p. 127

6 Finish the *Here and there* box with a partner. Then write it in your exercise book.

HERE AND THERE

In England
- Big supermarkets are sometimes open 24 ... a day.
- Lots of shops are open ... days a week.
- People use pounds (£).

In Germany
- Big supermarkets aren't ...
- Most shops are closed ...
- People use euros. They don't use ...

▶ W 33, 2–3

A NICE WEEKEND FOR EMMA?

1 It's Friday. What are Emma's parents doing at the weekend? Find out.

1 ⊙ 32

EMMA   Can you give me some money for town tomorrow, please?

MRS BAKER   I'm sorry, Emma! I didn't win the lotto last week!

EMMA   It's OK, Mum. I understand. I have an idea! Let's have a day in Exmouth. My friends have no time this weekend.

MRS BAKER   Oh, Emma, I have to drive my bus tomorrow morning.

EMMA   And in the afternoon?

MRS BAKER   I'm working for *Securex* in the afternoon.

EMMA   Oh, yes, you don't have only one job now. Poor Mum!

Now Emma is talking to her dad on the phone.

EMMA   Can we do something tomorrow, Dad?

MR BAKER   Sorry, Emma. I'm going to London with Dawn, my new girlfriend. I don't have time.

EMMA   But I wanted to see you. What about Sunday?

MR BAKER   Let's meet next weekend. We can hire canoes.

EMMA   Oh, Dad! I don't want to wait a week!

MR BAKER   I'm sorry, Emma. Dawn and I are in London all weekend.

EMMA   My friends don't have time, mum is working, you're going to London. But I can meet my new friend Sally.

2 Finish the sentences.

1 Mrs Baker didn't give Emma ...
2 Mrs Baker didn't win ...
3 She didn't have only one ... on Saturday.
4 And Mr Baker didn't have ...
5 Emma didn't want to wait ...

3 What do you think?

1 Emma's mum has/doesn't have lots of money.
2 Emma's dad is/isn't nice to Emma.
3 Emma thinks the weekend is going to be boring/very interesting.
4 Emma is/isn't happy.

4 Emma is talking to Sally on the phone. Listen. Put the sentences in the right order.

1 ⊙ 33

A Let's do something together.
B OK. Let's meet there at two o'clock.
C Where can we meet?
D I like Debenhams.
E What are you doing at the weekend?
F OK. Let's go to town tomorrow.
G Nothing.

▶ W 34, 4–5

5 Adverts

It's Friday evening. Emma is reading _Teen Page_ in the Exeter newspaper.
There are lots of adverts. Which advert (A–D) is for which of these places?

→ Dave's Disco • Debenhams • Mike's Music Shop • Odeon Cinema

A It's great!
The new CD by Mark
Marlowe
DID YOU SAY YES?

D **He's here in**
Exeter!
You didn't
dream it.
Next Saturday
DJ Terry Lee
Tickets £5

C DID YOU SEE
BIONIC BUNNY
LAST YEAR?

NOW SEE
BIONIC BUNNY 2!
STARTS FRIDAY

B Great T-shirts
in six different
colours £10

► W 34, 6

 ## 6 Rap: Buy, buy, buy!

1◉ 34 **a) Listen to the rap.**

 b) Write your own verse 1.

1 Buy my new book, then swim in our pool,
Wear our great jeans, and always be cool.
Eat super chips, then go fast by plane,
Drink cola, it's nice, forget all your pain.

2 Go to your nearest department store,
Buy lots of things, then buy many more.
Work very hard, then spend what you get,
Or go to your bank, then spend and forget!

3 Buy, buy, buy! You need something new.
Spend, spend, spend! The shops all need you.
You don't want to spend? Life isn't funny?
Take _Spendex_ now, and spend lots of money!

Buy my new ..., then swim in our pool,
Wear our great ..., and always be cool.
Eat super ..., then go fast by plane,
Drink ..., it's nice, forget all your pain.

STORY

1 Where are the people in the story? Only two pictures are right.

Exeter town centre

a jeans shop

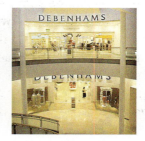
a department store

Alphington

2 Where's Emma's mum this afternoon? Find out.

DID YOU PAY FOR THAT?

1◉ 35

It was three o'clock on Saturday afternoon. Emma walked along Fore Street towards Sidwell Street. She was in the town centre. Her new friend Sally from school was at Debenhams department store.

5 "Hello, Sally," said Emma. "I'm sorry I'm late. Look at this terrible T-shirt! I need some new clothes."
"I need new clothes too," said Sally. "I have a big bag. Look."
"Yes, but I can't buy things this afternoon. I have no
10 money."
Sally didn't listen. "Did you read the advert for T-shirts in the newspaper yesterday? Let's go!"

The girls went into the department store. Sally looked at lots of different T-shirts but Emma didn't
15 want to look.
"Don't you like the T-shirts?" asked Sally.
"Yes, I do. I like the yellow T-shirt," said Emma.
"OK. Nobody is looking. I can put it in my bag," said Sally.
20 "No, Sally, no!"
But Sally put the yellow T-shirt in her bag.
"Let's go!" she said.
"Did you see the blue T-shirt? I have that in my bag too." Emma wasn't happy. "Wait. Sally, let's …"
25 "Stop the two girls!" It was a security guard. Sally pushed her bag into Emma's hands and ran towards the door. Then Emma was very stupid. She followed Sally out of the shop!

Sally turned left, Emma turned right. Emma ran along High
30 Street and into Fore Street, past all the shoppers. But the
security guard was fast. She was very near now. Emma turned
left into Market Street and then right. Suddenly there were
steps. Emma fell to the ground. The guard had her now!
"Did you pay for that?" she asked.
35 "Mum?!! What are you ...?"
"Give me the bag and go home now. We can talk this
evening."

In the evening, at the Bakers' flat:
"It isn't nice if your own daughter is a shoplifter. Why did
40 you do it?"
"I'm sorry, Mum. I didn't want to. Why were you at
Debenhams? You work for *Securex*."
"Yes, and *Securex* had a job for me at Debenhams today."
"What did you say to the people there, Mum?"
45 Mrs Baker looked at her daughter. "I said who the shoplifters
were, of course."
"Oh no!"
"And I said you'd be in the shop again tomorrow."
"I'm not going to Debenhams again!"
50 "You and Sally *are* going to Debenhams again," said Mrs
Baker. "You have to tell them what happened and say sorry."

3 **Right or wrong?**

1 Sally was late.
2 Emma said she needed some new clothes.
3 Sally looked at lots of T-shirts.
4 The girls didn't pay for the T-shirts.
5 Sally and Emma ran out of the
   department store.
6 The security guard was Sally's mum.

4 **Who said it?**

Look at pages 50 and 51.

1 "I have a big bag."
2 "I like the yellow T-shirt."
3 "Did you pay for that?"
4 "Why did you do it?"
5 "What did you say to the people there?"
6 "I'm not going to Debenhams again!"

5 **Finish Mrs Baker's report.**

Saturday, 3.30
One girl ... left, the other girl ... right. I ... along High Street and into Fore Street.
I ... fast. The girl ... left into Market Street and then right. I ... very near now.
Suddenly there ... steps. The girl ... to the ground. I ... her now.

▶ W 35, 7

1 What are they saying?

Look at the story on pages 50 and 51.

1 pay / Did you / for that / ? **2** do it / Why / did you / ? **3** did you / What / say / ?

4 see / the blue T-shirt / Did you / ? **5** the advert / Did you / read / ?

2 Pick the right words.

Check your answers in the story.

1 Emma walked at/along Fore Street.
2 Her friend was at/on the department store.
3 Sally looked with/at the T-shirts.
4 She put them in/out of her bag.
5 Emma ran with/past all the shoppers.
6 The security guard was near/past Emma now.

3 Who are the people from the story?

fr■■nd
d■■gh■er
g■rls
sh■■■er
■■■■lifter
security ■■■■■

4 What's in the bag?
Put in a, e, i or o.

c■k■   b■■k
m■n■y   n■wsp■p■r
t■ck■ts   T-sh■rt

5 Make dialogues in a department store.

The *List of numbers* on page 167 can help you.

YOU	YOUR PARTNER
Hello. Can I help you?	I'd like this ..., please.
That's ... pence/ ... pounds, please.	Here you are.
Thank you. Bye.	Bye.

► Wordbank 8, p. 128
► W 36, 8–10 ► W ⊙

£5
£79
£7
95p
£20
£2
£8
£9
50p
£20
£15
70p 85p

Reports

1 **Finish this report about shoplifters at Mike's Music Shop.**

1 The boys (come) into the shop.
2 They (look) at an expensive CD.
3 They (not see) me.
4 I (wait) near the window.
5 Suddenly they (put) the CD in a bag.
6 I (follow) them out of the shop.
7 First they (turn) left into Hill Street.
8 Then they (go) through the park.
9 They (run) very fast.
10 Then they (leave) in a car.

Tipp:
Berichte schreibt man im *simple past*. Du musst also für die Verben in Klammern die korrekte *simple past*-Form finden.
Siehe Seite 45 und 169.

2 **A shoplifter at the department store: Pick the right words.**

On Tuesday, April 7th/Next Monday at ten o'clock a girl came into the department store. She looked at a yellow/young T-shirt. She saw/didn't see me. I was near the dog/door. Suddenly she put the T-shirt in a box/bag. I followed her through the shop, past all the other drivers/shoppers. First she turned left/late, then she turned roads/right. Then she went through the doors/dogs and ran into Sidwell Street. I shouted/started, but the girl didn't stop/sing. So I ran/drank out of the shop and followed the girl through town. She stopped along/at the post office and I went back to the department store with her.

3 **Look at the pictures. What happened? Put the missing words in the report.**
Look at exercise 2.

1 A ... came into the department store.
2 He looked at ...
3 He put the ... in ...
4 I followed him ...
5 He went ... the doors and ran ... Sidwell Street.
6 He stopped at the ... and I ... back to the department store with him.

► W 37, 11–12   ► W ○

DID YOU HAVE A GOOD WEEKEND?

LISTENING

1 It's Monday afternoon. Did Emma like her present from London?
Listen and find out.

1⊙ 36

2 Match the questions and the answers.

1 Did you have a good weekend, Emma?
2 What did you do?
3 Did you meet your dad?
4 Did he bring you a T-shirt?
5 You don't like it?

A Yes, he did. But I don't want it.
B Nothing. I didn't go anywhere.
C I'm not very interested in T-shirts now!
D No, I didn't. He went to London.
E My weekend? It was OK.

3 Listen again and check your answers to 2.

1⊙ 36

4 PRONUNCIATION: Listen and repeat.

1⊙ 37

5 AND YOU? Talk to a partner.

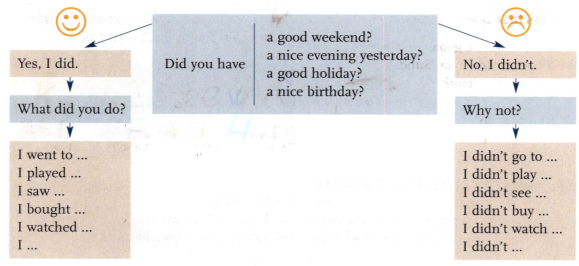

Did you have	a good weekend?
	a nice evening yesterday?
	a good holiday?
	a nice birthday?

Yes, I did.
↓
What did you do?
↓
I went to ...
I played ...
I saw ...
I bought ...
I watched ...
I ...

No, I didn't.
↓
Why not?
↓
I didn't go to ...
I didn't play ...
I didn't see ...
I didn't buy ...
I didn't watch ...
I didn't ...

▶ Wordbank 7, p. 127

▶ W 38, 13–14; W 39, 15

SPEAKING

 6 It's Monday evening. Emma is with her grandad.

1◉ 38 **a) Does he know about Debenhams on Saturday? Find out.**

GRANDAD	What did you do yesterday?
EMMA	I visited Sally.
GRANDAD	Did you stay long?
EMMA	No, I didn't. I left at eleven o'clock.
GRANDAD	Did you talk to Sally about the T-shirts?
EMMA	Yes, I did. We went back to the shop and said sorry.
GRANDAD	Poor Emma!
EMMA	Not "poor Emma", "stupid Emma"!

b) Practise the dialogue.

7 Now it's Tuesday morning.

a) Finish the dialogue. Look at exercise 6.

MRS BAKER	What did you do after school yesterday?
EMMA	... grandad.
MRS BAKER	... long?
EMMA	No, ... I ... at seven o'clock. I had lots of homework.
MRS BAKER	... talk to grandad about next Saturday?
EMMA	Yes, ... It's OK. Kevin can visit him. Then dad and I can go canoeing.

 b) Listen and check.
1◉ 39

c) Act the dialogue with a partner.

8 ROLE PLAY

Partner A:
Ask Partner B these questions.

1 Did you have a good weekend?
2 What did you do on Sunday?
3 Did you stay long?
4 Did you talk to your parents about next weekend?

Partner B:
Pick a boy or girl. Then look at page 124 and answer Partner A's questions.

Ryan   Lucy   Mike   Bina

9 Make funny dialogues with a partner.

YOU	YOUR PARTNER
Did you write an e-mail yesterday?	No, I didn't. But I wrote a book.
Did you buy a pen yesterday?	No, I didn't. But I bought a bus.
...	...

▶ W 39, 16–17 ▶ W ◉

TWO E-MAILS

1 **On Wednesday evening Emma got this e-mail from her dad.**

From:	John Baker
To:	Emma Baker
Subject:	next Saturday

Hi Emma,
Did you see the football match on TV yesterday? It was good.

>>>

I'm sorry I didn't see you and Kevin at the weekend. I didn't have much fun in London. Dawn worked on Saturday and Sunday!

>>>

Did I tell you what Dawn's job is? She works for BBC TV.

>>>

A young man from Exeter, I think his name is Harry Klone, is in a big show in London. Dawn made a film about him. She didn't know that singers work so hard!

>>>

Let's meet at ten o'clock next Saturday. We can hire canoes for three hours at *Saddles and Paddles* and then eat at *The Sun*.

>>>

Dawn doesn't want to come with us. She can't swim!

>>>

Lots of love, Dad

PS Do you like your new T-shirt? I'm sorry I didn't have more time on Sunday.

2 **What did Emma answer? Use these sentences.**

Tipp:
Achte auf die Reihenfolge in Mr Bakers E-Mail und halte dich auch bei Emmas Antwort daran.

A I didn't know that Dawn works for BBC TV. What a great job!

B Ten o'clock at *Saddles and Paddles* is OK.

C I'm sorry you didn't have much fun in London. I didn't have much fun in Exeter.

D Say hi to Dawn, please. But I have to talk to *you*, Dad. Bye, Emma.

E Did you get an autograph from Barry Stone (not Harry Klone!)? He's great!

F PS Thanks for the T-shirt. It's nice. But you know what happened on Saturday now.

G Hi Dad, I didn't see the match. I was at the sports centre.

3 WORD SEARCH

a) Find these words in the unit.

1 I ... the lotto last week! (p. 48)
2 He's here in Exeter! You ... it. (p. 49)
3 The girls ... for the T-shirts. (p. 51)
4 I'm sorry I ... you and Kevin at the weekend. (p. 56)
5 I ... much fun in London. (p. 56)
6 I ... that Dawn works for BBC TV. (p. 56)

b) Now find these words.

1 ... you ... yes? (p. 49)
2 ... you ... *Bionic Bunny*? (p. 49)
3 ... you ... for that? (p. 50)
4 ... you ... the blue T-shirt? (p. 50)
5 ... he ... you a T-shirt? (p. 54)
6 ... I ... you what Dawn's job is? (p. 56)

4 OVER TO YOU!
Finish the checkpoint.

CHECKPOINT

Simple past
Bei Fragen über die Vergangenheit verwendest du ...

Wenn du sagen willst, was nicht geschah, verwendest du ...

▶ Eine Übersicht über diese Regeln findest du auf der Summary-Seite 97.
▶ Extra practice, pp. 94 ff.
▶ W 40–41

NACH DIESER UNIT KANN ICH ...

über Öffnungszeiten sprechen.
▶ *The bank is closed on Sundays.*
The supermarket is open 24 hours a day.

sagen, was ich gern tun würde.
▶ *I'd like to go shopping.*
sagen, was ich nicht gern tun würde.
▶ *I wouldn't like to go to the park.*

um etwas bitten.
▶ *Can we do something tomorrow?*
Can you give me some money, please?

fragen, ob jemand etwas getan hat.
▶ *Did you read the newspaper?*
Did you pay for that?

sagen, was nicht geschehen ist.
▶ *I didn't have much fun.*
I didn't see the match.

mich für etwas entschuldigen.
▶ *I'm sorry I didn't see you.*
I'm sorry I didn't have more time.

Weitere Übungen: www.new-highlight.de
▶ W 42, Test yourself ▶ W 43–44, Portfolio ▶ W ◐
▶ Extra reading, pp. 112–113

Unit **5**

Outdoor activities

cycling

horse riding

skiing

jogging

swimming

1 **Listen. Which outdoor activities on pages 58 and 59 are the people talking about?**

2⊙1

2 **AND YOU? Talk to a partner about the activities in the pictures.**

YOU	YOUR PARTNER
Which activities do you do?	Camping/...
Which activity would you like to try?	Horse riding/...
Why?	I think it's exciting/fun/quiet/...
	Because I like horses/bikes/the country/sport/...

▶ W 45, 1

walking

camping

fishing

rock climbing

Trikke riding

PROJECT – A class survey about outdoor activities

a) Look at the survey for class 8R.

Outdoor activities in class 8R

The most popular outdoor activity in our class is cycling. Fourteen pupils like it. Football and swimming are very popular. Twelve pupils like football and eight pupils like swimming. Volleyball is popular too. Five pupils like it. But canoeing, table tennis, horse riding, camping and mountain biking aren't very popular.

Activity	Class 8R	
football	ℍℍℍ II	(12)
canoeing	I	(1)
horse riding	II	(2)
cycling	ℍℍℍℍ IIII	(14)
camping	II	(2)
table tennis	III	(3)
mountain biking	I	(1)
volleyball	ℍℍ	(5)
swimming	ℍℍ III	(8)

b) Now do a survey in your class.

1 Make a list of activities on the board. ► Wordbank 9, p. 128

2 Find out who likes what.

c) Write a report for your class.

What activities do you do?
football

Who likes football?

► W 45, 2

A CLASS TRIP

1 The pupils in 8R are planning a trip. What are they going to visit?
Look at the brochure.

2⊙2

Dartmoor is a national park near Exeter.
It's a moor – a wild and lonely place.
There are hills, rivers and woods.
There are nice villages too.

You can see lots of animals on
Dartmoor: sheep, cows – and wild ponies.

And you can do lots of activities on
Dartmoor, like walking, horse riding,
fishing, mountain biking and rock
climbing.

Visit our Information Centres.
They're open every day from
ten to five o'clock.

When you visit Dartmoor
• always take a jacket,
• wear good trainers
  or walking shoes,
• and don't forget your map.

If you have questions, you can ask
a Dartmoor ranger.

2 Dartmoor words: What can you see in the picture?

Work in groups. Which group can find the most words?

3 Answer the "Here
and there" questions in
your exercise book.

HERE AND THERE

• Are there national
  parks in Germany?
• Do you know the name
  of a national park in
  Germany?
• Is there a national park
  near you? What is it?

▶ W 46, 3

4 Dartmoor plans

2◉3 **a) Look at the pictures and listen to Mr Rooney. What's he talking about?**

 b) Listen again. Put the notes about the trip in the right order: d, f, …

2◉3

Class trip to Dartmoor
Saturday, May 13th

a) arrive in Postbridge
b) have a picnic
c) get back to school
d) meet at school
e) visit the Information Centre
f) leave school
g) walk to Hartland Tor
h) talk to rangers

5.00 10.00 9.15 9.00

c) Write the notes in the right order in your exercise book. Then listen again and write the times. ▸ W 46, 4

INTERNET PROJECT – More about Dartmoor

a) Use the Internet. Go to www.new-highlight.de, find the window for the webcode and put in NHL-2-61.

b) Find out more about Dartmoor and make notes.

1 Where's Dartmoor? – *In …*
2 What big towns are near Dartmoor?
3 What towns are on Dartmoor?
4 Where are the Information Centres?
5 What activities can you do on Dartmoor?

c) Work in groups and make a Dartmoor poster.

1 **Before you read: Answer these questions in your groups.**

1 Do you like walking?
2 Where can you go walking?
3 Would you like to visit Dartmoor?

2 **Now read and find out:**

1 What's the ranger's name? *Serina*
2 Who was the 'guide' for the day? *Jamie*
3 Who wasn't very happy? *Emma*
4 Did the pupils have a good day? *Yes they did*

🔊 A DAY ON DARTMOOR

2⊙4

Class 8R and the teachers were in the Information
Centre in Postbridge, a small village on Dartmoor.
There were lots of maps and brochures about Dartmoor.
"This is Serina, a Dartmoor ranger," Mr Rooney said.

5 "She's going to give us some rules for walkers."
"Hello and welcome to Dartmoor," Serina said.
"When you're walking on the moor, please stay on the
tracks. Don't feed the ponies. And please take your litter
home. Dartmoor is a great place! I'm sure you're going

10 to have lots of fun."
"I'm not going to have fun!" Emma said to Sarah.

The group left the Information Centre and walked along
the road. The weather was nice. It was sunny and warm.
Jamie was the 'guide' for the day.

15 "We're going to walk along this track," he said.
"I don't like walking," Emma complained.

The track went along a river. The children saw some wild
Dartmoor ponies.
"I'm going to feed the ponies," Emma said and she

20 opened her bag.
"Look at the sign," Jamie said.
Then he looked at his map. "OK, we're going to climb
that hill now. It's Hartland Tor," he said.
"I hate hills," Emma complained.

25 Then the weather started to change.
It was cold now and there were black clouds.
"It's going to rain, I think," Mr Rooney said.
"Oh no!" Emma said. "I left my jacket on the bus."
Jamie had big black bags for litter.

30 "Here's a jacket," he said.
Everybody laughed, but it was a good 'jacket'.
"The weather is terrible here," Emma complained.

The pupils arrived at Hartland Tor. There were lots of big rocks.

35 "Listen," Mr Rooney said. "Jamie has a great idea."
"We're going to go letterboxing," Jamie said.
" Letterboxing? What's that?" Tariq asked.
"It's like a treasure hunt. First we have to find a box. So let's go!" Jamie said.

40 "This is stupid," Emma complained.

The pupils looked everywhere. They had lots of fun. After fifteen minutes Emma and Sarah found a box. They opened it and saw a visitors' book and a Hartland Tor stamp. It was very exciting.

45 "Look, Mr Rooney has a Drake School stamp for the visitors' book. We can write our names too. And I have a letterboxing book. I got it at the Information Centre. Now I'm going to put the Hartland Tor stamp in our letterboxing book," Jamie said.

50 "This is fun. Are there more boxes?" Sarah asked. "Yes," Jamie answered. "There's a box on lots of hills." They climbed three more hills. Nobody complained. They found three more boxes and collected three more 55 stamps.

At half past one they had a picnic in a wood next to a river. "Dartmoor is nice," Tom said.
"Letterboxing is great," Tariq said.
"Walking on Dartmoor is OK too," Emma 60 said. Everybody laughed.

63

sixty-three

---

3 It's all wrong! But what's right?

1 An Information Centre is a hill on Dartmoor.
2 Postbridge is a great activity.
3 A ranger is a village on Dartmoor.
4 A Dartmoor pony works in a national park.
5 Hartland Tor is a place where you can get maps.
6 Letterboxing is an animal on Dartmoor.

4 What are the signs in German?

Don't feed the ponies.

Take your litter home.

Please stay on the tracks.

5 Finish Emma's postcard to her grandad.

The words are in the story.

Dear Grandad,
We had a great day on … . First we went to … and we met a … . On the moor we saw … . Then we collected … .
Letterboxing is … .
Lots of love,
    Emma

John Miller
32 Paris Street
Exeter EX1 1JN

▶ W 47, 5–6

1 What's letterboxing? The words are all in the story.

1 First go to ...

2 Then climb a ...

3 Look for a ...

4 Find a ...

5 Put your ... in the book.

6 And write your ...

2 Weather words

a) The weekend weather

TOMORROW

Tomorrow the weather is/isn't going to be terrible. It's going to be very cold/warm. You're going to see lots of black/white clouds. And it's/it isn't going to rain.

But on Sunday the weather is/isn't going to change. It's going to be nice/terrible. You're/You aren't going to see clouds. It's going to be very sunny/cold.

SUNDAY

b) Work with a partner. Make a weather network.

3 Activities and people

a) Make new words.

1 walk – a walker
2 help – ...
3 read – ...
4 sing – ...

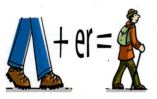

b) Make more words.

1 swim – a swim**mer**
2 run – ...
3 win – ...
4 plan – ...

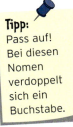

Tipp: Pass auf! Bei diesen Nomen verdoppelt sich ein Buchstabe.

c) What are these people? First think of the verbs.

a bus ...

a factory ...

a football ...

a rock ...

► W 48, 7–10 ► W ◯

Writing a letter

 Jamie is going to write a letter to Serina, the ranger.

a) He's making some notes for his letter. Match the notes on the right with the questions.

b) Now use the notes and write Jamie's letter to Serina.

1 Name?
2 School?
3 Class?
4 When?
5 Where?
6 Weather (morning)
7 Weather (afternoon)
8 Walked to?
9 Saw?
10 Activity?
11 How was the trip?

a) 8R
b) great
c) Saturday
d) Hartland Tor
e) Dartmoor ponies
f) Jamie Fraser
g) letterboxing
h) sunny and warm
i) Drake School
j) Postbridge
k) cold

Tipp:
Der Brief fängt immer mit *Dear* an. Dann schreibst du *Ms*, *Mrs* oder *Mr* und den Nachnamen – oder nur den Vornamen. Im Englischen verwendet man häufig den Vornamen. Danach folgt ein Komma und dann beginnst du mit einem großen Buchstaben.

Green Hill Farm,
Kenn,
Exeter EX6 7UQ

May 15th 20--

Dear Serina,
My name is (1) ... . I'm at (2) ... . And I'm in Class (3) ... .

We were on a class trip last (4) ... . We went to (5) ... .
Do you remember? We met you in the Information Centre.

In the morning the weather was (6) ... . But in the afternoon it was (7) ... . We walked to (8) ... . We saw some (9) ... . We went (10) ... . That was fun. The trip was (11) ... .

Best wishes,
    Jamie Fraser

PS I'm going to be a ranger when I'm older.
I hope you can give me some information about your job.

Tipp:
In englischen Briefen schreibst du immer deine Anschrift und das Datum oben rechts.

Tipp:
Der Brief endet immer mit einem Abschiedsgruß. Wenn du jemanden sehr gut kennst, schreibst du *Love* oder *Lots of love*. Sonst kannst du *Best wishes* verwenden.

 **Your letter**

a) Now make notes about a class trip.

The questions in 1 a) can help you.

 b) Write a letter to Jamie about your trip.

Name?
School?
Class?
When?
Where?
Weather?

▶W 49, 11 ▶W

COMMUNICATION

DESCRIPTIONS

LISTENING

1 **Jenny, Andy and Stacey are talking about their class trips.**

2◉5

a) Listen. Who's talking about picture A? Who's talking about picture B? And C?

b) Which picture is Princetown? Which picture is Plymouth? Which is Exmouth?

A

B

C

2 **Class trips**

2◉5

a) Write these notes in your exercise book.

Who?	Where?	Description?	Weather?
Jenny	...	big/...	cloudy/...
Andy	...	small/...	sunny/...
Stacey	...	not very big/...	terrible/...

b) Listen again to Jenny, Andy and Stacey and finish the notes about their trips. Use the words in the box.

Exmouth	boring	cold
Princetown	nice	warm
Plymouth	exciting	OK

3 **A family trip**

a) Make notes about a trip with your family.

Where?	Description?	Weather?
?	?	?

b) Talk to a partner about your trip.

We went to (where?) ...
It's (description) ...
It was (weather) ...

4 **PRONUNCIATION:**

2◉6

a) Listen. What places are they talking about?

b) Now listen to the names and repeat.

Alphington • Dartmoor
Exeter • Exmouth • Kenn
London • Plymouth
Postbridge

▶ W 50, 12–13

SPEAKING

5 **The Frasers live near Dartmoor, so Jamie's dad knows lots of rangers.**

2◉7   **a) Which ranger is Serina – A, B or C?**

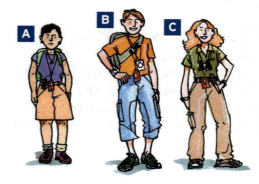

JAMIE	Dad, do you know Serina?
MR FRASER	What does she look like?
JAMIE	She's tall.
MR FRASER	How old is she?
JAMIE	About 20.
MR FRASER	What about her hair?
JAMIE	She has blonde hair.
MR FRASER	And is she nice?
JAMIE	Yes, she is. She's very friendly.
MR FRASER	Oh, yes! I think I know her.

b) Practise the dialogue with a partner.

6 **Another ranger**

a) Finish this dialogue.   Look at the pictures in exercise 5.

JAMIE	We met another ranger, a man.
MR FRASER	What does he look like?
JAMIE	He's …
MR FRASER	How old is he?
JAMIE	…
MR FRASER	What about his hair?
JAMIE	He has …
MR FRASER	And is he nice?
JAMIE	Yes, he is. He's …
MR FRASER	I think that's Ralph!

→ small • tall • very tall • about 20/30/40
blonde hair • black hair • brown hair
very friendly • terrible

b) Act the dialogue with a partner.

7 **Who is it? Work with a partner.**
Partner A: Think of a teacher at your
school. But don't say the name.
Partner B: Ask questions.

Use words in exercise 6 and Wordbank 10 on page 129.

A It's a woman/man.
B What does she/he look like?
A She's/He's …
B How old is she/he?
A About …
B What about her/his hair?
A She has … / He has …
B And is she/he nice?
A Yes, she/he is. She's/He's …. /
No, she/he isn't. She's/He's …

8 **AND YOU? Find an old picture of**
yourself. Write labels.

Put all the pictures and labels on the board.
Don't write your name on your picture.
Do the other pupils know who it is?

▸ Wordbank 10, p. 129
▸ W 51, 14–16   ▸ W ◉

DARTMOOR DIALOGUES

1 **Match the dialogues 1–6 with the pictures A–F.**

1 Are they going to feed the ponies?
– No, they aren't. They're going to have a picnic.

2 Is your dog going to eat our food?
– No, she isn't. She doesn't like cake!

3 Am I going to fall?
– No, you aren't going to fall. You're going to be OK!

4 Is the weather going to be OK?
– It isn't going to rain. But it's going to be cloudy!

5 Are we going to climb this hill?
– No, we aren't going to climb this hill. We're going to climb that hill!

6 Are you going to wear your jacket, Tom?
– I'm not going to wear it. I'm going to put it in my bag.

2 WORD SEARCH

a) **Find the missing words on pages 60–68.**

1 What ... they going to visit? (p. 60)
2 She'... going to give us some rules. (p. 62)
3 I'... not going to have fun! (p. 62)
4 We'... going to walk along this track. (p. 62)
5 ... I going to fall? (p. 68)
6 ... the weather going to be OK? (p. 68)
7 ... we going to climb this hill? (p. 68)
8 No, we ... going to climb this hill. (p. 68)

b) **Now find these words on pages 62–68.**

1 I'm sure you're ... lots of fun. (p. 62)
2 I'm ... the ponies! (p. 62)
3 I'm ... the Hartland Tor stamp in our letterboxing book. (p. 63)
4 Jamie is ... a letter to Serina. (p. 65)
5 They're ... a picnic. (p. 68)
6 Are you ... your jacket, Tom? (p. 68)

3 OVER TO YOU!

Finish the checkpoint.

Can you think of more examples?

Die Zukunft mit *going to*

Going to benutzt du, um zu sagen,
- was du vorhast oder
- dass etwas wahrscheinlich geschehen wird.

Vor *going to* brauchst du *I'm, you're,* ...
Nach *going to* steht immer das Verb im
Infinitiv, z.B. *have, be,* ...

▶ Eine Übersicht über diese Regeln
findest du auf der Summary-Seite 101.
▶ Extra practice, pp. 98 ff.
▶ W 52–53

NACH DIESER UNIT KANN ICH ...

Sportarten und Freizeitaktivitäten benennen.	▶ *rock climbing, cycling, swimming, ...*
Landschaften beschreiben.	▶ *There are hills, a moor, a wood, ...*
über Pläne sprechen.	▶ *We're going to visit Dartmoor.*
über das Wetter sprechen.	▶ *It's sunny and warm.*
Wettervorhersagen machen.	▶ *It's going to rain tomorrow.*
von einem Ausflug erzählen.	▶ *We went to Exeter. It's a big town.*
Personen beschreiben.	▶ *She's tall. She has brown hair.*
einen Brief schreiben.	▶ *Dear Thomas,* *...*

Goodbye to Exeter!

Exeter is in Devon. Devon is in England, of course!
England's neighbours are Scotland, Wales and Ireland.

1 Which neighbour are the people talking about? 1 … 2 … 3 …

2◉ 8

2 AND YOU? Talk to a partner about places near you.

Have you ever been to Stuttgart/Düsseldorf/France/…?

Dortmund

Yes, I have.

No, I haven't.

► W 55, 1

ACTIVITY – A poem

a) Read this poem.

> I've never been to Exmouth,
> I've never been to Rome,
> I've never been to Alphington,
> I always stay at home!

 b) Make your own poem.

> I've never been to ...,
> I've never been to Rome,
> I've never been to ...,
> I always stay at home!

Think of very small places for lines 1 and 3. It's funnier!

c) Listen to the poems in class. Who has the funniest poem?

ACTIVITY – Neighbours

a) Who are Germany's neighbours?

1 Denmark, 2 ...

→
- Austria
- Belgium
- ~~Denmark~~
- France
- The Netherlands
- Luxembourg
- Poland
- Switzerland
- The Czech Republic

b) Talk to a partner about Germany's neighbours.

– I've been to ...
– I've never been to ...
– I'd like to visit ...

 c) Draw a map of Germany and its neighbours. Write the names of the countries on the map.

► W 55, 2

THE INVITATION

1 Who's leaving Drake School? Find out.

2⊙ 9

EMMA I've finished exercise 1. What about you, Jamie?

JAMIE I've finished it too. It was easy – like a quiz. I love quizzes!

EMMA Yes, I know!

JAMIE I hope you haven't made plans for the last weekend in July. I'm going to have a goodbye party. I'll give you your invitations in the break.

TOM Goodbye? Are you leaving Devon?

JAMIE Yes, I am. I'm going to Oban.

SARAH You're leaving Drake School? Oh no! And where's Oban? Is it in England?

2 Why is he leaving? Find out.

TOM What has happened? Why are you going?

JAMIE It's my grandad. He's very old. He needs help.

EMMA And have your parents found a new house?

JAMIE Yes, they have. They've bought a house with lots of bedrooms!

SARAH But there are only three people in your family.

JAMIE The house is a hotel. Mum and dad want to do something different.

EMMA You're a good friend, Jamie. This is terrible!

SARAH Let's look at our invitations now.

TOM OK, but Jamie hasn't told us where Oban is.

JAMIE It's in Scotland – 600 miles from here!

ALL Oh no!

3 Questions

1 Has Jamie finished exercise 1?
2 What's Jamie going to have in July?
3 Does Sarah know where Oban is?

4 Who needs help?
5 Have Jamie's parents found a new house?
6 Where's Oban?

4 Jamie's invitation:
What do the three friends have?

 book • invitation card • magazine
map • postcard • poster • quiz

a ...,

and a ...!

Please come to my party on Saturday, July 31st, at two o'clock. Place: Green Hill Farm, Kenn Jamie

An ...,

5 ACTIVITY: Quiz time

With a partner help the friends with the quiz.

Jamie's quiz
A **different** way to Green Hill Farm

1 Saturday 10 o'clock. Come to **"SELDDAP dna SELDDAS"** in Exeter.

2 Come on your ■■■■S.
My first letter is in BOOK but not in LOOK. Letter 2 is in BIG but not in BAG. Letter 3 is in PARK but not in PART. Letter 4 is in EAT but not in CAT.

3 Follow the river track to this place: ■■■■ Cafe.
(You're going to get crisps and orange juice there.)
My first letter rhymes with SEA.
(not B, C, D, E, G, P, V!)
Letter 2 rhymes with NEW.
Letter 3 rhymes with CAR.
Letter 4 rhymes with JEFF.

4 When you leave the place in **3** there are dangerous things:
■■■■■■
The word for them starts with the last letter of the first word:
BUT RAIN STOPS

5 Go to this village: ■■■■■■
It has **my village in the name.**
There's lemonade for you at the cafe.

6 Meet me at the Green Hill ■■■■ ■■■■ for your prize.

You've done it!

> That's easy.

> Start with the last letter of the last word.

> It's "Sad ____ and _____."

TOM   That's B.
EMMA   Letter 2 is I.
SARAH   Letter 3 is ...
Letter 4 is ... . It's ■■■■S!

SARAH   The first letter is T.
TOM   It can't be Q. It's ...
EMMA   It's ■■■■! *The* ■■■■ *Cafe.*
Look at the English alphabet on page 167.

TOM   The first word is BUT.
EMMA   The last letter of BUT is T.
SARAH   It's TR■■■S!

TOM   Jamie's village is Kenn.
EMMA   We need a place with the letters K, E and two Ns in the name.
SARAH   It's ■■■■ON!
Look at the map on page 72.

> That's "f___ shop"!

What's the prize?
See page 79.

1 **Which is the best picture for the story?**

A

B

C

Tipp:
Lies die Geschichte einmal kurz durch. Du musst nicht jedes Wort verstehen. Du solltest nur erkennen, worum es geht.

2 **Who did something very dangerous, but helped a child? Find out.**

HAVE YOU EVER DONE THIS?

2⊙ 10

5

10

It was the day of Jamie's party. Emma, Sarah and Tom were on their bikes. It was great. In some places there were two tracks. One of the tracks was wide, but the other was narrow – and it was very near to the canal. Emma stayed on the wider track, but Tom and Sarah went on the narrow track. They wanted to be tough! But they were often very near to the canal, too near!

"Have you ever done this?" Tom shouted to Emma. "Look! No hands!"

"No, I haven't," Emma shouted back. "I don't want to fall in the canal."

"What was the name of the cafe?" asked Emma later.

"*Turf,*" said Sarah. "Look! That's it," said Sarah.

There was a small bridge across the canal to the cafe. Emma
15 and Sarah walked across. Tom was behind them.

"Have you ever done this?" he shouted. He was hanging from the bridge by his arms!

"No, we haven't," said Sarah. "We don't want to look stupid! And it's very dangerous." Tom climbed back onto the bridge
20 and the three friends went to the cafe.

The three friends had a glass of orange juice and crisps in the garden of *The Turf Cafe* and looked out across the River Exe. The river was very wide here, because it was near the sea.

"What were the dangerous things in question 4 again?" Tom
25 asked Emma.

"Trains," she said. "Our track goes across the railway line soon." Tom looked at her. "Ooh, exciting! Is it too exciting for you, Emma?"

30 Twenty minutes later they came to a gate. Behind it was the railway line from Exeter to Dawlish. A sign said, "Listen and watch for trains before you go across the line." They listened.

35 A train!

"I don't want to wait for the train," said Tom. "I'll open the gate."

"No," said Emma. "It's too dangerous. The train

40 is very near."

"OK, OK. We can wait," said Tom.

Then Emma saw a small boy on the other side of the line. He opened the gate. He was running after a football.

It was on the line. "Bang!" The gate closed behind the boy.

45 "Hurry!" Emma shouted and opened the gate on her side of the line. "The train is coming!" But the boy fell. Emma ran onto the line, picked up the boy and ran back to the others, just before the train came.

"Have you ever done *that*?" she shouted to Tom.

3 Who ...?

1 ... didn't go on the bike trip?
2 ... went on the narrow track?
3 ... was stupid on the bridge?
4 ... had orange juice and crisps?
5 ... didn't want to wait for the train?
6 ... helped the boy?

4 Pick the words.

1 Emma didn't want to be right/tough.
2 She didn't want to fall in the canal/cafe.
3 Tom was hanging from a bike/bridge.
4 There was a sign near the cafe/gate.
5 There was a small/big boy.
6 He was running after a friend/football.

5 What did Emma tell her mum?

There was a small ... . His friends were on the other ... of the line. The boy was ... after a football. But he ... . I ran ... the line. I picked up the ... and ... back to Tom and Sarah.

6 Talk to a partner about the text. Then tell the class. Here are some ideas.

Did Emma do the right thing?

YES: I think she did the right thing.
It was very dangerous.
She was very tough.
She only thought of the small boy.

NO: I think she did the wrong thing.
It was very dangerous.
She was very stupid.
She didn't think of her parents.

▶ W 56, 3–4

WORDPOWER

1 **Find the partners.** Look at the story on pages 74 and 75.

 road • canal
dangerous • gate
lemonade • wide

+

 door • street • river
long • juice • tough

road – street
canal – …

2 **ODD WORD OUT**

1 track, sea, street, road
2 canal, sea, ground, river
3 tough, friendly, nice, happy
4 arm, hand, glass, foot
5 lemonade, cola, tea, water
6 train, gate, bus, ship

3 **Match the words.**

Look at the story on pages 74 and 75.

1	the day	of the line
2	one	of the tracks
3	the name	of *The Turf Cafe*
4	a glass	of Jamie's party
5	the garden	of orange juice
6	the other side	of the cafe

4 **Match the words with the pictures.**

A Have you ever done this?
B Can you help me with this?
C Is that your dad?
D Is this your dog?
E Where did you buy that?
F What was that?

5 **What are they saying? – "I'll …"**

I'll

take your bag.
get the lemonade.
pick up the bike.
wait with the dog.
help you with the food.
open the gate.

► W 57, 5–7 ► W ○

An invitation to a party

Please come to my party on August 5th.

It's my goodbye party.
We're going to play football.
Then we're going to have a picnic.

The party starts at six o'clock.
It finishes at ten o'clock.
I live at 34 Exe Street, Exeter.
Phone: 01392 734537

Ben

1 Look at the photos. Write the invitation. Ben's invitation can help you.

 2 AND YOU: Write an invitation to your next birthday. Here's help with the dates:

1st	the **first**	11th	the eleventh	21st	
2nd	the **second**	12th	the **twelfth**		the **twenty-first**
3rd	the **third**	13th	the thirteenth	30th	
4th	the fourth	14th	the fourteenth		the thirtieth
5th	the **fifth**	15th	the fifteenth	31st	
6th	the sixth	16th	the sixteenth		the thirty-first
7th	the seventh	17th	the seventeenth		
8th	the **eighth**	18th	the eighteenth		
9th	the **ninth**	19th	the nineteenth		
10th	the tenth	20th	the **twentieth**		

January	July
February	August
March	September
April	October
May	November
June	December

22.12.
December 22nd
("December the
twenty-second")

▶ Wordbank 11, p. 129
▶ W 58, 8–9 ▶ W ⊙

AT A PARTY

LISTENING

 1 Jamie's party

2⊙11 **a)** It's the day of Jamie's party. Where are Jamie's friends? Listen and find out.

b) Match the sentences.

1 I've taken the prizes to the farm shop, Mum.
2 I've checked the quads.
3 I've taken the chairs to the farm shop too.
4 I've written all the questions for the party quiz.
5 I've made some of my home-made lemonade.
6 I've phoned Tom and the others.

A Great. Was quad 3 OK too?
B Where are they now? In Kenton?
C I hope your friends can find them!
D OK. People can sit there later.
E I hope the questions are easy!
F Great! Your friends are going to want a drink.

 c) Listen again and check your answers to b).

2⊙11

2 Party problems: Match the pictures and the sentences.

A I've just phoned Pete. He can't come.
B I've just checked the food.
   There are no crisps.
C I've just been to the living room.
   It's very cold in there.

D I've just talked to our neighbours.
   They don't like the music.
E I've just found out where the dog is!
F I've just tried the salad. It isn't OK!

▶ W 59, 10

SPEAKING

3 **The friends are all at the farm now.**

2◉12 **a)** **What are they going to do? Find out.**

JAMIE Have you all found your prizes in the farm shop?

EMMA Yes, we have. Great! Three books of quizzes!
Er, thanks, Jamie.

TOM Have your parents found a nice school for you
in Scotland?

JAMIE Yes, they have. It's near our new hotel.

SARAH And have you packed all your things, Jamie?

JAMIE No, I haven't. I don't want to start!

EMMA You've been a great friend, Jamie.

JAMIE Thanks. Hey, it's quad time now. Who wants to be first?

b) **Practise the dialogue with three partners.**

4 **An hour later**

a) **Finish the dialogue.**   Look at exercise 3.

JAMIE Have you all been on the quads?

EMMA ... Great! Thanks, Jamie.

TOM ... your parents ... a nice room for you in your hotel?

JAMIE Yes, of course they have – Room 007!

SARAH And ... you said goodbye to your friends in Kenn?

JAMIE ... I don't want to start!

b) **Listen and check.**   **c)** **Act the dialogue with partners.**

2◉13

5 **ROLE PLAY: After the party**
Partner A: You're a parent.
Talk to Partner B on the phone.

**Partner B: Pick a boy or girl. Then look at
page 124 and answer Partner A's questions.**

Have you ...

A done all the jobs in the kitchen?

B been to the park with the dog?

C talked to the neighbours?

D taken their chairs back?

E opened all the windows?

F written your "thank you" letters?

– Good!/

– Well, do it now, please!

LISA   BEN   LILLY   KEVIN

▶ W 59, 11–12 ▶ W ◉

JAMIE'S GOODBYE PARTY

1 What were the answers? Find the sentences for A–D.

1 I like quads too.
2 Yes, I have. They're very good.

3 No, I haven't.
   But I'd like to visit you, Jamie.
4 Try it. It's great.

2 More dialogues from the party. Match the sentences.

1 I've been to Scotland.
2 I've had too many hamburgers.
3 I've just played with Tess.
4 Have you seen Jamie?
5 Has Mrs Fraser ever ridden a quad?
6 Have your parents bought another farm?

A Yes, she has. Quad 3 is her favourite.
B No, they haven't. They've bought a hotel.
C Well, go again! You can visit me.
D Oh, Tom! You always eat too much.
E Yes, I have. He's in the farm shop, I think.
F Where is she? I want to play with her too.

3 WORD SEARCH
Find these words in the unit.

1 ... you ever been to Stuttgart? (p. 70)
2 What ... happened? (p. 72)
3 ... Jamie finished exercise 1? (p. 72)
4 ... Jamie's parents found a new house? (p. 72)
5 ... your parents found a nice school for you in Scotland? (p. 79)
6 ... Mrs Fraser ever ridden a quad? (p. 80)

4 WORD SEARCH

a) Find these words in the unit.

1 I've never ... to Rome. (p. 71)
2 Jamie hasn't ... us where Oban is. (p. 72)
3 I've ... the prizes to the farm shop, Mum. (p. 78)
4 I've ... the quads. (p. 78)
5 I've just ... with Tess. (p. 80)
6 They've ... a hotel. (p. 80)

b) Now find these words.

1 Have you ever ... that? (p. 75)
2 Have you all ... your prizes in the farm shop? (p. 79)
3 And have you ... all your things, Jamie? (p. 79)
4 Have you all ... on the quads? (p. 79)?
5 Have you ... Jamie? (p. 80)
6 Have your parents ... another farm? (p. 80)

5 OVER TO YOU!
Finish the checkpoint.

Can you find more examples?

CHECKPOINT

Present perfect
Mit dem *present perfect* sagst du,
• dass etwas soeben oder schon einmal geschehen ist:
  I've just seen Jim. I've been to Poland.
• dass etwas (noch) nicht oder (noch) nie geschehen ist:
  I haven't phoned mum. I've never been to London.
Du kannst auch fragen, ob etwas schon einmal geschehen ist:
Have you ever been to Rome?

Das *present perfect* bildest du mit *'ve* oder ... und einer besonderen Form des Verbs, dem Partizip Perfekt.
• Regelmäßige Verben haben die Endung *-ed*. Beispiel:
  work – worked; play – played; ...
• Einige Verben haben unregelmäßige Formen. Diese musst du lernen. Beispiel: *write – written; be – been; ...*

▶ Eine Übersicht über diese Regeln findest du auf der *Summary*-Seite 105

▶ Extra Practice, pp. 102 ff.

▶ W 60–61

NACH DIESER UNIT KANN ICH ...

sagen, was soeben geschehen ist.	▶ *I've just played football.*
sagen, was schon einmal geschehen ist.	▶ *I've been to France. I've ridden a quad.*
sagen, was (noch) nicht geschehen ist.	▶ *I haven't finished exercise 1.*
sagen, was (noch) nie geschehen ist.	▶ *I've never been to Belgium.*
fragen, ob etwas schon einmal geschehen ist.	▶ *Have you ever been to Rome?*
Deutschlands Nachbarländer nennen.	▶ *Austria, Belgium, Denmark, France, The Netherlands, Luxembourg, Poland, Switzerland, The Czech Republic*
spontan Hilfe anbieten.	▶ *I'll open the gate. I'll help you with the food.*
jemanden einladen.	▶ *Please come to my party.*

Weitere Übungen: www.new-highlight.de

▶ W 62, Test yourself ▶ W 63–64, Portfolio ▶ W ⊙

▶ Extra reading, pp. 120–121

1 It's Friday morning.
What's the right answer: a) or b)?

1 What's Emma doing?
a) She's going to bed.
b) She's getting up.

2 What's Jamie doing?
a) He's going to school.
b) He's going home.

3 What are the Prices doing?
a) They're having breakfast.
b) They're playing football.

4 Sarah, what are you doing?
a) I'm visiting my grandma.
b) I'm saying goodbye to Sammy.

5 Jake and Amy, what are you doing?
a) We're going to the cinema.
b) We're walking to the bus.

6 **Teacher**: And what am I doing now?
a) You're speaking English now.
b) You're speaking French now.

2 It's half past three on Friday afternoon.
Write the text and put in 'm, 're or 's.

The first red box on page 85 can help you.

School is over and all the pupils are in the playground. They... going home. "Where's Tom?" Jamie asks Tariq. "He... talking to Ms Trevor in the teachers' room." Sarah is next to the door and she... looking at Tom. "Hurry up, Tom. We... waiting for you," she says. Ms Trevor says, "Ah Sarah, you... listening to me too – good! I... explaining a maths exercise. Come and sit next to Tom."

3 It's eight o'clock on Friday evening. Write the dialogue in your exercise book.

Sarah is at home. She (talk) ... to Emma on the phone.
SARAH What are you doing, Emma?
EMMA I (do) ... my homework. What about you?
SARAH We (watch) ... TV. It's *Mr Bean* and he's great.
Listen to mum: "Ha, ha, ha!" She (laugh) ... now.
EMMA My mum and brother aren't here.
They (visit) ... my grandma this evening.
SARAH Oh, you (stay) ... at home alone this evening!
EMMA No, I (come) ... to your house! Is that OK?
SARAH Yes, great! I can ask my mum and dad.

4 Which text is right: a or b? Look at the picture.

a) TOM

I'm not feeling very happy. My friends aren't talking to me. Jamie isn't sitting next to me. And I'm not reading a book about bikes – I'm reading a book about school!

b) TOM

Tariq and Jamie are sitting next to me. Tariq is laughing. We're making plans for the weekend. And I'm reading a great book – it's a book about bikes!

5 That's nonsense!

→ going • reading • feeling • singing

a) Can you find the right verb?

1 I'm eating a book.
   – That's nonsense! You aren't eating a book. You're reading a book.
2 You're walking a song about school now.
   – That's nonsense! I'm not walking a song. I'm … a song.
3 Tom is talking tired.
   – That's nonsense! Tom isn't … tired. He's … tired.
4 It's half past three and we're sitting home now.
   – That's nonsense. We aren't … home now. We're … home now.

b) What's right?

1 I'm standing breakfast now. – That's nonsense! You aren't … You're …
2 You're eating TV. – That's nonsense! I'm …
3 Sarah is sleeping next to Emma in class 8R. – That's nonsense! She …
4 The girls are sharing their friends after school. – That's nonsense! They …

6 Write sentences for the pictures.

I'm not …

Sarah isn't …

Tom and Tariq aren't …

7 **Questions – but which is the right answer: a, b or c?**

1 What are you doing?
a) She's doing her homework.
b) We're playing a game.
c) They're talking.

2 Why are you laughing?
a) I'm watching *Mr Bean* on TV.
b) I'm going to bed.
c) I'm not feeling very well.

3 Is Tom coming?
a) Yes, they are.
b) No, she isn't.
c) Yes, he is.

4 Are you feeling OK?
a) Sarah is feeling tired.
b) I'm fine, thanks.
c) Thanks.

5 Are we going to town now?
a) Yes, we are. Hurry up!
b) No, he isn't. He's helping his mum.
c) No, she isn't. She's staying at home.

8 **Make questions for the answers.**

1 What / ? / you / are / doing — I'm writing an e-mail.
2 ? / eating / Are / chocolate / you — Yes, I am. Do you want some?
3 your English homework / Are / doing / ? / you — No, I'm not. I'm doing my maths homework.
4 are / What / ? / looking at / you — I'm looking at you!
5 now / we / Are / ? / going home — Yes, we are. It's half past three.

9 **AND YOU?**

a) **Make six questions about people in your class.**

Are	you / the boys / the girls / we	feeling OK / laughing / talking / speaking English / doing homework / making plans / eating chocolate / going home	listening to the teacher / singing / using your ruler / working / reading a magazine / sleeping	now?
Is	Alex / Anna / your partner / the teacher			

b) **Practise the questions and answers with a partner.**
Look at the box *Fragen und Kurzantworten* on page 85.

→ Yes, I am. • No, I'm not. • Yes, she is. • No, he isn't. • Yes, we are. • No, we aren't.
Yes, they are. • No, they aren't. • …

PRESENT PROGRESSIVE

Mit der Verlaufsform der Gegenwart (*present progressive*) sagst du, was gerade geschieht oder nicht geschieht.

Mit dieser Form kannst du auch sagen, was du planst.

Are you making a cake?
– Yes, I am. I'm making a chocolate cake.

Am I going to school with you?
– No, you aren't. You're staying at home.

Aussagen

I'm You're She's He's We're They're	doing homework.

Verneinungen

I'm not You aren't She isn't He isn't We aren't They aren't	singing.

Fragen und Kurzantworten

Am	I	
Are	you we they	singing?
Is	he she	

Yes,	I am. you are. we are. they are. he is. she is.

No,	I'm not. you aren't. we aren't. they aren't. he isn't. she isn't.

Tipp:
Ein stummes **e** am Ende des Verbs fällt bei der **-ing**-Form weg.

arriv**e** – arriving   mak**e** – making
com**e** – coming   rid**e** – riding
hav**e** – having   shar**e** – sharing
invit**e** – inviting   writ**e** – writing

Tipp:
Bei manchen Verben wird der letzte Buchstabe verdoppelt.

ge**t** – ge**tt**ing   sto**p** – sto**pp**ing
si**t** – si**tt**ing   ru**n** – ru**nn**ing

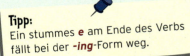

EXTRA PRACTICE

1 **Pick the right word.**

1 Germany is bigger/faster than England.
2 English is smaller/easier than German.
3 Planes are faster/smaller than trains.
4 England is nearer/older to Germany than Florida.
5 Saturdays are nicer/bigger than Mondays.
6 Bike tracks are faster/quieter than roads.

2 **Match the slogans with the pictures.**

a) Our newest shop!

b) Our smallest CD player!

c) Our quietest plane!

d) Our cheapest cola!

e) Our fastest car!

f) Our biggest hamburger!

3 **Make three lists.**   Pages 32 and 89 can help you with this exercise.

good	...	...
...	worse	...
early	...	...
...	dirtier	...
...	...	easiest

sporty   sportier   sportiest

4 **Say it in English!**

1 „Das rote Auto war schneller."
– *The red car was ...*

2 „Dies ist das hungrigste Tier auf dem Bauernhof."
– *This is the ... on the farm.*

3 „Ich bin sportlicher als meine Schwester."
– *I'm ... than ...*

4 „Motorräder sind schlimmer als Autos."
– *Motorbikes are ...*

5 „Dies ist der beste Laden in der Straße."

6 „Dies ist die ruhigste Straße in Berlin."

5 Harry and Sally went on two different tours to Exeter. Finish the sentences.

most boring • more interesting
most dangerous • more expensive

Sally's guide was ... than Harry's guide.

Harry's bus driver was the ... driver in England!

The museum was the ... place on the tour for Harry.

Harry's tour was ... than Sally's tour.

6 ODD WORD OUT

Tipp:
Du findest die Lösung, wenn du die Adjektive steigerst. Je ein Adjektiv wird nach einem anderen Muster gesteigert.

cool, old, *expensive*, new

1 easy, early, hungry, interesting
2 expensive, dangerous, young, frightened
3 big, small, cheap, exciting
4 small, hungry, fast, boring
5 important, exciting, big, boring

7 Jutta and Tom: Finish the sentences.

Tipp:
Benutze das Lösungswort aus *exercise 6* in der richtigen Vergleichsform.

It's the *most expensive* T-shirt in the shop.

1 This isn't the ... exercise in the book!
2 Sal is ten. She's the ... girl in the class.
3 Pete says *Shrek* is the ... film in Exeter.
4 But I think it's the ... film in the world!
5 Debenhams? It's the ... shop in Exeter.

8 Find six different things in picture B.

1 The DVD is more exciting in picture B.
2 The girl is ...
3 The dog is ...
4 The CD is ...
5 The boy is ...
6 The DVD player is ...

● **9** **From Krefeld to Exeter**
Lots of things are wrong on this page from the Drake School magazine.
a) **Read the text.**

FROM KREFELD TO EXETER

1 Tom Price in class 8R has a visitor from Germany. It's his sister Jutta. She works in Krefeld. Her teachers thought a trip to Exeter was a good idea.

2 Jutta is having a terrible time in Exeter. She went to town with Tom and his father. She saw the Exe. She said the Exe was a very big town. "The Rhine is much smaller than the Exe," she said.

3 Jutta went to the Underground Passages with Mr Price. The teacher said, "This is our smallest street. Who wants to go in?" Jutta went in, but it was too boring for her! So she went to a field with Tom and had a nice cup of English water!

b) **Make a list of the wrong things.**

1 *sister – works – …*
2 *terrible – … – … –*
3 *Mr Price – … – … – … – … –…*

c) **Find the right things.**
Look at pages 24, 26 and 27 again.

1 *cousin – …*
2 *nice – …*
3 *Tom – …*

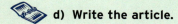

d) **Write the article.**

1 *Tom Price in class 8R has a visitor from Germany. It's his cousin Jutta. She …*

e) **Draw Jutta for your article.**

VERGLEICHE

Personen und Sachen kann man miteinander vergleichen.

The blue bag is cheap.

The red bag is cheaper than the blue bag.

The green bag is the cheapest bag in the shop.

Expensive, ...

... more expensive, ...

... the most expensive bike.

Sarah is younger than Tom. She's the youngest girl in the class.
Sarah ist jünger als Tom. Sie ist das jüngste Mädchen in der Klasse.
Heathrow is more important than Exeter Airport. It's the most important airport in England.
Heathrow ist wichtiger als der Flughafen Exeter. Es ist der wichtigste Flughafen Englands.

Bei den meisten Adjektiven hängst du *-er* bzw. *-est* an das Adjektiv, um die Vergleichsformen zu bilden.

Manchmal musst du bei der Schreibweise aufpassen:

Diese Formen musst du auswendig lernen:

cool	cool**er**	cool**est**
new	new**er**	new**est**
old	old**er**	old**est**
fast	fast**er**	fast**est**

big	bi**gg**er	bi**gg**est
easy	easi**er**	easi**est**
nice	nic**er**	nic**est**

good	**better**	**best**
bad	**worse**	**worst**

Bei einigen, meist längeren Adjektiven setzt du *more* bzw. *most* vor das Adjektiv, um die Vergleichsformen zu bilden.

boring	**more** boring	**most** boring
frightened	**more** frightened	**most** frightened

Hier sind alle anderen Adjektive, die du bis jetzt kennst, die mit *more* bzw. *most* gesteigert werden.

→ dangerous • exciting • expensive • important • interesting • modern • terrible

1 **My day: Write the sentences for Sarah.**

1 I / at half past seven / got up
2 had breakfast / Jake and I / At quarter to eight
3 we / went to school / Then
4 in the break / had some fruit / I
5 came home / At four o'clock / I
6 played with Sammy / I / in the afternoon
7 we / watched TV / In the evening
8 went to bed / at nine o'clock / Amy and I

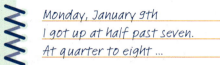

Monday, January 9th
I got up at half past seven.
At quarter to eight ...

Tipp:
Zeitangaben wie *at four o'clock*, *in the break* oder *in the afternoon* stehen am Anfang oder am Ende des Satzes.

2 **Mum's day: Now write these sentences.**
Exercise 1 can help you.

Yesterday mum ... up at six o'clock. She ... breakfast alone. Then she ... to town on her motorbike. She ... a salad at dad's restaurant at one o'clock. At half past five mum ... home. She ... a game with Amy. In the evening she ... TV with Jake, Amy, dad and me. She ... to bed at half past ten.

3 **Dad's day: Look at the pictures. Write eight sentences about Sarah's dad.**
Exercise 2 can help you.

1 Yesterday dad got up at .... 2 He ...

4 **Your day: Write about your day yesterday.**

Yesterday I got up at ...

5 **A day in *The Sun* (1): Pick the right verb.**

It was/were Saturday morning. Sarah, Amy, Jake and Mrs Johnson was/were in bed. Mr Johnson left/laughed the house at seven o'clock. He shared/stopped at a shop in Church Road. He bought/borrowed a magazine. Then he opened/closed his restaurant at half past seven.

6 **A day in *The Sun* (2): Put in the verbs.**

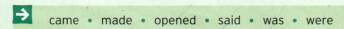

➜ came • made • opened • said • was • were

At eleven o'clock the door ... . Two people ... in. They ... young people – a boy and a girl. "Two salad rolls," the girl ... . Mr Johnson ... very quiet. He ... the rolls.

7 **A day in *The Sun* (3): Use the simple past forms of the verbs.**

The two people ... (eat) their rolls. Then they ... (get) up. They ... (go) to the door. They ... (leave) *The Sun*. "Wait!" Mr Johnson ... (say). He ... (go) to the door. He ... (open) the door and he ... (shout), "Come back!" But the young people only ... (laugh). Then something ... (happen).

8 **A day in *The Sun* (4): Finish the story.**   Use the simple past.

A

young people – go – to – car

B

go – to – Church Street – traffic lights – red

C

then – they – have – accident

D

police officer – arrive – Mr Johnson – come – too – he – not happy

9 **Sarah's postcard: It's a long weekend and Sarah is in London.**

a) Read her postcard to Emma.

Dear Emma,
We're in London. The weather is terrible.
We arrived here on Friday. The trip was OK
– we went by car.
We visited my grandma. We had lunch in a
small restaurant yesterday. I had pizza. It
was nice.
In the evening we went to the cinema.
See you soon. Bye,
        Sarah

Emma Baker

75 Queens Road

Alphington

Exeter EX2 9EW

b) Read the postcard again. Then match the questions and the answers.

1	Where?
2	Weather?
3	Arrived when?
4	Trip?
5	Visited?
6	Food?
7	In the evening?

a	Terrible!
b	OK – by car.
c	Cinema.
d	Lunch – small restaurant – pizza.
e	London.
f	Grandma.
g	On Friday.

10 **Jamie's postcard: Write Jamie's postcard in your exercise book.**

1	Where?	Newcastle.
2	Weather?	Nice.
3	Arrived when?	Yesterday.
4	Trip?	Long – by train.
5	Visited?	Mum's friends.
6	Food?	Lunch – fish and chips.
7	In the evening?	Walked in town.

Dear Tom,
We're in
arrived here
went by
lunch in a
It was nice
See you,
        Jamie

11 **Your postcard: It's a long weekend and you're in a nice place.**
Write a postcard in your exercise book
to Jamie or Sarah.

Before you write your postcard make some notes.
Look at exercise 10.

Jamie Fraser
Green Hill Farm
Kenn
Exeter EX6 7UQ
England

Sarah Johnson
11 Fairfield Road
Alphington
Exeter EX2 3QR
England

SIMPLE PAST (1)

Mit der einfachen Vergangenheit *(simple past)* sagst du, was in der Vergangenheit geschah.

Yesterday I went to school
in Sarah's bag.

The pupils saw me
and they laughed.

Regelmäßige Verben haben die Endung *-ed*.

Last Saturday I helped my dad.
Letzten Samstag habe ich meinem Vater geholfen./
Letzten Samstag half ich meinem Vater.
Yesterday we played football.
Gestern haben wir Fußball gespielt./
Gestern spielten wir Fußball.

arrive – arriv**ed**	like – lik**ed**
close – clos**ed**	live – liv**ed**
finish – finish**ed**	play – play**ed**
follow – follow**ed**	talk – talk**ed**
invite – invit**ed**	wait – wait**ed**
learn – learn**ed**	walk – walk**ed**

Unregelmäßige Verben haben besondere Vergangenheitsformen.

We came to England last May.
Wir sind letzten Mai nach England gekommen./
Wir kamen letzten Mai nach England.
I went to my grandma's house at Christmas.
Weihnachten bin ich zu meiner Oma gegangen./
Weihnachten ging ich zu meiner Oma.

buy – **bought**	know – **knew**
come – **came**	leave – **left**
fall – **fell**	make – **made**
get – **got**	meet – **met**
go – **went**	say – **said**
have – **had**	see – **saw**
hurt – **hurt**	sit – **sat**

▶ Look at the list on page 169.

Diese *time words* findest du oft in Sätzen im *simple past:*

last week	**in** January	**on** January 1st	**at** one o'clock
last month	in May	on May 2nd	at quarter past two
last year	in August	on August 3rd	at half past three
last Sunday	in December	on December 4th	at quarter to four

after a month • yesterday • in the summer holidays •
at Christmas • at the weekend • on Monday

o 1 At a department store: Match the pictures and the questions.

A Did you bring your money?
B Did you see our teacher?
C Did you buy the yellow T-shirt?
D Did you like the cake?
E Did you speak German?
F Did you pay for that, young man?

o 2 At school: Put the words in the right order.

1 his homework / yesterday / Pete / Did / do / ?
2 you / Did / the rolls / make / ?
3 you / with Sally Lee / on Saturday / see / Did I / ?
4 Did / win / the football match / the boys / ?
5 last week / the story / Did we / finish / ?
6 Tom and Philip / last week / go to judo club / Did / ?

● 3 At school: Say it in English.
Exercise 2 can help you.

1 Hast du gestern deine Hausaufgaben gemacht?
2 Hat deine Mutter die Brötchen gemacht?
3 Hat Jane dich gestern mit Sally Lee gesehen?
4 Hat Toms Team das Spiel gewonnen?
5 Habt ihr letzte Woche die Geschichte zu Ende gelesen?
6 Bist du letzte Woche zum Judo gegangen?

● 4 What were the police officer's questions about the *Securex* report?

Securex report
The boy looked at the caps. He had a big bag. He talked to a friend. His friend helped. They put six caps in the bag. They ran out of the store.

1 Did you look at the caps? – Yes, I did.
2 Did you ...? – Yes, I did.
3 Did you ...? – Yes, I did.
4 Did your friend ...? – Yes, he did.
5 Did you ...? – Yes, we did.
6 Did you ...? – Yes, we did.

Tipp:
Fragen werden mit *did* und der Grundform (*buy, go, watch*) des Verbs gestellt.

5 A bad weekend: Match the sentences with the pictures.

1 I didn't like my present from London.
2 I didn't see my dad.
3 I didn't go to Exmouth with mum.
4 I didn't go to the cinema.
5 I didn't play football.
6 I didn't meet my best friends.

6 A good weekend: Write the sentences.

1 didn't have / I / homework
2 at home / didn't help / I
3 in my room / I / didn't work
4 in town / my teachers / I / didn't see
5 the match / Liverpool / didn't win / on Saturday
6 I / my grandma / didn't visit

7 Sarah's bad weekend: What's she saying?

1 JAMIE   I went to Exmouth.
  SARAH   I didn't go to Exmouth.
2 JAMIE   I went to the sports centre.
  SARAH   I didn't ...
3 JAMIE   I saw my friends.
  SARAH   I ...

4 JAMIE   I played games with my dad.
  SARAH   ...
5 JAMIE   I watched a good TV programme.
  SARAH   ...
6 JAMIE   I had fun at the weekend.
  SARAH   ...

8 AND YOU? Did you have a good or a bad weekend? Write what didn't happen.

 I had a good weekend.

 I had a bad weekend.

I didn't
My mum didn't
My dad didn't
... didn't

go to ...
watch ...
do ...
play ...
see ...
help ...
have ...

○ **9** **Make three groups with 1–12.**

1 Dad bought the tickets.
2 We didn't have fun.
3 Did you see the shoplifters?
4 Mum didn't feel OK.
5 Did the train go fast?
6 I went to London.

7 I didn't go anywhere.
8 I saw two girls with bags.
9 She didn't see the T-shirts.
10 The man left the shop.
11 Did you go to Oxford Street?
12 What did you do on Sunday?

+	**—**	**?**
Dad bought the tickets. I ...	We didn't have fun. Mum didn't ...	Did you see the shoplifters? Did ...?

○ **10** **Jamie's day: What are the right words?**

1 Jamie played / didn't play football.
2 He met / didn't meet Tom.
3 He helped / didn't help his mum.
4 He checked / didn't check the quads.
5 He did / didn't do his homework.
6 He watched / didn't watch *Teen Scene*.

○ **11** **Questions for Sammy: Put in *do* or *did*.** The answers can help you.

1 ... you have a holiday every year, Sammy? – Yes, I do. I like the sea.
2 ... you go to the sea last year, Sammy? – Yes, I did, with my friend Sarah.
3 Where ... you go last summer? – I went to Exmouth with Sarah.
4 ... you go to school with Sarah? – Yes, I do. And I work too.
5 Where ... you work? – In a school book, *New Highlight*.
6 ... you go to school in London? – Yes, I did, *Spider Academy*.

● **12** **A teacher's bad holiday: Put in the right form of the verb.**

1 I (not have) a good holiday.
I didn't have a good holiday.
2 I ... (have) an accident. *I had an accident.*
3 I ... (go) mountain biking in Germany.
4 I ... (fall) on the first day! But I was OK.
5 So I ... (not go) to hospital.

6 But I ... (not want) to go biking again after the accident.
7 I ... (stay) in my room and ... (watch) TV.
8 But it was terrible. I ... (not understand) the programmes! I don't speak German.

 ● **13** **My last holiday**

Write about your last holiday. Say what happened and what didn't happen.

SIMPLE PAST (2)

Du kannst nun sagen, was in der Vergangenheit geschah.

I went to town yesterday.

Tom checked his bike.

Sammy bought a magazine.

Mit *didn't* sagst du, was **nicht** geschah.

The Bakers didn't go to town.

Josh didn't clean his bike.

Sammy didn't buy a new bag.

My parents didn't work yesterday.
Meine Eltern haben gestern nicht gearbeitet. / Meine Eltern arbeiteten gestern nicht.
I didn't see Jamie last week.
Ich habe Jamie letzte Woche nicht gesehen. / Ich sah Jamie letzte Woche nicht.

Mit *did* **fragst** du, was geschah.

Did you watch TV yesterday?
Hast du gestern ferngesehen?
Did Sarah visit her grandma last week?
Hat Sarah letzte Woche ihre Oma besucht?
Did the boys buy a nice present?
Haben die Jungen ein nettes Geschenk gekauft?

Did you do that?

97

ninety-seven

1 **What are you going to be when you're older?**

1 JAMIE

I'm going to be a ...   I'm not going to be a ...

2 EMMA

I'm ...   I'm not ...

3 TOM

I'm ...   I'm not ...

4 SARAH

I'm ...   I'm not ...

2 **AND YOU? Write about your plans.**

When I'm older ...	be	a horse/a motorbike/a quad/...
	live	lots of countries/England/Spain/...
	work	Trikke riding/rock climbing/...
... I'm going to/	ride	in a town/in a village/in the country/...
I'm not going to	drive	lots of children/lots of money/a nice house/...
	have	a teacher/a police officer/...
	visit	a fast car/a bus/a train/...
	try	in a factory/in a shop/in a restaurant/...

3 **Saturday plans**

a) Look at the notes and finish the dialogue for Sarah and Tom.

	morning	afternoon	evening
Sarah	work in the restaurant	play with Sammy	stay at home
Tom	visit Tariq	meet mum in town	stay at home ✗ play tennis
Jamie	get up late work on the farm ✗	help dad in the shop	watch TV do my homework ✗

b) What's Jamie going to say?

TOM   What are your plans for Saturday, Sarah?

SARAH   In the morning I'm going to ... in the restaurant with dad. And in the afternoon I'm ... with Sammy. In the evening I'm ... at home. What about your plans, Tom?

TOM   I'm ... Tariq in the morning. Then I'm ... mum in town in the afternoon. In the evening I'm not ... at home. I'm ... tennis at the youth club.

JAMIE   In the morning I'm ...

4 Oh, no! Finish the sentences.

A — Oh no! I'm ...!

... going to

... take our clothes!
... rain!
... sit on the cat!
... fall!
... eat my lunch!

B — Oh no! It's ...!

C — Oh no! You're ...!

D — Oh no! He's ...!

E — Oh no! They're ...!

5 Sunday plans: Finish Jamie's e-mail. Use

→ 'm • 's • 're

> Hi Tariq,
> I have a surprise. I... going to visit Dartmoor again next Sunday. Dad has to work.
> He... going to stay in the shop. But mum wants to come. She... going to drive so we
> don't have to go on the bus.
> I saw Tom, Sarah and Emma yesterday. They... going to come. I hope you... going to
> come too! We... going to go letterboxing. I... going to bring my new stamp. And now
> I... going to watch the weather on TV.
>
> Best wishes,
> Jamie

6 Draw this weather map in your exercise book.
Put in: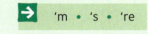

7 Write a weather report for Monday.

Good evening.
This is the weather for
Sunday. It isn't going to be
very nice near Exeter. It's
going to rain. And it's going
to be cold.
In London the weather isn't
going to be so bad. It isn't
going to rain. It's going to be
cloudy and cold. But it's going
to be sunny in Newcastle.
And it's going to be warm too.

8 **What's the best question (a, b or c) for the answer?**

1 a) What are you going to do before school?
  b) What are you going to do after school?   – I'm going to go home.
  c) What are you going to do at home?

2 a) How are you going to get home?
  b) When are you going to leave?   – By bus.
  c) What are you going to buy?

3 a) Where are you going to do your homework?
  b) Who's going to do your homework?   – At about five o'clock.
  c) When are you going to do your homework?

4 a) What are you going to do in the evening?
  b) Who's going to visit you in the evening?   – I'm going to watch TV.
  c) Who are you going to see in the evening?

5 a) What are you going to read?
  b) What are you going to listen to?   – A James Bond film.
  c) What are you going to watch?

9 **Nonsense words: Find the right words and make the questions.**

1 When are you going to ZONK up? – At seven o'clock.
2 ZONK are you going to leave the house? – At half past seven.
3 How are you ZONK to get to school? – By bus.
4 What are you going ZONK do in the evening? – I'm going to help mum.
5 Are ZONK going to meet your friends on Saturday? – Yes, I'm going to meet Jenny.
6 ZONK are you going to do this summer? – I'm going to visit London.

10 **In ten years …**

a) Make some sentences for your partner.

Exercise 2 on page 98 can help you.

You're going to …   be …
You aren't going to …   have …
              live …
              play …
              drive …
              …

b) Read your partner's sentences about you.

GOING TO

Mit *going to* sagst du, was in der Zukunft wahrscheinlich geschehen wird.
Es kann um Pläne und Vorhaben gehen oder um etwas, das bald geschehen wird.

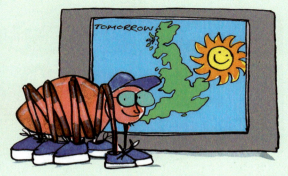

I'm going to make a salad.

It's going to be sunny in England tomorrow.

We're going to have a picnic on Saturday.
Wir haben vor, am Samstag ein Picknick zu machen.
Oh no, he's going to fall!
Oh nein, er fällt gleich herunter!
Are you going to invite Andy to your party?
Wirst du Andy zu deiner Party einladen?
The weather isn't going to be very nice at the weekend.
Das Wetter wird am Wochenende nicht sehr schön sein.

Aussagen

I'm You're He's She's It's We're They're	going to fall!

Verneinungen

I'm not You aren't He isn't She isn't It isn't We aren't They aren't	going to fall.

Fragen und Kurzantworten

Are you going to visit us tomorrow?	– Yes, I am. / – No, I'm not.

1 Holidays: Match the pictures and the sentences.

A I've cleaned the kitchen.
B I've packed my bag.
C I've closed the windows.

D I've talked to the neighbours.
E I've phoned grandma.
F I've checked the car.

2 A youth club party: Match the words.

1 I've checked
2 I've opened
3 I've asked
4 I've phoned
5 I've planned
6 I've helped

A the windows.
B Ms Brown for help.
C the music.
D everybody in the club.
E in the kitchen.
F the CD player.

3 AND YOU? Pick the right word.

1 I've/I haven't been to France.
2 Mum has/hasn't tried rock climbing.
3 I've/I haven't made a cake.
4 I've/I haven't checked a bike.
5 My friend has/hasn't stayed at my house.
6 I've/I haven't watched English TV.

4 AND YOU? Make six sentences.

I've I haven't	been to ... checked ... had ... made ... read ... seen ...

5 Say it in English.

1 Ich bin schon oft in Frankreich gewesen.
  – *I've often ...*
2 Ich habe schon oft Fußball gespielt.
3 Ich habe schon oft *Teen Scene* gekauft.
4 Ich habe schon oft die falschen Hausaufgaben gemacht.
5 Ich bin schon oft ins Kino gegangen.
6 Ich habe schon oft Oma angerufen.

6 **Have you ever ...? Match the pictures and the sentences.**

A Have you ever played football?
B Have you ever done this?
C Have you ever checked a VERY important car?

D Have you ever worked with older children?
E Have you ever been to Germany?
F Have you ever arrived at nine o'clock?

7 **Questions and answers**

a) **Finish the questions with the right form of the verb.**   Look at the list on page 169.

1 Have you ever (have) a dog?
2 Have you ever (watch) *Lindenstraße?*
3 Have you ever (play) volleyball?

4 Have you ever (walk) ten kilometres?
5 Have you ever (write) a story?
6 Have you ever (ride) a mountain bike?

b) **Now ask about ...**

1 ... a cat.
2 ... *GZSZ.*

3 ... beach volleyball.
4 ... ten miles.

5 ... a letter.
6 ... a quad.

c) **Answer the questions in a) and b).**   Use *Yes, I have* or *No, I haven't.*

8 **Ask a partner.**

Have you ever ...	been bought checked had made	played read ridden seen written	...?

– Yes, I have.

– No, I haven't.

9 **Put the words in the right order.**

just seen / I've / something!

a salad / made / I've often

to Wales / I've never / been

a quad / ridden / He has just

to hospital / She has often / been

They've / never had / hamburgers

10 **What's the missing word?**

1 I've just/often seen a great match.
2 Lee played again. He has often/never played for England.
3 Our team was super! They've often/never played better.
4 I've often/never seen matches with the German team, so I know how bad they were today.
5 What's wrong? What have I often/just said?

11 **AND YOU? Finish the sentences.**

1 I've often …
2 I've never …
3 I've just …
4 My partner has just …
5 Our teacher has just …
6 My parents have often/never …

12 **INTERPRETING: Help an English friend. What are the people saying?**

Ich habe deinen Hund noch nie gesehen.

I've …

Ich bin gerade angekommen.

I've …

Ich bin schon in Schottland gewesen.

I've …

PRESENT PERFECT

Mit der vollendeten Gegenwart *(present perfect)* kannst du sagen, was soeben oder schon einmal geschehen ist.

I've just found your bag.

I've just talked to a friend.

Sammy has often been to school with Sarah.

Mit der verneinten Form sagst du, was (noch) nicht oder (noch) nie geschehen ist:
I haven't tried the cake.
I have never been to Scotland.

Du kannst auch fragen, ob etwas schon einmal geschehen ist:
Have you ever been to Wales? – Yes, I have.

Aussagen

I've You've We've They've	checked the bike.
She has He has	

Verneinungen

I You We They	haven't bought the tickets.
She He	hasn't bought the tickets.

Fragen und Kurzantworten

Have you bought the tickets?	- Yes, I have.
Has Peter phoned Sue?	- No, he hasn't.

Das *present perfect* bildest du mit *'ve/has* und dem Partizip Perfekt.

Regelmäßig: *-ed*
worked, arrived, started

Unregelmäßig:
seen, made, found

Look at the list on page 169.

I've found my shoes.

Verwende das *present perfect* immer dann, wenn etwas
- soeben geschehen ist,
- schon einmal geschehen ist,
- (noch) nicht oder (noch) nie geschehen ist.

Folgende Wörter kommen oft in Verbindung mit dem *present perfect* vor:
just, often, never.

EXTRA READING

DRAKE SCHOOL BUDDIES

2⊙ 14

A

What are buddies? They're pupils. They help new pupils at Drake School. They're in year 10. Every pupil in year 7 has a buddy.

How can buddies help? On your first day at school you can do a tour with your buddy. You can ask your buddy lots of questions about the school, your homework, your subjects. And your buddy can help you with problems.

When can you talk to your buddy? You can meet your buddy in the break on Fridays. You can have lunch with your buddy on Mondays.

What are playground buddies? Four buddies (two boys and two girls) are in the playground every day in the break. They wear buddy badges. You can talk to them. They can help you.

And who helps the buddies? Mr Rooney talks to the buddies on Wednesdays. They meet after lunch. Mr Rooney helps the buddies with their problems.

A buddy badge

B I'm in year 10 and I'm a buddy. I look after a boy in year 7. He's a nice boy. But he's very quiet. He doesn't have many friends and he's often alone. I meet him in the break and we talk. On Monday he had a problem. There's a girl in year 7 and she's horrible. She took some things from him. I talked to Mr Rooney and he talked to the girl. Things are OK now, I think. Being a buddy is OK, but sometimes it isn't easy and sometimes it's boring.

C I'm in year 7 and I have a buddy. She's in year 10. She's great. Sometimes she comes to my classroom in the break and talks to me. When I have a problem, we talk about it. On Monday I had a problem with a girl in my class. She was horrible. She took my things. My buddy talked to Mr Rooney. And that was the end of the problem. I think buddies are great. I want to be a buddy when I'm in year 10.

1 What do you think?
Who wrote text A, text B, text C?

Robert Ryan, year 7   Sandra Holt, year 10   Mr Rooney, teacher

2 Who says what –
Robert, Sandra or Mr Rooney?

I'm a buddy. It isn't always easy.

Buddies help new pupils in our school. And I help buddies.

My buddy is great. She often helps me.

3 New words in the texts
Can you guess what these words are in German?

1 ask questions: Fragen stellen / Fragen beantworten
2 wear: verkaufen / tragen
3 look after: sich anschauen / sich kümmern um
4 sometimes: manchmal / jemand
5 horrible: toll / scheußlich
6 end: beenden / Ende

Tipp:
• Manchmal kennst du schon einzelne Bestandteile einer Redewendung und kannst so ihre Bedeutung erraten.
• Bei anderen hilft dir der Zusammenhang: Suche die Redewendung in den Texten auf Seite 106 und versuche, ihre Bedeutung durch den umgebenden Text zu erschließen.
• Und manche Wörter klingen auf Deutsch ähnlich. Im Zweifelsfall schau im *Dictionary* (Seite 147–157) nach.

4 Drake School buddies
Finish the network in your exercise book.

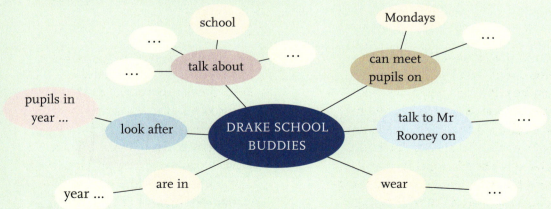

5 Finish this text about Drake School buddies.
The network in exercise 4 can help you.

Drake School has buddies. The buddies are in … . They look after … . Buddies talk to year 7 pupils. They talk about lots of things: … Buddies can meet year 7 pupils … . And they talk to Mr … . Buddies always wear …

THAT'S ENGLAND FOR YOU!

 1 **Was the bike trip in Exeter easy for Jutta?**
2⊙15 **Find out.**

Tom and Jutta were in Exeter on bikes. Jutta thought it
was great.
"Careful, Jutta!" Tom shouted.
A boy was on the zebra crossing.
5 "Jutta! You didn't see that boy!" Tom said.
"Of course I saw him," Jutta said. "In Germany people
check if it's safe first. He ran across the road."
"That's England for you," said Tom. "People on the
zebra crossing are always right."
10 "Yes," said Jutta. "And I was wrong. It isn't fair."

Later ...
"Careful, Jutta!" Tom shouted.
The traffic lights were green for cars and bikes, but two
girls were on the road.
15 "But it's red for them!" said Jutta.
"Oh, Jutta," said Tom. "Lots of English people don't
wait for green."
"I see," said Jutta. "So I was wrong again! What a
strange country!"

20 "Turn right!" Tom shouted. "Careful! Keep left!"
Jutta was on the wrong side of the road.
"Hmm," said Jutta. "I don't like this. I always do the
wrong thing."
"OK," said Tom. "Let's have a cola at this cafe."

25 Jutta locked her bike. Tom saw a fast car in the street.
He thought it was interesting.
"Is your bike OK?" asked Jutta.
"It's OK," said Tom. "My bike is as safe as houses
here."
30 "That's England for you!" said Jutta. "This big sign is
just for fun."
"What sign?"
"This sign," Jutta said. "*Careful! Bikes are often stolen
here!*"

2 **Who was it? Finish the sentences.**

1 ... were on bikes.
2 ... was on the zebra crossing.
3 Lots of ... don't wait for green.
4 ... was on the wrong side of the road.
5 ... locked the bike.
6 ... saw a big sign.

3 **Right or wrong?**

1 In England people on a zebra crossing are always right.
2 English people always wait for green.
3 Jutta was "wrong" three times.
4 Tom said, "Let's have a hamburger."
5 Tom saw a new car.
6 Tom saw a sign about houses.

4 **Finish the sentences with the right words.**

1 "That's England for you" = "That's OK/That's terrible in England."
2 A zebra crossing is on a farm/in a street.
3 Traffic lights are white and blue/red and green.
4 "It's as safe as houses" = "It's/It isn't very safe."
5 "Bikes are often stolen here" = Bikes are/aren't usually safe here.

5 **What are these words in German?**
Check the words in the *Dictionary* (pages 147–157).

1 Careful! – Volles Auto! Kehren! Vorsicht!
2 safe – Seife, Safe, sicher
3 strange – streng, merkwürdig, stretchen
4 side – Seite, seit, Seide

Tipp:
Du kannst die Bedeutung neuer Wörter oft aus dem Zusammenhang erschließen. Manchmal gibt es ähnliche Wörter im Deutschen. Aber Vorsicht: Es gibt auch Wörter, die zwar ähnlich aussehen, aber eine ganz andere Bedeutung haben.

6 **Pick one sentence for the picture.**

• Bikes are often stolen here!
• It's as safe as houses!
• That's Germany for you!

SPECIAL DAYS

2 ⊙ 16

MIKE (13)

Christmas is great.
I love Christmas decorations, Christmas cards and Christmas trees.
On Christmas Eve (December 24th) we often go to town and get the last Christmas presents.

On Christmas Day (December 25th) I get up early and look for my Christmas stocking. In the stocking there are small presents – like a book, a game, a CD ... and chocolate.

We usually go to church.
I like Christmas music and songs. When we come home, we all go to the living room and sit next to the Christmas tree. Everybody gets presents. It's great!

We have Christmas dinner in the afternoon – at two or three o'clock. And then we have Christmas pudding – I love that!
In the evening we watch TV and play games. And we eat again – Christmas cake.

1 **Find the words in the text for these things.**

Guess what these Christmas things are. Then check in your dictionary.

110

one hundred and ten

2⊙ 17

I love Eid food. And there are special Eid cakes. We eat all day. We talk, laugh and have lots of fun with our family. We visit friends too.
And we give food and money to poor people.

BINA (12)

I'm a Muslim.
So we have Ramadan every year.

In Ramadan we don't eat in the day – only at night. It's a very special time. And after a month Ramadan is over. Then we celebrate Eid.

For Eid we always get new clothes. We go to the mosque in the morning. Then we always go to my grandma's house. All the family is there.
We get presents – usually money.

2 **Find the sentences in the text for these pictures.**

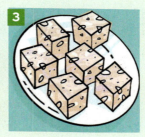

3 **AND YOU? What do you celebrate?**
Write some sentences in your exercise book.

We celebrate ...   We usually eat ...
I like ...   We get ...
I love ...   We play ...
We always go to ...   We visit ...

Tipp:
Du kannst dir ganze Sätze aus beiden Texten „ausleihen".
Schmücke deine Sätze mit Farben, Bildern und Zeichnungen aus.

🔊 EMMA'S ENORMOUS EASTER EGG

2⊙ 18

"Bye, Grandad! Thanks again for the Easter egg!"
It was eleven o'clock in the morning on Easter Sunday.
It was raining again. It usually only rained on Good
Friday, her grandad said. But then it was often nice
5   weather two days later on Easter Sunday. Not this year!
Emma left her grandad's flat and walked along the
street towards Tom's house. She looked into the
houses. She saw children with enormous chocolate
Easter eggs. Like the egg in her bag. It was the biggest
10 egg in the world!

She turned right into Tom's street. Tom and his two
brothers were in the garden. They had umbrellas and
they were looking for something.
"Happy Easter, Emma!" said Tom.
15 "What are you doing?" asked Emma. "Looking for your
homework? Can I help?"
Tom looked at his two brothers.
"Yes, please," Tom said. "We're looking for something.
In fact, we're looking for lots of things. They're small
20 and blue, or red or ..."
"Like an egg?" said Emma.
"Yes," said Josh, and laughed.
"Oh no! You're looking for chocolate eggs. I didn't
think of that," said Emma. "We don't have a garden,
25 you see."
"It makes mum happy if we look for the eggs," said
Tom. "She says it's an old German custom."
"Yes," said Josh. "Mum says when she came to
England, nobody in England looked for eggs."
30 "Yes, like fireworks on New Year's Eve. They come from
Germany too," said Sam. "Dad says they didn't have
fireworks on New Year's Eve when he was a boy."
"That's right, Sam." It was Mr Price. "Halloween is
new here too. But that comes from America, not from
35 Germany."
"Did you hide the eggs, Mr Price?" asked Emma.
Tom's dad laughed. "No, it was the Easter bunny, of
course, Emma."
Emma put her hand in her bag and showed everybody
40 the enormous Easter egg. "It's good that the Easter
bunny didn't have this in his bag!" she said.

1 **Put the sentences in the right order.**

1 Emma showed her egg to everybody.
2 The young people talked about customs.
3 They were looking for something.
4 Emma saw Tom and his brothers.
5 Emma saw her grandad.
6 Emma left her grandad's flat.

2 **Right or wrong?**

1 Emma walked along the street towards Tom's house.
2 She saw shops with enormous Easter eggs.
3 She turned left into Tom's street.
4 Tom and his two brothers were in the garden.
5 Tom said, "We're looking for something."
6 Mr Price said, "Easter is new here too."

Tipp:
Finde die Stelle in der Geschichte. Dann vergleiche die Sätze.

3 **Pick the right words.** The answer to 5 isn't in the text.

1 It was in the morning/afternoon.
2 The boys were looking for homework/eggs.
3 Mr Price/The Easter bunny hides the eggs every year.
4 Halloween comes from England/America.
5 New Year's Eve is December 31st/January 1st.

4 **What are the words in German?**
You can check your answers in the *Dictionary* on pages 147–157.

1 enormous? – normal, riesengroß, ökologisch
2 umbrella? – Regenschirm, Umweg, Ungeheuer
3 custom? – Kunde, Brauch, Kostüm
4 fireworks? – Frühschicht, Feuerwerk, Feiertage
5 hide? – verstecken, häuten, Heide

Tipp:
In welchem Zusammenhang kommt das Wort in der Geschichte vor?

5 **ODD WORD OUT**

1 German, Halloween, New Year's Eve, Easter
2 America, England, Good Friday, Germany
3 enormous, raining, interesting, exciting
4 egg, chocolate, cake, umbrella
5 show, no, go, follow

6 **Make a network with the words.**
You can draw pictures for your network.

Easter – Easter egg – present –
Good Friday – Easter bunny –
chocolate – Easter Sunday –
Easter Monday – Easter Saturday

THE HOUND OF THE BASKERVILLES

by Sir Arthur Conan Doyle

2◉19

Baskerville Hall was a big, lonely house. It was near Grimpen, a village on Dartmoor.
In 1904 Sir Charles Baskerville lived there
5 with his servant Barrymore and his cook Mrs Barrymore.

It was a cold night and Sir Charles was at home. He heard a terrible sound on the moor. He was frightened. He went into the garden but he didn't come back. 10
Later Barrymore found Sir Charles in the garden. He was dead.

What happened? What did Sir Charles see in the garden? What killed him? The police
15 officers didn't know. Nobody knew. It was time to go to 221b Baker Street in London and talk to the famous detective Sherlock Holmes and his friend Doctor Watson.

Sir Henry Baskerville, Sir Charles' nephew and the new owner of Baskerville Hall, lived 20 in London too. He visited Holmes and Watson there. He had a note:
"Don't come to Baskerville Hall, Sir Henry. It's dangerous for you!"

1 **People in the story: Who's who?**

Sherlock Holmes

Doctor Watson

Sir Charles

Sir Henry

Barrymore

Mrs Barrymore

… was the old owner of Basker-ville Hall. He was dead.
… was a cook.
… was Sherlock Holmes' friend.
… was a servant.
… was a famous detective.
… was Sir Charles' nephew.

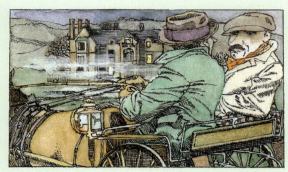

25 The next day Watson and Sir Henry left London and went to Dartmoor by train. Holmes stayed in London. The two men got to Baskerville Hall in the evening. The weather was terrible. It was cold and there 30 was a mist on the moor.

In the morning Watson walked to Grimpen. He met Mr Stapleton in the village. Stapleton talked about a terrible animal on the moor, "It's the Hound of the Baskervilles. I think that Sir Charles saw this hound and 35 was very frightened. That's why he died."

Stapleton invited Watson to his house. They walked across Grimpen Moor. "If you leave the track here, you can fall into the moor 40 and never come out," Stapleton said. "It's a very dangerous place."

At Stapleton's house Watson met a young woman. "This is my sister Beryl," Stapleton said. Beryl was nice, but very nervous. When her brother wasn't near, she 45 whispered to Watson, "Go back to London."

2 **Who – or what – are they?** The answers are on this page.

In the evening, back at Baskerville Hall, Sir Henry had some news. "In Princetown, a town near here, there's a famous prison –
50 Dartmoor Prison. Last week a man escaped. His name is Seldon and he's very dangerous."

That night, when Watson was in bed, he heard a sound. He went to Sir Henry's bedroom. The two men walked along the 55 hall. They saw a light. They followed it. Suddenly they saw Barrymore. He was next to a window.

On the moor they could see another light.
60 "Who's out there?" Sir Henry asked. Barrymore said nothing. Then Mrs Barrymore came. "It's Seldon, Sir. He's my brother," she said. "He's hungry and it's cold, so we gave him some food and some
65 of your clothes. I'm sorry, Sir Henry."

"Seldon is dangerous. We have to find him," Watson said. But Seldon was very fast and he knew the moor. The moon came out and they saw another man. He was on Black Tor. "Who's that?" Sir Henry asked. 70
"I don't know, but I'm going to find out," Watson answered.

3 **Places in the story: What and where are they?** Look at pages 114, 115 and 116.

1 Baskerville Hall is ...
2 Grimpen is ...
3 Grimpen Moor is ...
4 221b Baker Street is ...
5 Princetown is ...
6 Dartmoor prison is ...

a big house on Dartmoor.
a town near Baskerville Hall.
a dangerous place near Grimpen.
in Princetown.
where Sherlock Holmes lives.
a village on Dartmoor.

The next day Watson walked to Black Tor.
There were old houses on the hill. He
75 waited in one house. He had his gun in his
hand. After two hours he heard something.
"It's a nice evening, my dear Watson."
It was Holmes.

Nobody knew that Holmes was on
Dartmoor. He wanted to watch everything. 80
Suddenly they heard a terrible sound on the
moor. "I think it's near the rocks," Holmes
shouted. "Let's go."
The two men started to run.

85 Then they saw a man on the ground. There
was blood everywhere. "We're too late! It's
Sir Henry. I know his jacket," Watson said.
"The hound has killed him."
"No, Watson. It's Sir Henry's jacket, but it
90 isn't Sir Henry," Holmes said.

Holmes was right. It was Seldon.
"He had Sir Henry's jacket. So the hound
thought that he was Sir Henry," Watson
said.
"Hurry up, Watson!" Holmes said. "We have 95
to get back to Baskerville Hall!"

4 **Something is wrong. But what's right?**   Look at pages 116 and 117.

1 Sir Henry escaped from Dartmoor Prison.
2 Seldon was Barrymore's brother.
3 There was a woman on Black Tor.
4 Holmes was in London now.
5 Sir Henry was dead.
6 Seldon had Barrymore's jacket.

2⊙ 23

At Baskerville Hall Holmes and Watson were in a big room. Barrymore was there too. There were lots of old pictures.
100 "Who's that?" Holmes asked.
"It's Sir Hugo Baskerville, Sir Henry's grandfather," Barrymore answered.
"Look, Watson," Holmes whispered. "Sir Hugo looks like Stapleton. Can you see it?"

"Yes, Holmes. You're right! So Stapleton is 105 Sir Henry's cousin!" Watson said.
"Yes, my dear Watson! Now he wants Sir Henry's house – and all his money!" Holmes answered.
"So Stapleton killed Sir Charles and now 110 he wants to kill Sir Henry," Watson said.
"We need a plan," Holmes answered.

That evening Sir Henry wanted to visit the Stapletons. Holmes told Sir Henry that he 115 and Watson had to go back to London. They went to Grimpen, but they didn't take the train to London.

At ten o'clock Holmes and Watson walked to the Stapletons' house. They waited near some rocks and watched. There was a 120 terrible mist and it was very cold on the moor.

5 **Right or wrong?** Look at this page.

1 Sir Charles Baskerville was Sir Hugo's grandfather.
2 Stapleton looked like Sir Hugo.
3 Stapleton killed Sir Charles.
4 Holmes and Watson went to London by train.
5 Sir Charles went to the Stapletons' house.
6 Holmes and Watson stayed in Grimpen that night.

They waited and waited. Then a door opened. They heard Sir Henry. He said good night to Stapleton and started to walk home across Grimpen Moor. Then Stapleton opened a door. Something big ran out.

It was terrible. It was very big. It was the Hound of the Baskervilles and it was behind Sir Henry! Holmes and Watson fired their guns. Bang, bang, bang, bang! The hound fell. It was dead. Sir Henry was very frightened but he was OK.

They all ran to the Stapletons' house. Beryl Stapleton was there. She was tied up. "Where's your brother?" Watson asked. "I don't know. But he has a small house on Grimpen Moor," she said. "I can take you there."

Beryl Stapleton knew the dangerous moor very well. They went along small tracks. At last they came to an old house. But nobody was there. Then they found something on the moor. It was Stapleton's hat. He was gone forever.

6 **Finish the sentences.**   You have to look at pages 114–119.

1) Sir Charles Baskerville lived at … **2)** Barrymore found Sir Charles in the garden – he was … **3)** Sir Henry Baskerville visited Sherlock Holmes and Doctor Watson in … **4)** Watson and Sir Henry went to … **5)** Watson walked to Grimpen and he met … **6)** At Stapleton's house Watson met Stapelton's … Beryl. **7)** Seldon escaped from … Prison. **8)** Seldon was Mrs Barrymore's … **9)** It was cold so she gave him Sir Henry's … **10)** The next day Watson went to Black Tor and met … **11)** Holmes and Watson heard a terrible sound and they saw a man on the ground – it was … **12)** Then Holmes and Watson found something out – Stapleton was Sir Henry's … **13)** That evening Holmes and Watson went to … **14)** Then they walked to the Stapletons' … **15)** Stapleton opened a … **16)** Suddenly the hound was behind … **17)** Holmes and Watson fired their … **18)** The hound was … **19)** They looked for Stapleton, but they only found his … **20)** He was gone …

YOU'RE HISTORY, MAN!

2 ◉ 25

At Drake School: Pupils from class 8R are on their way to the next lesson.

TOM	Hurry up! We're late!
EMMA	It's OK. It's only Ms Hill.
SARAH	Ms Hill? Is it history or geography?
JAMIE	History. We're finding out more about Sir Francis Drake today.
5 **TOM**	Boring! Why do we have to find out about old things?
MAN	Because they're important today, young man.
EMMA	Who are you?
MAN	Who am I? Well, I don't have – what's the name? – jeans, or a sea-shirt, ...
SARAH	T-shirt.
10 **MAN**	Right. Thank you. Tea-shirt. I don't have a tea-shirt, so I'm very old.
TOM	I like your light sabre. Did you see *Star Wars* too?

MAN	Light sabre? This, young man, is a sword. And I saw **sea** wars, not star wars, with hundreds of ships and sailors and ...
SARAH	I know. You're an actor – for our history project.
MAN	An actor? One of Shakespeare's men? No, no, no! What's the name of your school?
EMMA	Drake School.
MAN	Yes. **Drake** School. That's my name.
SARAH	You're Francis Drake, the pirate!
25 **DRAKE**	**Sir** Francis Drake, favourite of Queen Elizabeth. That's Queen Elizabeth the First, of course.
TOM	But you died on your ship in 1596. What are you doing here?
30 **DRAKE**	I want to tell you what a nice, er, cool man I was.
SARAH	You're history, man! We're late!
JAMIE	Yes, bad history. You took slaves on your ships.
35 **DRAKE**	Yes, yes. But I did lots of good things too. I did a world trip – and it wasn't "last-minute" in a, er, plane. I went in my ship.
SARAH	Cool!

40 **JAMIE** Yes, but what about the Spanish? You weren't very nice to them.

DRAKE Well, I didn't think the Spanish were, er, cool.

EMMA No, you didn't. You stole their gold.

DRAKE Yes, yes. But I did it for England.

JAMIE And for the money. You bought your house in Devon with Spanish gold.

45 **DRAKE** Yes, but I shared the money with the Queen.

EMMA Yes, that's why the Spanish say you were The Queen's Pirate.

DRAKE That's only because I beat all the Spanish ships, their Armada.

JAMIE I have a question. People say you finished your game of bowls in Plymouth before you beat the Spanish Armada. Is that right?

50 **DRAKE** Everybody in England wants to believe that, the cool hero. Well, ...

QUEEN Sir Francis!

DRAKE I'm sorry. I have to go. It's my queen. Goodbye and have a nice history lesson. Please don't believe everything.

55 **EMMA** Well! Nobody is going to believe us.

SARAH So we're going to say nothing. OK?

They walk into the classroom.

TOM Sorry, Ms Hill. We had to help an old sailor.

MS HILL That's OK. Today we're going to find out about Sir Francis Drake. Was he a hero or a criminal? What do you think?

1 **Right or wrong?**

1 The next lesson is geography.
2 Drake didn't wear T-shirts.
3 Drake died in 1596.
4 He only did good things.
5 He didn't like the Spanish.
6 Ms Hill saw Drake too.

2 **Pick the right word.**

1 Drake had a sword/light sabre.
2 He lived in Spain/Devon.
3 Drake bought/beat the Spanish Armada.
4 Drake stole gold/a game of bowls.
5 Drake bought a school/house in Devon.
6 Was Drake a hero/history teacher or a criminal?

3 **Act *You're history, man!* in your class.**

**INTERNET PROJECT –
Hero or criminal?**

a) Go to www.new-highlight.de, put in the webcode NHL-2-121 and find out more about Sir Francis Drake:

• his family
• his first job
• the name of his ship
• the Spanish Armada
• his world trip
• Queen Elizabeth I

b) Write a text about Drake. Then say what you think about him:

– *He was a great sailor and a cool hero.*
– *I think Drake was a bad man. He stole things and took slaves on his ships.*

PARTNER PAGES

Unit 1 (page 19)

Are you Daniel, Sophie, Emily or Thomas?
Listen to Partner A. Then answer his/her questions.

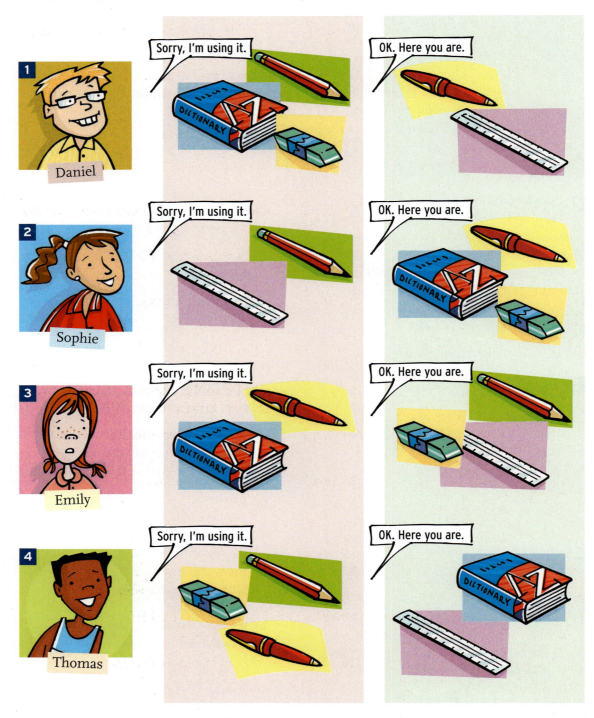

Unit 3 (page 43)

Are you Alex, Kylie, Lynn or Justin?
Look at "your" weekend and yesterday and answer your partner's questions.

Weekend	Terrible. I worked at home on Saturday. I helped mum.
Yesterday	I was at the hospital. I had an accident. I fell off my bike. I hurt my arm.
OK now?	No, I feel terrible!

Alex

Weekend	Great. I went to the cinema on Saturday. And I went to *Quad World* on Sunday.
Yesterday	I had an accident. I fell off my quad. I hurt my foot.
OK now?	Yes, I'm fine, thanks.

Kylie

Weekend	OK. I stayed at home on Saturday and Sunday. I watched TV.
Yesterday	I had an accident. I fell off a chair. I hurt my hand.
OK now?	Yes, I'm OK, thanks.

Lynn

Weekend	Fine. I visited my grandma on Saturday. I read a book on Sunday.
Yesterday	I had an accident. I fell off my horse. I hurt my head.
OK now?	Yes, I'm fine now, thanks.

Justin

Unit 4 (page 55)

Are you Ryan, Lucy, Mike or Bina?
Look at "your" weekend and answer your partner's questions.

Ryan

weekend?	Yes, I did. It was great.
Sunday?	I went to the park.
stay long?	Yes, I did. I left at five o'clock.
talk to parents?	Yes, I did. It's OK.

Lucy

weekend?	Yes, I did. It was OK.
Sunday?	I went to town.
stay long?	No, I didn't. I left at two o'clock.
talk to parents?	No, I didn't.

Mike

weekend?	Yes, I did. It was OK.
Sunday?	I went to a football match.
stay long?	Yes, I did. I left at four o'clock.
talk to parents?	Yes, I did. It's OK.

Bina

weekend?	No, I didn't. It was terrible.
Sunday?	I went to the sports centre.
stay long?	No, I didn't. I left at one o'clock.
talk to parents?	No, I didn't.

Unit 6 (page 79)

Are you Lisa, Ben, Lilly or Kevin? Look at "your" list and answer your partner's
questions: *Yes, I have. / No, I haven't.*

- done all the jobs in the kitchen ✔
- been to the park with the dog ✔
- talked to the neighbours
- taken their chairs back ✔
- opened all the windows
- written my "thank you" letters ✔

Lisa

- done all the jobs in the kitchen ✔
- been to the park with the dog
- talked to the neighbours
- taken their chairs back
- opened all the windows ✔
- written my "thank you" letters

Ben

- done all the jobs in the kitchen
- been to the park with the dog
- talked to the neighbours ✔
- taken their chairs back ✔
- opened all the windows
- written my "thank you" letters

Lilly

- done all the jobs in the kitchen
- been to the park with the dog
- talked to the neighbours ✔
- taken their chairs back ✔
- opened all the windows ✔
- written my "thank you" letters ✔

Kevin

WORDBANKS

WORDBANK 1

B bag, board, book; **C** chair, computer, cupboard; **D** dictionary, door; **E** exercise book;
H homework diary; **P** pen, pencil, pencil case, picture, poster, pupils; **R** rubber, ruler;
S shelf; **T** table, teacher; **U** uniform; **W** window

chalk

plant

sponge

clock

waste-paper basket

blinds

curtains

map

pinboard

WORDBANK 2

art, computers, English, French, geography, German, history, maths, science

sport (PE)

RE

technology

woodwork

WORDBANK 3

art room, classroom, computer room, French room, gym, hall, head teacher's office,
library, science room, secretary's office, teachers' room, boys' toilet/girls' toilet

• **WOODWORK ROOM**

• **CAFETERIA**[1]

• **PLAYGROUND →**

• **CLOAKROOM**[2]

• **CARETAKER'S ROOM**[3]

• **MAP ROOM**

[1]*cafeteria* Cafeteria, Kantine; [2]*cloakroom* Garderobe; [3]*caretaker's room* Hausmeisterbüro

WORDBANKS

WORDBANK 4 Unit 2

milk, orange juice, tea, water

bread	roll	butter	jam	egg
cheese	ham	cornflakes	honey	cocoa

WORDBANK 5 Unit 3

JOB?
baker (Bäcker/in)
beautician (Kosmetiker/in)
builder (Bauarbeiter/in)
caretaker (Hausmeister/in)
cleaner (Raumpfleger/in)
dentist's assistant (Zahnarzthelfer/in)
doctor's assistant (Arzthelfer/in)
electrician (Elektriker/in)
firefighter (Feuerwehrmann/-frau)
florist (Florist/in)
labourer (Arbeiter/in)
mechanic (Mechaniker/in)
nurse (Krankenschwester/-pfleger)
office worker (Angestellte/r)
painter (Maler/in)
plumber (Klempner/in)
receptionist (Empfangsdame/-chef)
road worker (Straßenbauarbeiter/in)
secretary (Sekretär/in)
soldier (Soldat/in)
tiler (Fliesenleger/in)

WHERE?
bakery (Bäckerei)
beauty salon (Kosmetikstudio)
building site (Baustelle)
garage (Autowerkstatt)
hotel (Hotel)
surgery (Arztpraxis)

WORDBANK 6   Unit 3

chicken, chips, crisps, fruit, hamburger, ice cream, pizza, salad, vegetables

pastries

hot dog

sausage with curry sauce

bagel

doner kebab

sausage

sandwich

pretzel

cheeseburger

doughnut

chocolate bar

chicken nuggets

WORDBANK 7   Unit 4

What can you buy in shops?
· clothes
· magazines
· books
· CDs
· toys
· cosmetics
· games
· sweets

Where can you go?
· park
· river
· shop
· cafe
· restaurant
· museum
· cinema
· theatre

What can you have at a cafe?
· tea
· coffee
· orange juice
· water

· cake
· ice cream
· waffles

What can you hire?
· quads
· bikes
· canoes
· boats
· ice skates
· in-line skates

WORDBANKS

WORDBANK 8   Unit 4

£7
scarf

£5
mug

£19
skirt

£4
calendar

£8
DVD

£26
sweatshirt

£3
eyeshadow

£12
perfume

WORDBANK 9   Unit 5

camping, cycling, football, fishing, horse riding, jogging, mountain biking, rock climbing, skiing, swimming, table tennis, Trikke riding, volleyball, walking

surfing

badminton

in-line skating

diving

rafting

orienteering

ice skating

canoeing

skateboarding

windsurfing

WORDBANK 10   Unit 5

What does he/she look like?
He's/She's ...
· small – tall
· young – old

· thin   –   heavy

Is he/she nice?
Yes, he's/she's ...
· friendly, funny,
  great, cool

No, he's/she's ...
· boring, stupid, terrible,
  not my type*

*type Typ

What about his/her hair?
He/She has ...
· blonde, red, brown, black, grey hair

· long hair – short hair

**He's/She's
bald.**

His/Her clothes:
· headscarf
· baggy pants
· boots
· shirt and tie
· dress
· sandals

WORDBANK 11   Unit 6

We're going to ...
· play football
· listen to music
· do a quiz
· play games
· dance
· sing songs
· watch a film

Then we're going to have ...
· a picnic
· fish and chips
· lots of cake
· waffles
· sandwiches
· hamburgers
· a barbecue

Dieses Wörterverzeichnis enthält alle neuen Wörter des Buches in der Reihenfolge, in der sie im Buch zum ersten Mal vorkommen.

Mit den **gelben** Kästen am Anfang kannst du bekannte Wörter wiederholen.

Do you know these words?

ball • class • classroom • collect • fan • find out • football match
help • holidays • homework • lesson • listen • make • play
pupil • read • talk • teacher • team • work • write • year

Test yourself
Write the lists in your exercise book.
a) Verbs: **collect,** …, …, …, …, …, …, …, …, …
b) Football: **ball,** …, …, …
c) School: **class,** …, …, …, …, …, …, …, …, …, …

Tipp:
Schau dir die W…
in den oberen…
noch einmal a…

Diese Zahl gibt die Seite an, auf der die Wörter zum ersten Mal vorkommen.

Ein **blauer** oder **roter** Pfeil heißt: Schau dir den **blauen** oder **roten** Kasten rechts an.

Der **graue** Pfeil heißt: Schau in die rechte Spalte.

In den **roten** Kästen stehen wichtige Hinweise.

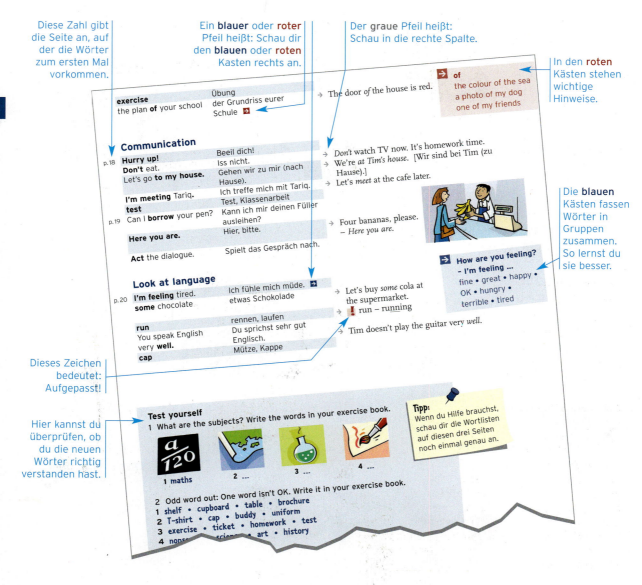

exercise	Übung	
the plan **of** your school	der Grundriss eurer Schule →	

→ The door *of* the house is red.

of
the colour of the sea
a photo of my dog
one of my friends

Communication

p.18
Hurry up!	Beeil dich!
Don't eat.	Iss nicht.
Let's go **to my house.**	Gehen wir zu mir (nach Hause).
I'm meeting Tariq.	Ich treffe mich mit Tariq.
test	Test, Klassenarbeit
Can I **borrow** your pen?	Kann ich mir deinen Füller ausleihen?
Here you are.	Hier, bitte.
Act the dialogue.	Spielt das Gespräch nach.

→ *Don't* watch TV now. It's homework time.
→ We're *at* Tim's house. [Wir sind bei Tim (zu Hause).]
→ Let's *meet* at the cafe later.

→ Four bananas, please.
 – *Here you are.*

How are you feeling?
 – **I'm feeling …**
fine • great • happy •
OK • hungry •
terrible • tired

Die **blauen** Kästen fassen Wörter in Gruppen zusammen. So lernst du sie besser.

Look at language

p.20
I'm feeling tired.	Ich fühle mich müde. →
some chocolate	etwas Schokolade
run	rennen, laufen
You speak English very **well.**	Du sprichst sehr gut Englisch.
cap	Mütze, Kappe

→ Let's buy *some* cola at the supermarket.
→ ! run – ru**nn**ing
→ Tim doesn't play the guitar very *well.*

Dieses Zeichen bedeutet: Aufgepasst!

Test yourself
1 What are the subjects? Write the words in your exercise book.

Tipp:
Wenn du Hilfe brauchst, schau dir die Wortlisten auf diesen drei Seiten noch einmal genau an.

a/120

1 maths 2 … 3 … 4 …

Hier kannst du überprüfen, ob du die neuen Wörter richtig verstanden hast.

2 Odd word out: One word isn't OK. Write it in your exercise book.
1 shelf • cupboard • table • brochure
2 T-shirt • cap • buddy • uniform
3 exercise • ticket • homework • test
4 nons… scie… • art • history

Unit 1

Lerntipp 1: Wiederholung

Weißt du noch? Jeder Mensch lernt anders. Was wirkt bei dir am besten?

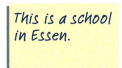

● **Lesen und schreiben**   ● **Zeichnen**   ● **Ordnen und sortieren**

● **Hören und sprechen**   ● **Spielen**

Probiere aus, was dir am meisten liegt – oder mache von allem etwas.

❗ Das Allerwichtigste: Beschäftige dich möglichst **jeden Tag** mit den englischen Wörtern!

Do you know these words?

ball • class • classroom • collect • fan • find out • football match •
help • holidays • homework • lesson • listen • make • play •
pupil • read • talk • teacher • team • work • write • year

Test yourself
Write the lists in your exercise book.
a) Verbs: **collect,** …, …, …, …, …, …, …, …, …
b) Football: **ball,** …, …, …
c) School: **class,** …, …, …, …, …, …, …

Are your answers right? Check on page 170.

Tipp:
Scháu dir die Wörter in den oberen Reihen noch einmal an.

---

p.10	**Put** them in the right order.	Bringe sie in die richtige Reihenfolge.	→	*Put* the books in alphabetical order, please.
	ask questions	Fragen stellen	→	Can I *ask* you *a question*, Mum?
	Can you …? – **Yes, I can./No, I can't.**	Kannst du …? – Ja./Nein.	→	Can you help me with German? – *Yes, I can.*
	uniform	(Schul-)Uniform	→	Our *uniform* is boring: It's blue and black.
p.11	**close**	zumachen, schließen	→	Let's *close* the window.
	label	Schildchen, Etikett		
	shelf, shelves	Regal, Regale		
	homework diary	Hausaufgabenheft; Schülerkalender	→	❗ one diary – two diar<u>ies</u>
	Sit here, please.	Setze dich bitte hierhin.		

p.12	The holidays are **over.**	Die Ferien sind vorbei.		→	Look! Dan *is arriving* at home.	**→ -ing**
	they're arriving	sie treffen (gerade) ein →		→	**!** arrive – arriving	I'm reading.
	arrive	ankommen, eintreffen		→		He isn't playing.
	laugh	lachen		→	l**a**u**g**h a, ha, ha!	Are you eating?
	class teacher	Klassenlehrer, Klassen-lehrerin				
	all the pupils	alle Schüler und Schüle-rinnen		→	It's spring and *all the* birds are singing.	
	timetable	Stundenplan				
	subject	(Schul-)Fach				**→ Sprachen**
	French	Französisch; franz.; Fran-zose(n), Französin(nen) →		→	Do you speak *French*? / Let's buy a *French* car. / Yvonne is *French*.	English French German
	maths	Mathe(matik)				
	history	Geschichte				
	geography	Erdkunde, Geografie		→	My favourite subject is *geography*.	
	science	Naturwissenschaft				
	art	Kunst				
p.13	**break**	Pause		→	Let's play ball in the *break*.	
	lunch	Mittagessen				
	first	zuerst		→	Can you wait? I have to finish my homework *first*.	
	brochure	Broschüre				
	club	Klub, Arbeitsgemeinschaft		→	I go to judo *club* at school.	
	buddy, buddies	„Kumpel" *(ältere Schüler/ Schülerinnen, die jüngeren helfen)*		→	My *buddy*'s name is Lisa.	
	Give the book **to** Tim.	Gib Tim das Buch.		→	*Give* the pen *to* your partner.	

Story

p.14	**happen**	passieren, geschehen		→	The film is boring. Nothing *happens*!	
	Where's the boy **from?**	Woher kommt der Junge?		→	*Where* are you *from*? – I'm from Kenn.	
	in the playground	auf dem Schulhof				**→ Kurzantworten**
	alone	allein				Yes, I am./No, I'm not.
	Are you ...? – **Yes, I am./No, I'm not.**	Bist du ...? – Ja./Nein. →		→	Is Sarah from London? – *Yes, she is.*	Yes, I can./No, I can't. Yes, I do./No, I don't.
	we moved here **from** Somalia	wir sind aus Somalia hier-her gezogen				
	Well, ...	Nun/Tja, ...				
p.15	**so**	also; daher		→	I'm tired, *so* I'm going to bed now.	
	in the evening	abends, am Abend →				**→**
	shout	laut rufen, schreien				in the morning
	he's on the phone	er ist am Telefon				in the afternoon
	ticket	Eintrittskarte; Fahrkarte, Flugschein				in the evening
	That's OK.	Schon gut./Bitte.		→	My favourite band! Thanks, Alan! – *That's OK.*	

Wordpower

| p.16 | **nonsense** | Unsinn, Blödsinn | | → | Spiders are great pets. – That's *nonsense*! |

Training

| p.17 | **different** | anders; verschieden | | → | You can buy the T-shirt in three *different* colours. This is a *different* shop. [ein anderer Laden] |

| exercise | Übung |
| the plan **of** your school | der Grundriss eurer Schule 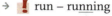 |

→ The door *of* the house is red.

of
the colour of the sea
a photo of my dog
one of my friends

Communication

p.18	**Hurry up!**	Beeil dich!
	Don't eat.	Iss nicht.
	Let's go to my house.	Gehen wir zu mir (nach Hause).
	I'm meeting Tariq.	Ich treffe mich mit Tariq.
	test	Test, Klassenarbeit
p.19	Can I **borrow** your pen?	Kann ich mir deinen Füller ausleihen?
	Here you are.	Hier, bitte.
	Act the dialogue.	Spielt das Gespräch nach.

→ *Don't* watch TV now. It's homework time.
→ We're *at Tim's house.* [Wir sind bei Tim (zu Hause).]
→ Let's *meet* at the cafe later.

→ Four bananas, please. – *Here you are.*

Look at language

p.20	**I'm feeling** tired.	Ich fühle mich müde. 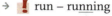
	some chocolate	etwas Schokolade
	run	rennen, laufen
	You speak English very **well.**	Du sprichst sehr gut Englisch.
	cap	Mütze, Kappe

→ Let's buy *some* cola at the supermarket.
→ ❗ run – ru**nn**ing
→ Tim doesn't play the guitar very *well.*

How are you feeling?
– I'm feeling ...
fine • great • happy •
OK • hungry •
terrible • tired

Test yourself

1 What are the subjects? Write the words in your exercise book.

1 maths   **2** ...   **3** ...   **4** ...

Tipp:
Wenn du Hilfe brauchst, schau dir die Wortlisten auf diesen drei Seiten noch einmal genau an.

2 Odd word out: One word isn't OK. Write it in your exercise book.
1 shelf • cupboard • table • brochure
2 T-shirt • cap • buddy • uniform
3 exercise • ticket • homework • test
4 nonsense • science • art • history

3 Write the sentences in your exercise book and finish them.
1 It's September now and the holidays are ... .
2 Where's the new girl ... ? – London.
3 We're late for the cinema, Sam. ... up!
4 Can I borrow your ruler, Alan? – Of course. ... you ... .
5 I don't speak French very ... , but I can speak German.

Are your answers right? Check on page 170.

Unit 2

Lerntipp 2: Freunde und Bekannte

Wahre Freunde: Englisch = Deutsch; Vorsicht bei der Aussprache!
• *basketball, camping, computer, hamburger, poster* …

Gute Bekannte: Englisch ähnlich wie Deutsch; im Zusammenhang kannst du die Bedeutung erraten.
• *banana, December, family, garden, postcard* …

Falsche Freunde: Englisch ≠ Deutsch, obwohl es so aussieht.
• *art* heißt nicht „Art", sondern „Kunst": *Our art teacher is very nice.*
• *programme* heißt nicht „Programm", sondern „Sendung":
  My favourite TV programme is 'Good times'.
• *spring* heißt nicht „springen", sondern „Frühling": *Spring is here.* usw.
Am besten markierst du diese Wörter beim Abschreiben mit einem Warndreieck: ⚠

Do you know these words?

apple • arrived • banana • bike • bus • cake • car • chicken • chocolate • eight o'clock • fish • five to nine • had • half past seven • hamburger • ice cream • motorbike • orange • plane • quarter past two • quarter to ten • said • ten past eleven • thought • train • was • went • were

Test yourself
Write the lists in your exercise book.
a) *Verkehrsmittel:* **bike,** …, …, …, …, …
b) *Zeitangaben:* **eight o'clock,** …, …, …, …, …
c) *Vergangenheitsformen:* **arrived,** …, …, …, …, …, …
d) *Lebensmittel:* **apple,** …, …, …, …, …, …, …

Are your answers right? Check on page 170.

Tipp:
Schau dir die Wörter in den oberen Reihen noch einmal an.

I'm the fastest!

p.22	**ship**	Schiff
	tunnel	Tunnel
	through the tunnel	durch den Tunnel
	the **fastest** way	der schnellste Weg →
p.23	**when**	wenn
	drive	fahren
	on the left	auf der linken Seite
	mile	Meile
	kilometre	Kilometer
	to	bis
	on the right	auf der rechten Seite
p.24	The text is **about** trains.	Der Text handelt von Zügen.
	cousin	Cousin, Cousine
	They thought it **was** a good idea.	Sie dachten, es wäre eine gute Idee.
	the **nearest** airport	der nächste Flughafen
	more expensive	teurer

→ **left** [links]

→ ❗ one kilometre – two kilometres

**right** [rechts]

→ The song is *about* friends.

→ 'Cafe Cool' is the *nearest* cafe to our school.

→ fast
   fast**er**
   fast**est**
new
   new**er**
   new**est**
old
   old**er**
   old**est**

In fact, it was better.	Es war sogar besser.	→ The book isn't too boring. *In fact,* it's OK.
cheap	billig, preiswert	
the **most** expensive trip	die teuerste Reise	**→** expensive **more** expensive **most** expensive
important	wichtig →	important **more** important **most** important
only	nur, bloß; erst	
long	lang; lange	→ *long*
hour	Stunde →	→ hour
mobile (phone)	Mobiltelefon, Handy	day

p.25

I left	ich verließ	week
I waited	ich wartete	month
I sat	ich setzte mich, ich saß	year
dream	Traum	
get	bekommen	→ Mandy often *gets* expensive presents. ! get
Learn it **by heart**.	Lerne es auswendig.	getting
exciting	aufregend, spannend	! more exciting – most exciting
underground	unterirdisch	
passage	Gang, Korridor	
water	Wasser	
guide	Führer, Führerin *(für Sehenswürdigkeiten)*	
crawl	kriechen	→

crawl   walk   run

Story

p.26

Rhine	Rhein	
a cup of tea	eine Tasse Tee	
the worst drink	das schlimmste Getränk	→ The *drinks* aren't very good here. Cola is the *worst*.
in the world	auf der (ganzen) Welt	→ My new job is the best job *in the world*.
You're right.	Du hast Recht.	
something different	etwas anderes	→ Can I ask you *something*?
I'd like a cup of tea.	Ich hätte gern eine Tasse Tee. →	**→** ...'d like
		I'd like
go **in**, crawl **in**	hineingehen, hineinkriechen	→ I'm not *going in* there,

p.27

he was frightened	er hatte Angst	→ I'm *frightened*!
she stopped	sie blieb stehen	you'd like
Are you OK?	Ist alles in Ordnung bei dir?	she'd like

we'd like
they'd like

Training

p.29

interpreting	Dolmetschen

Communication

p.30

visitor	Besucher/Besucherin, Gast →	**→** visit
		visitor
Nice to meet you.	Schön, dich kennen zu lernen.	
I don't like tea, **you see**.	Ich mag keinen Tee, verstehen Sie.	→ I can't come. We have visitors. – Oh, *I see*. [ich verstehe]
interesting	interessant	→ ! more interesting – most interesting
What do you think of England?	Was hältst du von England?	
singer	Sänger, Sängerin	

p.31

food	Essen	
a glass of milk	ein Glas Milch →	**→** a cup of tea
		a glass of milk
milk **instead of** tea	Milch statt Tee	→ Can I have a glass of milk *instead of* tea, please?

of course	natürlich
bad	schlecht; schlimm
I miss her	ich vermisse sie
for breakfast/for lunch	zum Frühstück/zum Mittagessen

→ Loulou *misses* our parents.

→ I always have juice *for breakfast*.

Look at language

p. 32	**worse**	schlimmer; schlechter ⇥

→ The weather is very bad again. In fact, it's *worse* than yesterday!

→ bad
worse
worst

Test yourself

1 Find and write in your exercise book:
a) *4 Wörter für Personen:* c..., g..., v..., s...
b) *4 Wörter, die etwas mit Wasser zu tun haben:* t..., s..., w..., R...
c) *3 Wörter zum Messen von Entfernungen oder Zeit:* m..., k..., h...

2 *Schreibe die Wörter in dein Heft und ergänze dabei jeweils den Buchstaben, der dem Wort zweimal fehlt. Nacheinander aufgeschrieben ergeben die 7 Buchstaben ein weiteres neues Wort.*
exc-t-ng, i-teresti-g, the fa-te-t way, impor-an-, kilom-tr-, p-ss-ge, un-ergroun-

3 A postcard: Write the sentences in your exercise book and finish them.
Dear Sam,
I'm in Germany now! We went the f... way, t... the tunnel. Here we have to d... on the ... . It's exciting. We're doing the most i... part of the trip now, along the River ... . The weather isn't b.... How's my hamster? I m... him!
See you soon,
Lucy
PS: You're r...: My bike is the w... bike in the ... :-(

Are your answers right? Check on page 170.

Tipp:
Schau dir die Wortlisten auf diesen drei Seiten genau an.

Unit 3

Lerntipp 3: Merkhilfen

Kannst du dir manche Wörter besonders schlecht merken?

Dann schreibe ein oder zwei solcher Wörter deutlich auf einen Zettel, vielleicht mit einer Zeichnung dazu.

Diesen Zettel hängst du an Stellen, wo du häufig hinschaust: an den Spiegel im Badezimmer, an deine Schreibtischlampe oder an den Kühlschrank, zum Beispiel.

Nun begegnest du diesen Wörtern immer wieder. Lies sie, sprich sie, mach dir klar, was sie bedeuten – und bald wirst du sie nicht mehr vergessen!

Test yourself
Write the lists in your exercise book.
a) Verbs: buy, …, …, …, …, …, …, …, …
b) In the kitchen: chair, …, …
c) Jobs: baggage handler, …, …, …
d) Places: airport, …, …, …, …, …, …, …, …, …, …, …

Are your answers right? Check on page 170.

Tipp:
Schau dir die Wörter in den oberen Reihen noch einmal an.

p. 34	cook	Koch, Köchin
	gardener	Gärtner, Gärtnerin
	hairdresser	Friseur, Friseurin
	police officer	Polizist, Polizistin
	security guard	Wachfrau, Wachmann
	shop assistant	Verkäufer, Verkäuferin
p. 35	factory	Fabrik
	hospital	Krankenhaus
	restaurant	Restaurant
p. 36	move: I moved	umziehen: ich zog um, ich bin umgezogen →
	last year	letztes Jahr →
	have: I had	haben: ich hatte
	get: I got	bekommen: ich habe bekommen
	hard	hart, schwer
	courier	Kurier/Kurierin, Bote/Botin
	look for a job	eine Stelle suchen
	go: I went	gehen: ich bin gegangen
	fast food	Fastfood (schnell verzehrbare Gerichte)
	healthy	gesund
p. 37	love	lieben, sehr mögen
	vegetable	(ein) Gemüse
	chips	Pommes frites
	salad	Salat
	crisps	Kartoffelchips
	fruit	Obst, Früchte
	lip	Lippe
	if	wenn, falls

→ My father is a *security guard*.

→ I have to move every year.
I *moved* to Exeter in August.

→ I have English lessons every day.
Last year I *had* French lessons too.

→ I *got* a new pen from my grandad on Monday.

→ I *went* to the museum last Sunday.

I love vegetables!

! Vegetables are healthy.
[Gemüse ist gesund.]

→ We can go home now *if* you like.

→ **-ed**
I watched
you helped
it happened
we played
they asked

→ last year
this year
next year

Story

p. 38	project	Projekt, Projektarbeit
	open	sich öffnen, aufgehen
	come in: I came in	hereinkommen: ich bin hereingekommen
	say: I said	sagen: ich sagte

→ "Come in," I shouted. The door openeed and a girl *came in*.

→ "Hallo," I *said*. – "Good morning," she answered.

hate	hassen, nicht ausstehen können →	→ I *hate* coffee, but I love tea.	→ like love hate
leave: I left	verlassen, weggehen (von): ich habe verlassen, ich bin weggegangen (von)	→ I usually *leave* the flat at 8 o'clock. On Monday I *left* at 9.	
There was lots of food.	Es gab viel Essen. →		→ there's / there are there was / there were
need	brauchen		

p. 39

rent	mieten →		→ borrow rent buy sell
buy: I bought	kaufen: ich habe gekauft	→ I *bought* a judo magazine last week.	
ready	fertig, bereit	→ Lunch is *ready*.	
in the street	auf der Straße		
nobody	niemand		
make: **I made**	machen: ich habe gemacht	→ Last week I *made* an apple cake.	
roll	Brötchen		
It's going to be OK.	Es wird gut werden.		
Let's wait and see.	Warten wir's ab.		

Training

p. 41

Writing a story	Eine Geschichte schreiben		
see: **I saw**	sehen: ich habe gesehen	→ On Friday I *saw* the new film with Sam Sheldon.	
follow	folgen, verfolgen		
into the street	auf die Straße (hinaus)	→ The shop assistant followed the boy *into the street*.	

Communication

p. 42

What's up?	Was gibt's?		
yesterday	gestern		
Poor you!	Du Arme!/Du Armer!		
Thanks for calling.	Danke für den Anruf.		
the same	derselbe, dieselbe, dasselbe	→ We're at the *same* school.	

p. 43

accident	Unfall		
It's Sarah.	Hier spricht Sarah.	→ Lucy? *It's* Ben.	
today	heute →		→ yesterday today tomorrow
fall: **I fell**	fallen: ich bin gefallen		
fall **off** a quad	vom Quad fallen	→ I fell *off* my bike yesterday.	
hurt: I hurt my hand	verletzen, wehtun: ich habe mir die Hand verletzt	→ My lips *hurt* when I drink. I *hurt* them in my bike accident last week.	
arm	Arm		
foot, feet	Fuß, Füße		
head	Kopf →		→ **Körper** head lip arm hand foot

Look at language

p. 44

remember	sich erinnern (an)	→ I'm sorry, I don't *remember* your name. – That's OK. I'm Mark.	
I can't wait for it.	Ich kann es kaum erwarten.	→ The children *can't wait for* the holidays.	
know: **I knew**	wissen: ich wusste	→ I *knew* that I was right!	
meet: **I met**	treffen: ich habe getroffen	→ I often meet Sam. In fact, I *met* him yesterday.	
on September 9th	am 9. September	→ School starts again *on January 8th*.	
Shut up!	Halt den Mund!		
funny	lustig, komisch		
date	Datum	→ What *date* is it today? – It's November 10th.	
simple past	einfache Vergangenheit		

p. 45

form	Form

one hundred and thirty-eight

Test yourself

1 Write the lists in your exercise book.
a) *Adjektive:* **hard,** ..., ..., ...
b) *Gegensätze:* **love – hate, arrive –** ..., **everybody –** ..., **tomorrow –** ..., **forget –** ...
c) *Lebensmittel:* **vegetable,** ..., ..., ..., ..., ...

2 *Finde die richtige Vergangenheitsform zur Grundform (oder umgekehrt) und schreibe die Liste in dein Heft.*

have:	I had	...:	I left	...:	I hurt
get:	I ...	buy:	I ...	know:	I ...
go:	I ...	make:	I ...	meet:	I ...
come in:	I ...	see:	I ...		
say:	I ...	...:	I fell		

Tipp:
Wenn du bei Aufgabe 2 Hilfe brauchst, kannst du auch in der Liste *Irregular verbs* auf S. 169 nachsehen.

Are your answers right? Check on page 170.

Unit 4

Lerntipp 4: Irregular verbs (Unregelmäßige Verben)

In der Liste **Irregular verbs** (S. 169) kannst du die besonderen Formen der unregelmäßigen Verben nachschlagen.

Steht ein Wort **nicht** in der linken Spalte, ist es **regelmäßig**. Solche Wörter brauchen für die einfache Vergangenheitsform *(simple past form)* meist nur ihre Grundform und *-ed,* z. B. *laugh: I laughed.*

Die besonderen Formen der **unregelmäßigen** Verben musst du dir jedoch gut merken, z. B. *buy: I bought.*
Schreibe sie immer zu den Grundformen, auch zu solchen, die du bereits kennst.
Nimm dabei für Buchstaben, die in der Grundform **nicht** vorkommen, eine andere Farbe:

see	know	make	hurt
I saw	I knew	I made	I hurt

Do you know these words?
at the weekend • bag • buy • go canoeing • go to the river • in the afternoon • meet friends • money • next week • on Sundays • ride a quad bike • shop • supermarket • this Saturday • tomorrow • town centre • visit people

Test yourself
Write the lists in your exercise book.
a) *Einkaufen:* **bag,** ..., ..., ..., ...
b) *Freizeitaktivitäten:* **go canoeing,** ..., ..., ..., ...
c) *Zeitangaben:* **at the weekend,** ..., ..., ..., ..., ...

Tipp:
Schau dir die Wörter in den oberen Reihen noch einmal an.

Are your answers right? Check on page 170.

p. 46	**tell: I told**	erzählen, sagen: ich habe erzählen, ich habe gesagt	→	I *told* Melissa about the party. Can you *tell* Paul?
	It's **different from** Germany.	Es ist anders als in Deutschland.		
	department store	Kaufhaus		
	open	offen, geöffnet	→	
	post office	Post(amt)		
	closed	geschlossen, zu	→	
	24 hours **a** day	24 Stunden am Tag	→	The shop is open five days *a* week.
	man, men	Mann, Männer		
	woman, women	Frau, Frauen →		

→ boy – man
  girl – woman

p. 47	**go shopping**	einkaufen gehen		
	hire	mieten, vermieten	→	! hire a car – rent a flat
	canoe	Kanu		
	I'd (= I would) like to go.	Ich möchte gehen.	→	*I'd like to* talk to you, Ben.
	I wouldn't (= would not) like to go.	Ich möchte nicht gehen.	→	*I wouldn't like to* leave this town.
	sometimes	manchmal →		
	pound (£)	Pfund *(britische Währung)*	→	£4 = four *pounds*
	most shops	die meisten Geschäfte	→	*Most* people here are very nice.
	euro (€)	Euro	→	€6.20 = six *euros* twenty

→ sometimes
  often
  usually
  always

p. 48	**I didn't win the lotto.**	Ich habe nicht im Lotto gewonnen. →	→	Tim *didn't go* to school yesterday.
	win: I won	gewinnen: ich habe gewonnen	→	I sometimes *win*, but last week I *won* nothing.
	understand: I understood	verstehen: ich habe verstanden	→	I *understand* more French now. Yesterday I *understood* a French song!
	girlfriend	(feste) Freundin		
	all weekend	das ganze Wochenende →		
	together	zusammen		

→ didn't
  I didn't shout
  he didn't say
  we didn't go

→ all day
  all week
  all year

p. 49	**advert**	Anzeige		
	newspaper	Zeitung		
	by Mark Marlowe	von Mark Marlowe		
	Did you say yes?	Hast du ja gesagt? →	→	*Did I tell* you about the book by Nick Mill? It's great!
	start	anfangen, beginnen		
	dream	träumen		
	swim: I swam	schwimmen: ich bin geschwommen	→	I *swim* every day. On Sunday I *swam* one kilometre.
	wear jeans: **I wore** jeans	Jeans tragen: ich habe Jeans getragen	→	At school I *wear* a uniform. But at the school party last week I *wore* jeans.
	drink: I drank	trinken: ich habe getrunken	→	I *drink* lots of juice. Yesterday I *drank* apple juice.
	pain	Schmerzen	→	After the accident I didn't feel much *pain*.
	spend: I spent	ausgeben: ich habe ausgegeben	→	I often *spend* £5 a week. Last week I only *spent* £3.
	take: I took	nehmen; bringen: ich habe genommen/gebracht	→	I *take* Karen to the station every Friday. Yesterday I *took* her to the airport.

→ Did ... ?
  Did I forget?
  Did she ask?
  Did we know?

Story

p. 50	**pay: I paid**	zahlen, bezahlen: ich habe gezahlt, ich habe bezahlt	→	I usually *pay* £3 here, but yesterday I only *paid* £2.80.
	walk **along** the street	die Straße entlanggehen		
	walk **towards** the house	in Richtung Haus gehen, auf das Haus zugehen	→	

towards

I'm sorry I'm late.	Tut mir leid, dass ich zu spät komme.	
into the shop	in das Geschäft (hinein)	→ She went *into* the department store.
put: I put	tun, legen: ich habe getan, ich habe gelegt	→ I *put* my bag here yesterday. Now I can't find it!
push	drücken	
run: I ran	rennen: ich bin gerannt	→ Last month I *ran* ten miles!
stupid	dumm, blöd	
out of the shop	aus dem Geschäft (hinaus)	→ He went *out of* the shop.
p. 51 **turn left/right (into** Market Street)	nach links/rechts (in die Market Street) abbiegen	
past the people	an den Menschen vorbei	
shopper	Käufer, Käuferin	
suddenly	plötzlich	
step	Stufe	
fall to the ground	auf den Boden fallen	→ The mobile *fell to the ground.*
daughter	Tochter	
shoplifter	Ladendieb, Ladendiebin	
job	Aufgabe, Arbeit	
I said **you'd be** in the shop tomorrow.	Ich habe gesagt, du wärst morgen im Laden.	
You have to **say sorry.**	Ihr müsst euch entschuldigen.	→ That wasn't very nice of Matt. – No, but later he *said sorry.*
report	Bericht	

Wordpower

p. 52 **That's two pounds, please.**	Das macht zwei Pfund, bitte.	→ One bottle of cola, please. – Here you are. *That's one pound, please.*
pence (p)	Pence	→ A postcard? That's fifty *pence*, please.

Communication

p. 54 I did**n't** go **anywhere.**	Ich bin nirgendwohin gegangen.	→ I ca*n't* see her *anywhere.* [nirgendwo]
interested in T-shirts	an T-shirts interessiert	→ I'm very *interested in* planes.
p. 55 write: **I wrote**	schreiben: ich habe geschrieben	→ I *wrote* four pages of my new book yesterday.

Look at language

p. 56 I know **that** ...	Ich weiß, dass ...	→ I didn't know *that* dogs can swim.
so hard	so hart	
What a great job!	Was für ein toller Beruf!	→ Let's buy a new house. – *What a* stupid idea!
Say hi to Dawn**, please.**	Grüße Dawn, bitte.	
autograph	Autogramm	

Test yourself

1 Odd word out: One word isn't OK. Write it in your exercise book.

1 always • sometimes • stupid • often
2 euro • pound • money • canoe
3 along • pain • past • towards
4 shopper • report • daughter • man

Hinweis:
Auf der nächsten Seite gibt es noch mehr Aufgaben.

Test yourself Unit 4 (Fortsetzung von S. 141)

2 Write the sentences in your exercise book and finish them.
1 This house is very different ... our house in Germany.
2 My girlfriend and I are interested ... the same things.
3 Say hi ... Jeremy, please.

3 *Finde die richtige Vergangenheitsform zur Grundform (oder umgekehrt) und schreibe die Liste in dein Heft.*

tell:	I told	swim: I ...	...: I took	put: I ...
win:	I ...	...: I wore	...: I spent	run: I ...
understand:	I ...	...: I drank	pay: I ...	

Are your answers right? Check on page 170.

Unit 5

Lerntipp 5: Nachschlagespiele

In diesen Listen sind Wörter in alphabetischer Reihenfolge sortiert:
Dictionary (Englisch – Deutsch) und **Wörterverzeichnis** (Deutsch – Englisch).
Wie gut seid ihr im Nachschlagen? Spielt die folgenden Spiele mit 2–4 Personen.
Wer zuerst die richtige Antwort nennt, hat die Runde gewonnen.
(Ein „Eintrag" beginnt immer mit einem blauen Wort am linken Rand der Spalte.)

Dictionary (S. 147–157)
1 Wie viele Einträge gibt es ... **a)** unter dem Buchstaben **J**? **b)** unter **K**? **c)** unter **V**?
2 Wie viele Einträge gibt es ... **a)** zwischen den Einträgen **closed** und **cold**?
  b) zwischen **Goodbye** und **guess**? **c)** zwischen **poem** und **programme**?

Wörterverzeichnis (S. 158–166)
1 Wie viele Einträge gibt es ... **a)** unter **A** vor dem Wort **alles**? **b)** unter **Z** vor **Zeit**?
2 Wie viele Einträge ... **a)** fangen mit **Fl/fl** an? **b)** mit **Mon**? **c)** mit **Str**?

... und natürlich auch sehr wichtig: die Seitenzahlen!
Wie lautet der erste Eintrag auf ... **a)** *page one hundred and forty-seven*?
b) *page one hundred and fifty*? **c)** *page one hundred and sixty-three*?

Auf Seite 170 könnt ihr überprüfen, ob eure Antworten richtig sind.

Do you know these words?

animals • big • boring • cows • exciting • football • go canoeing •
go swimming • happy • interesting • mountain biking • nice •
quiet • rivers • sheep • small • tennis • tracks • villages •
volleyball • wild

Test yourself
Write the lists in your exercise book.
a) *Adjektive:* big, ---, ---, ---, ---, ---, ---, ---, ---
b) *Freizeitaktivitäten:* football, ---, ---, ---, ---, ---
c) *Auf dem Land:* animals, ---, ---, ---, ---, ---

Tipp:
Schau dir die Wörter in den oberen Reihen noch einmal an.

Are your answers right? Check on page 170.

p.58	**outdoor activity**	Beschäftigung im Freien	→ I love sport and all *outdoor activities*.
	cycling	Radfahren	
	horse riding	Reiten	
	skiing	Skifahren	→ My favourite outdoor activity is *skiing*.
	jogging	Jogging	
	try	versuchen, (aus)probieren	❗ try: she's trying, she <u>tries</u>, she <u>tried</u>
	It's fun.	Es macht Spaß.	
	because	weil	→ Why do you like horse riding? – *Because* it's fun.
p.59	**walking**	Spazierengehen, Wandern	
	fishing	Fischen, Angeln	
	rock climbing	Klettern	→ I'd like to try *rock climbing*. I'm sure it's exciting.
	Trikke/quad/... riding	Trikkefahren/Quadfahren/...	
	survey	Umfrage, Untersuchung	→ We used a questionnaire for our *survey*.
	popular	beliebt	→ Chips are the most *popular* food in our class.
p.60	**plan**	planen, vorhaben	→ What are your holiday plans?
	they're going to visit it	sie werden es besuchen, sie besuchen es ➡	– I'm *going to try* fishing.

➡ **Plans**
I'm going to watch TV
he's going to read
we're going to play

national park	Nationalpark	
moor	(Hoch-)Moor	
lonely	einsam	
hill	Hügel, (kleiner) Berg	
wood	Wald	
on Dartmoor	in Dartmoor	
information	Informations-, Informationen	→ Can you give me more *information* about the trip, please?
Take a jacket.	Nimm/Bring eine Jacke mit.	
trainer	Sportschuh	→
walking shoe	Wanderschuh ➡	→
map	Landkarte, Karte	
ranger	Ranger *(Aufseher/in in Nationalparks)*	

trainers   *walking shoes*

➡ cap
jacket
jeans
shoes

p.61	**have a picnic**	ein Picknick machen	→ We *had a picnic* in the park last Sunday.

➡ walk
walking
walker

Story

p.62	**rule**	Regel, Vorschrift	
	walker	Wanderer, Wanderin ➡	
	litter	Abfall	→ People leave too much *litter* in the parks.
	sunny	sonnig	
	warm	warm	
	complain	sich beschweren	→ My dad works too much, but he doesn't *complain*.
	climb a hill	auf einen Hügel klettern	→ We *climbed* hills and crawled through tunnels.
	I started to run	ich begann zu rennen	→ Dan always *starts to* shout when he sees a spider.
	change	(sich) ändern, (sich) verändern	→ When the village started to *change*, we moved.
	cold	kalt	
	cloud	Wolke	
	rain	regnen	
p.63	**rock**	Fels, großer Stein	
	letterboxing	„Letterboxing" *(eine Art Schatzsuche)*	
	treasure hunt	Schatzsuche	
	everywhere	überall	→ Look, there are flowers *everywhere*!
	minute	Minute ➡	
	find: I found	finden: ich habe gefunden	
	stamp	Stempel	→

➡ minute
hour
day

Training

p. 65	**Best wishes, ...**	Viele Grüße ...
	I'm going to be a ranger.	Ich werde Ranger.
	hope	hoffen

→ **!** Best wishes, ... [Viele Grüße ...]
Lots of love, ... [Viele liebe Grüße ...]

→ What are you *going to be* later?
– *I'm going to be a* hairdresser.

Communication

p. 66	**description**	Beschreibung
	cloudy	bewölkt
p. 67	**What does she look like?**	Wie sieht sie aus?
	tall	groß *(bei Personen)*
	about 20	ungefähr 20
	hair	Haar, Haare
	blonde	blond
	friendly	freundlich
	another ranger	noch ein Ranger
	a picture **of yourself**	ein Bild von dir

→ **cloudy**
tall

→ How much money do we need? – *About* £5.

→ Tina's *hair* is pink now!

→ I'd like *another* glass of cola, please.

Test yourself

1 Write the lists in your exercise book.
a) Weather words: **sunny,** ..., ..., ..., ..., ...
b) *(Andere) Eigenschaften:* **popular,** ..., ..., ..., ...

> **Tipp:**
> Wenn du Hilfe brauchst, schau dir die letzten beiden Seiten noch einmal an.

2 oe, oo or ou? Write the words in your exercise book and finish them.
- - td - - r activity, m - - r, w - - d, walking sh - -, cl - - d, ab - - t

3 *Finde die verwandten Wörter und schreibe die Paare in dein Heft.*
jogger – jogging, fish – ..., walk – ..., sun – ..., cloud – ..., friend – ...

4 Write the sentences in your exercise book and finish them.
1 **Why do you like jogging? – ... it's easy.**
2 **What are your weekend plans? – We're ... to have a picnic on Sunday.**
3 **This brochure has lots of ... about the trip.**
4 **I'm going to be ... gardener later.**
5 **What does your friend look ...? – He's tall and blonde.**

Are your answers right? Check on page 170.

Unit 6

Lerntipp 6: Präpositionen

Diese kleinen Wörter *(at, in, on, to, ...)* haben oft mehrere Bedeutungen. *on* heißt z. B. nicht nur „auf", sondern manchmal auch „am" *(on Saturday, on the phone)*, „im" *(on the bus, on TV)* oder „zu" *(on foot)*.

Deshalb merke dir solche Wörter immer im Zusammenhang. Am besten beginnst du eine Sammlung: Schau dir die Wendungen im *Dictionary* (S. 147–157) an und notiere sie. Ergänze deine Sammlung, wenn du auf neue Vorkommen triffst.

> **at**
> at eight o'clock
> at Exeter station
> at home
> at night

> **in**
> in 1596
> in Fairfield Ro...
> in German
> in the country
> in the day
> ...kend

> **on**
> on August 5th
> on Dartmoor
> on foot
> on holiday

Do you know these words?

climbed • England • Exeter • fell • finish at 11 o'clock • Germany •
have a picnic • have a quiz • invite • Kenn • London • play football •
ran • shouted • Somalia • Spain • start at 6 o'clock • stayed • went

Test yourself
Write the lists in your exercise book.
a) Places: England, ..., ..., ..., ..., ..., ...
b) Verbs in the simple past: climbed, ..., ..., ..., ..., ...
c) A party: finish at 11 o'clock, ..., ..., ..., ..., ...

Are your answers right? Check on page 170.

→ **Ordnungszahlen**
1st   first
2nd   second
3rd   third
4th   fourth
5th   fifth
6th   sixth
7th   seventh
8th   eighth
9th   ninth
10th   tenth

Auf S. 167 gibt es
weitere Zahlen.

p.70	neighbour	Nachbar, Nachbarin
	Scotland	Schottland
	Wales	Wales
	Ireland	Irland
	Have you ever ...? – Yes,	Bist/Hast du schon
	I have./No, I haven't.	einmal ...? – Ja./Nein.
	be: **I've (= I have) been**	sein: Ich bin (schon einmal)
	to France.	in Frankreich gewesen.

→ *Have you ever been to* Scotland?
No, I haven't, but ...

→ ... *I've been to* Ireland. It's great.

p.71	**never**	(noch) nie, niemals
	Rome	Rom
	Austria	Österreich
	Belgium	Belgien
	Denmark	Dänemark
	Luxembourg	Luxemburg
	Poland	Polen
	Switzerland	Schweiz
	Czech Republic	Tschechische Republik
	Netherlands	Niederlande
	its	sein, seine; ihr, ihre

→ I've *never* been to Wales.

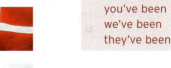

→ **have been**
I've been
you've been
we've been
they've been

p.72	**invitation**	Einladung
	finish: **I've (= I have)**	beenden: ich habe beendet
	finished	
	I haven't finished	ich habe nicht beendet
	make: **I've made**	machen: ich habe gemacht
	I'll give you your	Ich gebe euch eure Einla-
	invitations in the break.	dungen in der Pause.
	it has happened	es ist passiert
	help	Hilfe
	find: **I've found**	finden: ich habe gefunden
	buy: **I've bought**	kaufen: ich habe gekauft
	hotel	Hotel
	tell: **I've told**	ich habe erzählt
	card	Karte

 I like their house, but <u>its</u> colour is terrible.
I like their house. <u>It's</u> (= It is) pink!

→ *I've finished* my homework. Let's play now.

→ *I haven't talked* to Mel. Let's phone her now.

→ **I've** finished – **I haven't** finished
he **has** made – he **hasn't** made

→ Look! *I've found* a bag!

→ *I've bought* lots of food. Let's have a party!

→ *I've told* my mum that I'll help her.

p.73	**letter**	Buchstabe
	rhyme (with)	(sich) reimen (auf)
	lemonade	Limonade
	prize	Preis, Gewinn
	do: **I've done**	machen: ich habe gemacht

→ 'I' *rhymes with* 'my', but not with 'say'.

→ It rhymes!
Hi. - Bye.
day - they
see - tea

→ Don't look at me – *I've done* nothing!

Story

p.74	do: **I did**	machen: ich machte
	wide	breit

→  **WIDE**

narrow	schmal, eng	→	
canal	Kanal		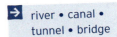
tough	hart, zäh, stark		river • canal • tunnel • bridge
bridge	Brücke →		
across the canal	über den Kanal	→	We walked *across* the new bridge.
behind	hinter		
he was hanging	er hing (gerade)		
by his arms	an den Armen		
onto the bridge	auf die Brücke hinauf	→	Sammy is climbing *onto* the box.
railway line	Eisenbahnstrecke, Gleis		

p. 75	gate	Tor		
	side	Seite	→	Let's walk on the sunny *side* of the street.
	he was running	er rannte (gerade)		
	after a ball	hinter einem Ball her	→	I shouted *after* him, but he didn't hear me.
	she picked up the boy	sie hob den Jungen hoch	→	Always *pick up* the litter in the playground!
	just before	kurz bevor		
	the right/best thing	das Richtige/Beste	→	Camping is cheap. And *the best thing* is: It's fun!
	think: I thought	denken: ich dachte		

Communication

p. 78	take: I've taken	bringen, nehmen: ich habe gebracht, genommen		
	write: I've written	schreiben: ich habe geschrieben	→	*I've written* her a letter.
	home-made	selbst gemacht	→	The cake is *home-made*!
	phone	anrufen, telefonieren		
	just	gerade, soeben	→	I've *just* talked to Kim. She's fine.
p. 79	pack	packen, einpacken	→	Let's *pack* some clothes and drive to France.
	say: I've said	sagen: ich habe gesagt		

Look at language

p. 80	have: I've had	haben: ich habe gehabt	→	*I've* just *had* breakfast.
	see: I've seen	sehen: ich habe gesehen	→	*Have you seen* the new film with Emily Watson?
	ride: I've ridden	fahren: ich bin gefahren	→	*I've* never *ridden* a quad bike.

Test yourself

1 *Finde das richtige Partizip Perfekt und schreibe die Liste in dein Heft.*

be:	I've been	tell:	I've ...	say:	I've ...
make:	I've ...	do:	I've ...	have:	I've ...
find:	I've ...	write:	I've ...	see:	I've ...
buy:	I've ...	take:	I've ...	ride:	I've ...

Tipp:
Wenn du bei Aufgabe 1 Hilfe brauchst, kannst du auch in der Liste *Irregular Verbs* auf S.169 nachsehen.

2 Write the sentences in your exercise book and finish them.
1 Have you ever ... to Spain? – No, I ... .
2 Which word ... with 'laugh' – 'half' or 'love'?
3 We're going on holiday tomorrow. I have to ... my clothes.
4 I like cycling, but I've ... ridden a mountain bike.

Are your answers right? Check on page 170.

DICTIONARY

Alphabetische Liste der Wörter aus Band 1 und 2 (Englisch - Deutsch)

mit Fundstellenangaben für den Lernwortschatz aus Band 2, z. B. U3: 48 = Unit 3, S. 48

WF (wahlfrei) = nicht zum Lernwortschatz gehörende Wörter

→ = verweist auf die Grundform eines Wortes

A

a [ə] ein, eine; **she's a bus driver** sie ist Busfahrerin; **24 hours a day** 24 Stunden am/pro Tag U4: 46

about [ə'baʊt] **1** über; **The text is about ...** Der Text handelt von ... U2: 24; **What about you?** Und du?/Was ist mit dir? **2** ungefähr U5: 67

accident ['æksɪdənt] Unfall U3: 43

across [ə'krɒs] über; hinüber, herüber U6: 74

act [ækt]: **Act the dialogue.** Spielt das Gespräch nach. U1: 19

action film ['ækʃnfɪlm] Actionfilm

activity [æk'tɪvəti] Beschäftigung, Aktivität U5: 58

actor ['æktə] Schauspieler/in WF

advert ['ædvɜːt] Anzeige U4: 49

after ['ɑːftə] nach; **after school** nach der Schule; **after a ball** hinter einem Ball her U6: 75

afternoon ['ɑːftə'nuːn] Nachmittag; **in the afternoon** am Nachmittag, nachmittags U1: 15

again [ə'gen] noch einmal, (schon) wieder

airport ['eəpɔːt] Flughafen; **at Exeter Airport** am Flughafen Exeter

all (the) [ɔːl] alle U1: 12; **all weekend** das ganze Wochenende U4: 48; **all the family** die ganze Familie WF

alone [ə'ləʊn] allein U1: 14

along [ə'lɒŋ] entlang U4: 50

alphabet ['ælfəbet] Alphabet U6: 73

alphabetical [ælfə'betɪkl] alphabetisch

always ['ɔːlweɪz] immer

am [æm] bin; **I'm (= I am) Sarah.** Ich heiße Sarah. **I'm from London.** Ich komme aus London. **How are you? – I'm fine, thanks.** Wie geht's? – Danke, gut. **Are you ...? – Yes, I am./No, I'm not.** Bist du ...? – Ja./Nein. U1: 14

America [ə'merɪkə] Amerika WF

an [ən] ein, eine

and [ænd, ənd] und

animal ['ænɪml] Tier

another [ə'nʌðə] noch ein, eine, einer, eins U5: 67

answer ['ɑːnsə] **1** antworten, beantworten; **2** Antwort

anywhere ['eniweə]: **not ... anywhere** nirgendwo, nirgendwohin, nirgendwoher U4: 54

apple ['æpl] Apfel

April ['eɪprəl] April

are [ɑː] bist; seid; sind; **aren't (= are not)** bist nicht; seid nicht; sind nicht; **How are you?** Wie geht's? **What are they in German?** Wie heißen sie auf Deutsch?

area ['eəriə] Gegend

arm [ɑːm] Arm U3: 43

arrive [ə'raɪv] ankommen U1: 12

arrived [ə'raɪvd]: **it arrived** er/sie/es kam an

art [ɑːt] Kunst U1: 12

as [əz]: **as safe as houses** vollkommen sicher WF

ask [ɑːsk] fragen; **ask a question** eine Frage stellen U1: 10

asked [ɑːskt]: **she asked** sie fragte

assistant [ə'sɪstənt]: **shop assistant** Verkäufer/in U3: 34

at [æt, ət] bei; an; in; **at eight o'clock** um acht/zwanzig Uhr; **at Exeter Station** im Bahnhof Exeter; **at home** zu Hause, daheim; **at night** nachts, in der Nacht WF; **at the weekend** am Wochenende; **she's at school** sie ist in der Schule; sie geht zur Schule

August ['ɔːgəst] August; **August 20th** 20. August

Austria ['ɒstriə] Österreich U6: 71

autograph ['ɔːtəgrɑːf] Autogramm U4: 56

B

back [bæk] zurück; **back from school** aus der Schule zurück; **I'm back!** Ich bin wieder da!

bad [bæd] schlecht; schlimm U2: 31

badge [bædʒ] Abzeichen; Button WF

badminton ['bædmɪntən] Badminton, Federball(spiel)

bag [bæg] (Schul-)Tasche

bagel ['beɪgl] Bagel (eine Art ringförmiges, festes Brötchen) WF

baggage handler ['bægɪdʒhændlə] Gepäckabfertiger, -abfertigerin

baggy pants ['bægipænts] Baggy Pants (modisch weite Hose) WF

baker ['beɪkə] Bäcker, Bäckerin WF

bakery ['beɪkəri] Bäckerei WF

bald [bɔːld]: **He's bald.** Er hat eine Glatze. WF

ball [bɔːl] Ball

banana [bə'nɑːnə] Banane

band [bænd] Band, (Musik-)Gruppe

bank [bæŋk] Bank, Sparkasse

barbecue ['bɑːbɪkjuː] Grill(fest) WF

basketball ['bɑːskɪtbɔːl] Basketball

bathroom ['bɑːθruːm] Badezimmer, Bad

be [biː, bi] (I/he was, you were; I've been) sein U4: 49

beach [biːtʃ] Strand

beat [biːt]: **I beat** ich schlug, ich habe geschlagen WF

beautician [bjuː'tɪʃn] Kosmetiker, Kosmetikerin WF

beauty salon ['bjuːtisælɒn] Kosmetikstudio WF

because [bɪ'kɒz] weil U5: 58

bed [bed] Bett

bedroom ['bedruːm] Schlafzimmer

been [biːn, bɪn] (→ be): **I've been** ich bin gewesen U6: 70

before [bɪ'fɔː] bevor

behind [bɪ'haɪnd] hinter U6: 74

being ['biːɪŋ]: **Being a buddy is OK.** „Kumpel" zu sein ist okay. WF

Belgium ['beldʒəm] Belgien U6: 71

believe [bɪ'liːv] glauben WF

best [best] beste, bester, bestes; **Best wishes, ...** Viele Grüße ... U5: 65

better ['betə] besser

big [bɪg] groß

bike [baɪk] Fahrrad, Rad

bird [bɜːd] Vogel

birthday ['bɜːθdeɪ] Geburtstag; **It's my birthday.** Ich habe Geburtstag.

black [blæk] schwarz

blind [blaɪnd] Rolladen, Jalousie WF

blonde [blɒnd] blond U5: 67

blood [blʌd] Blut WF

blue [bluː] blau

board [bɔːd] Tafel

boat [bəʊt] Boot, Schiff WF

book [bʊk] Buch; Heft

bookshop ['bʊkʃɒp] Buchhandlung

boot [buːt] Stiefel WF

boring ['bɔːrɪŋ] langweilig

borrow ['bɒrəʊ]: **borrow a pen** sich einen Füller (aus)leihen U1: 19

bought [bɔːt] (→ buy): **I bought** ich kaufte, ich habe gekauft U3: 39; **I've bought** ich habe gekauft U6: 72

bowls [bəʊlz] Bowls *(Kugelspiel, ähnl. wie Boule oder Boccia)* WF

box [bɒks] Kiste, Kasten

boy [bɔɪ] Junge

bread [bred] Brot WF

break [breɪk] Pause U1: 13

breakfast ['brekfəst] Frühstück; **have breakfast** frühstücken

bridge [brɪdʒ] Brücke U6: 74

bring [brɪŋ] (I brought, I've brought) bringen

brochure ['brəʊʃə] Broschüre U1: 13

brother ['brʌðə] Bruder; **brothers and sisters** Geschwister

brown [braʊn] braun

buddy ['bʌdi] „Kumpel" *(ältere/r Schüler/in, der/die jüngeren hilft)* U1: 13

builder ['bɪldə] Bauarbeiter/in WF

building site ['bɪldɪŋsaɪt] Baustelle WF

bunny ['bʌni] Hase, Häschen WF

bus [bʌs] Bus

bus driver ['bʌsdraɪvə] Busfahrer, Busfahrerin

but [bʌt] aber

butter ['bʌtə] Butter WF

buy [baɪ] (I bought, I've bought) kaufen

by [baɪ] von; durch U4: 49; **by bike/bus/car/...** mit dem Rad/Bus/Auto/...; **by his arms** an den Armen U6: 74; **Learn it by heart.** Lerne es auswendig. U2: 25

Bye. [baɪ] Tschüs. Wiedersehen.

C

cafe ['kæfeɪ] Café

cafeteria [kæfə'tɪərɪə] Cafeteria, Kantine WF

cake [keɪk] Kuchen

calendar ['kælɪndə] Kalender WF

calling ['kɔːlɪŋ]: **Thanks for calling.** Danke für den Anruf. U3: 42

came [keɪm] (→ come): **I came** ich kam, ich bin gekommen U3: 38

camping ['kæmpɪŋ] Camping

can [kæn, kən] können, dürfen; **can't** [kɑːnt] nicht können; **Can you ...? – Yes, I can./No, I can't.** Kannst du ...? – Ja./Nein. U1: 10

canal [kə'næl] Kanal U6: 74

canoe [kə'nuː] Kanu U4: 47

canoeing [kə'nuːɪŋ] Kanu fahren, Paddeln

cap [kæp] Kappe U1: 20

car [kɑː] Auto

card [kɑːd] Karte U6: 72

Careful! ['keəfl] Vorsicht! WF

caretaker ['keəteɪkə] Hausmeister, Hausmeisterin WF; **caretaker's room** Hausmeisterbüro WF

car park ['kɑːpaːk] (großer) Parkplatz

cat [kæt] Katze

CD [siː'diː] CD

celebrate ['selɪbreɪt] feiern WF

centre ['sentə] Zentrum; Mitte

chair [tʃeə] Stuhl; Sessel

chairperson ['tʃeəpɜːsn] Vorsitzende, Vorsitzender

chalk [tʃɔːk] Kreide WF

change [tʃeɪndʒ] (sich) ändern, (sich) verändern U5: 62

cheap [tʃiːp] billig, preiswert U2: 24

check [tʃek] kontrollieren, überprüfen

cheese [tʃiːz] Käse WF

cheeseburger ['tʃiːzbɜːgə] Cheeseburger WF

chicken ['tʃɪkɪn] Huhn; (Brat-)Hähnchen

chicken nuggets ['tʃɪkɪn'nʌgɪts] Chicken Nuggets *(kleine, panierte Geflügelfleischstücke)* WF

child, children [tʃaɪld, 'tʃɪldrən] Kind, Kinder

chips [tʃɪps] Pommes frites U3: 37

chocolate ['tʃɒklət] Schokolade

chocolate bar ['tʃɒklətbaː] Schokoladenriegel WF

Christmas ['krɪsməs] Weihnachten; Weihnachts- WF

Christmas Day [krɪsməs'deɪ] Erster Weihnachtsfeiertag WF

Christmas Eve [krɪsməs'iːv] Heiligabend WF

Christmas pudding [krɪsməs'pʊdɪŋ] Plumpudding *(heiß servierte Nachspeise)* WF

church [tʃɜːtʃ] Kirche WF

cinema ['sɪnəmə] Kino

class [klɑːs] Klasse

classroom ['klɑːsruːm] Klassenzimmer

class teacher ['klɑːstiːtʃə] Klassenlehrer, Klassenlehrerin U1: 12

cleaner ['kliːnə] Raumpfleger, Raumpflegerin WF

climb [klaɪm]: **climb a hill** auf einen Hügel klettern U5: 62

cloakroom ['kləʊkruːm] Garderobe WF

clock [klɒk] Uhr WF

close [kləʊz] zumachen, schließen U1: 11

closed [kləʊzd] geschlossen, zu U4: 46

clothes [kləʊðz] Kleidung, Kleider

cloud [klaʊd] Wolke U5: 62

cloudy ['klaʊdi] bewölkt U5: 66

club [klʌb] Klub, Arbeitsgemeinschaft U1: 13

cocoa ['kəʊkəʊ] Kakao WF

coffee ['kɒfi] Kaffee WF

cola ['kəʊlə] Cola U2: 27

cold [kəʊld] kalt U5: 62

collect [kə'lekt] sammeln

colour ['kʌlə] Farbe; **What colour is your room?** Welche Farbe hat dein Zimmer?

come [kʌm] (I came, I've come) kommen; mitkommen; **come in** hereinkommen U3: 38; **come out** herauskommen WF

complain [kəm'pleɪn] sich beschweren U5: 62

computer [kəm'pjuːtə] Computer, Rechner

cook [kʊk] Koch, Köchin U3: 34

cool [kuːl] cool, toll

cornflakes ['kɔːnfleɪks] Cornflakes WF

cosmetics [kɒz'metɪks] Kosmetika WF

could [kʊd]: **I could** ich konnte WF

country ['kʌntri] Land; **in the country** auf dem Land

courier ['kʊrɪə] Kurier/Kurierin, Bote/Botin U3: 36

course [kɔːs]: **of course** natürlich, selbstverständlich U2: 31

cousin ['kʌzn] Cousin, Cousine U2: 24

cow [kaʊ] Kuh

crawl [krɔːl] kriechen U2: 25; **crawl in** hineinkriechen U2: 26

criminal ['krɪmɪnl] Kriminelle, Krimineller WF

crisps [krɪsps] Kartoffelchips U3: 37

crossing ['krɒsɪŋ]: **zebra crossing** Zebrastreifen WF
cup [kʌp] Tasse U2: 26; **a cup of tea** eine Tasse Tee U2: 26
cupboard ['kʌbəd] Schrank
curry sauce ['kʌrɪsɔːs]: **sausage with curry sauce** Currywurst WF
curtain ['kɜːtn] Vorhang WF
custom ['kʌstəm] Brauch WF
cycling ['saɪklɪŋ] Radfahren U5: 58
Czech Republic [tʃekrɪ'pʌblɪk] Tschechische Republik U6: 71

D

dad [dæd] Papa, Vati
dancing ['dɑːnsɪŋ]: **go dancing** tanzen gehen
dangerous ['deɪndʒərəs] gefährlich
date [deɪt] Datum U3: 44
daughter ['dɔːtə] Tochter U4: 51
day [deɪ] Tag
dead [ded] tot WF
deal [diːl]: **deal with bags** sich um Taschen kümmern
dear [dɪə]: **Dear ...** Liebe/Lieber ...; **my dear Watson** mein lieber Watson WF
December [dɪ'sembə] Dezember
decoration [dekə'reɪʃn] Dekoration, Schmuck
Denmark ['denmɑːk] Dänemark U6: 71
dentist's assistant ['dentɪstsə'sɪstənt] Zahnarzthelfer, Zahnarzthelferin WF
department store [dɪ'pɑːtməntstɔː] Kaufhaus U4: 46
description [dɪ'skrɪpʃn] Beschreibung U5: 66
detective [dɪ'tektɪv] Detektiv/Detektivin WF
dialogue ['daɪəlɒg] Dialog, Gespräch
diary ['daɪəri]: **homework diary** Hausaufgabenheft; Schülerkalender U1: 11
dictionary ['dɪkʃənri] Wörterbuch; Wörterverzeichnis
did [dɪd] (→ do): **I did** ich machte, ich habe gemacht U6: 74; **you didn't see him** du hast ihn nicht gesehen WF
die [daɪ] sterben WF
different ['dɪfrənt] verschieden; anders U1: 17; andere, anderer, anderes U1: 17; **different from** anders als U4: 46
dinner ['dɪnə] Festessen WF

dirty ['dɜːti] schmutzig
diving ['daɪvɪŋ] Springen *(vom Sprungbrett)* WF
DJ ['diːdʒeɪ] DJ (= Discjockey) U4: 49
do [duː] (he does; I did, I've done) **1** tun, machen; schaffen; **2 I don't (= do not)/He doesn't (= does not) live here.** Ich wohne/Er wohnt nicht hier. **Do you/Does he live here? - Yes, I do./No, I don't. / Yes, he does./No, he doesn't.** Wohnst du/Wohnt er hier? - Ja./Nein. **Don't eat.** Iss nicht. U1: 18
doctor's assistant ['dɒktəzə'sɪstənt] Arzthelfer, Arzthelferin WF
does [dʌz] → do
dog [dɒg] Hund
doing ['duːɪŋ]: **What are you doing?** Was machst du (da)?
done [dʌn] (→ do): **I've done** ich habe gemacht U6: 73
doner kebab [dɒnəkɪ'bæb] Döner-kebab WF
door [dɔː] Tür
doughnut ['dəʊnʌt] Donut *(ring-förmiges Hefegebäck)* WF
drank [dræŋk] (→ drink): **I drank** ich trank, ich habe getrunken U4: 49
draw [drɔː] (I drew, I've drawn) zeichnen
dream [driːm] **1** träumen U4: 49; **2** Traum U2: 25
dress [dres] Kleid WF
drink [drɪŋk] **1** (I drink, I've drunk) trinken U4: 49; **2** Getränk U2: 26
drive [draɪv] (I drove, I've driven) fahren U2: 23
driver ['draɪvə] (Auto-)Fahrer/in
DVD [diːviː'diː] DVD

E

early ['ɜːli] früh
Easter ['iːstə] Ostern; Oster- WF
easy ['iːzi] einfach, leicht
eat [iːt] (I ate, I've eaten) essen; fressen
egg [eg] Ei WF
Eid [iːd] Eid *(muslimisches Fest)* WF
electrician [ɪlek'trɪʃn] Elektriker, Elektrikerin WF
electronic [ɪlek'trɒnɪk] elektronisch
e-mail ['iːmeɪl] E-Mail U1: 15
end [end] Ende WF

England ['ɪŋglənd] England
English ['ɪŋglɪʃ] englisch; Englisch; Engländer/in(nen)
English teacher ['ɪŋglɪʃtiːtʃə] Englischlehrer/in
enormous [ɪ'nɔːməs] riesengroß WF
escape [ɪ'skeɪp] ausbrechen, (ent)fliehen WF
euro (€) ['jʊərəʊ] Euro U4: 47
evening ['iːvnɪŋ] Abend; **in the evening** am Abend, abends U1: 15
ever ['evə] schon einmal, jemals U6: 70
every ['evri] jede, jeder, jedes
everybody ['evribɒdi] jeder, alle
everything ['evriθɪŋ] alles WF
everywhere ['evriweə] überall U5: 63
example [ɪg'zɑːmpl] Beispiel
exciting [ɪk'saɪtɪŋ] aufregend, spannend U2: 25
exercise ['eksəsaɪz] Übung U1: 17
exercise book ['eksəsaɪzbʊk] Schulheft
expensive [ɪk'spensɪv] teuer
explain [ɪk'spleɪn] erklären
eyeshadow ['aɪʃædəʊ] Lidschatten WF

F

fact [fækt]: **In fact, it was better.** Es war sogar besser. U2: 24
factory ['fæktri] Fabrik U3: 35
fair [feə] fair, gerecht WF
fall [fɔːl] (I fell, I've fallen) fallen U3: 43; **fall to the ground** auf den Boden fallen U4: 51
family ['fæməli] Familie
famous ['feɪməs] berühmt WF
fan [fæn] Fan, Anhänger/in
farm [fɑːm] Bauernhof, Hof
farmer ['fɑːmə] Bauer, Bäuerin
fast [fɑːst] schnell
fast food [fɑːst'fuːd] Fastfood *(schnell verzehrbare Gerichte)* U3: 36
father ['fɑːðə] Vater
favourite ['feɪvərɪt] Lieblings-; Liebling
February ['februari] Februar
feed [fiːd] (I fed, I've fed) füttern, zu essen geben
feel [fiːl] (I felt, I've felt) sich fühlen U1: 20
feet [fiːt] Füße (→ foot) U3: 43
fell [fel] (→ fall): **I fell** ich fiel, ich bin gefallen U3: 43

field [fiːld] Feld, Wiese
film [fɪlm] Film
find [faɪnd] (I found, I've found) finden; **find out** herausfinden
fine [faɪn] gut, schön U3: 42; **How are you? – I'm fine, thanks.** Wie geht's? – Danke, gut.
finish ['fɪnɪʃ] aufhören (mit); beenden
fire ['faɪə]: **fire a gun** mit einer Pistole schießen WF
firefighter ['faɪəfaɪtə] Feuerwehrfrau, Feuerwehrmann WF
fireworks ['faɪəwɜːks] Feuerwerk WF
first [fɜːst] **1** erste, erster, erstes; **2** zuerst U1: 13
fish [fɪʃ] Fisch, Fische
fish and chip shop [fɪʃən'tʃɪpʃɒp] Schnellimbiss für Fisch und Pommes frites
fishing ['fɪʃɪŋ] Fischen, Angeln U5: 59
flat [flæt] Wohnung
floor [flɔː] **1** Fußboden WF; **2** Stockwerk WF; **on the first floor** im ersten Stock(werk) WF; **ground floor** Erdgeschoss, Parterre WF
florist ['flɒrɪst] Florist, Floristin WF
follow ['fɒləʊ] folgen, verfolgen U3: 41
food [fuːd] Essen; Lebensmittel U2: 31
foot, feet [fʊt, fiːt] Fuß, Füße U3: 43; **on foot** zu Fuß
football ['fʊtbɔːl] Fußball
for [fɔː, fə] für; **for breakfast/ lunch** zum Frühstück/Mittagessen U2: 31; **just for fun** nur zum Spaß WF; **That's England for you!** So ist England eben! WF
forever [fər'evə] für immer WF
forget [fə'get] (I forgot, I've forgotten) vergessen
form [fɔːm] Form U3: 45
found [faʊnd] (→ find): **I found** ich fand, ich habe gefunden U5: 63; **I've found** ich habe gefunden U6: 72
France [frɑːns] Frankreich U6: 70
French [frentʃ] französisch; Französisch; Franzose(n), Französin(nen) U1: 12
Friday ['fraɪdeɪ, 'fraɪdi] Freitag
friend [frend] Freund, Freundin
friendly ['frendli] freundlich U5: 67

frightened ['fraɪtnd]: **I'm frightened** ich habe Angst U2: 27
from [frɒm, frəm] aus; von; **I'm from London.** Ich komme aus London.
fruit [fruːt] Obst, Früchte U3: 37
fun [fʌn] Spaß; **It's fun.** Es macht Spaß. U5: 58
funny ['fʌni] lustig, komisch U3: 44

G

game [geɪm] Spiel; **a game of bowls** eine Partie Bowls WF
garage ['gærɑːʒ] Autowerkstatt WF
garden ['gɑːdn] Garten
gardener ['gɑːdnə] Gärtner, Gärtnerin U3: 34
gate [geɪt] Tor U6: 75
gave [geɪv]: **I gave** ich gab, ich habe gegeben WF
geography [dʒi'ɒgrəfi] Erdkunde, Geografie U1: 12
German ['dʒɜːmən] deutsch; Deutsch; Deutsche, Deutscher
Germany ['dʒɜːməni] Deutschland
get [get] (I got, I've got) **1** bekommen U2: 25; **2** holen; **3** kommen, gelangen; **I have to get out of this place.** Ich muss hier raus. **get up** aufstehen
girl [gɜːl] Mädchen
girlfriend ['gɜːlfrend] (feste) Freundin U4: 48
give [gɪv] (I gave, I've given) geben; **Give the book to Tim.** Gib Tim das Buch. U1: 13; **give money to people** Geld an Menschen verschenken WF
glass [glɑːs] Glas, Trinkglas U2: 31
go [gəʊ] (I went, I've gone) gehen; fahren; fliegen U2: 24; führen U5: 62; **go in** hineingehen U2: 26
going to ['gəʊɪntu, 'gəʊɪntə]: **I'm going to win** ich werde gewinnen, ich gewinne U5: 60; **I'm going to be a ranger.** Ich werde Ranger. U5: 65; **It's going to be OK.** Es wird gut werden. U3: 39
gold [gəʊld] Gold WF
gone [gɒn]: **he was gone** er war verschwunden WF
good [gʊd] gut; **Good evening/ morning/night.** Gute(n) Abend/ Morgen/Nacht. **Good Friday** Karfreitag WF

Goodbye. [gʊd'baɪ] Auf Wiedersehen.
got [gɒt] (→ get): **I got** ich bekam, ich habe bekommen U3: 36
grandad ['grændæd] Opa, Großvater
grandfather ['grænfɑːðə] Großvater WF
grandma ['grænmɑː] Oma, Großmutter
great [greɪt] toll, großartig
green [griːn] grün
grey [greɪ] grau WF
ground [graʊnd] Boden U4: 51
ground floor [graʊnd'flɔː] Erdgeschoss, Parterre WF
group [gruːp] Gruppe
guard [gɑːd]: **security guard** Wachfrau, Wachmann U3: 34
guess [ges] raten; erraten
guide [gaɪd] Führer, Führerin (für Sehenswürdigkeiten) U2: 25
guitar [gɪ'tɑː] Gitarre
gun [gʌn] Pistole WF
gym [dʒɪm] Turnhalle WF

H

had [hæd, həd] (→ have): **I had** ich hatte, ich habe gehabt U3: 36; **I've had** ich habe gehabt U6: 79
hair [heə] Haar, Haare U5: 67
hairdresser ['heədresə] Friseur, Friseurin U3: 34
half [hɑːf]: **half past nine** halb zehn
hall [hɔːl] **1** Aula WF; **2** Flur WF
Halloween [hæləʊ'iːn] Halloween (31. Oktober) WF
ham [hæm] Schinken WF
hamburger ['hæmbɜːgə] Hamburger
hamster ['hæmstə] Hamster
hand [hænd] Hand
hand signal ['hændsɪgnəl] Handzeichen
hanging ['hæŋɪŋ]: **he was hanging** er hing (gerade) U6: 74
happen ['hæpən] passieren, geschehen U1: 14
happy ['hæpi] glücklich, froh; **Happy birthday!** Herzlichen Glückwunsch zum Geburtstag! **Happy Easter!** Frohe Ostern! WF
hard [hɑːd] hart; schwer U3: 36
has [hæz, həz] → have
hat [hæt] Hut WF
hate [heɪt] hassen, nicht ausstehen können U3: 38

have [hæv, həv] (he has; I had, I've had) **1** haben; **have a cola** eine Cola trinken; **have a party** eine Party geben; **have a picnic** ein Picknick machen U5: 61; **have an ice cream** ein Eis essen; **have breakfast** frühstücken; **2 I've (= I have)/he has finished** ich habe/er hat beendet U6: 72; **I haven't (= have not)/he hasn't (= has not) finished** ich habe/er hat nicht beendet U6: 72; **Have you ever ...? – Yes, I have./No, I haven't.** Bist/Hast du schon einmal ...? – Ja./Nein. U6: 70

have to ['hævtu, 'hævtə] (I had to, I've had to) müssen

he [hiː] er; **he's (= he is)** er ist

head [hed] Kopf U3: 43

headscarf ['hedskɑːf] Kopftuch WF

head teacher [hed'tiːtʃə] Schulleiter, Schulleiterin WF

healthy ['helθi] gesund U3: 36

heard [hɜːd]: **I heard** ich hörte, ich habe gehört WF

heart [hɑːt]: **Learn it by heart.** Lerne es auswendig. U2: 25

heavy ['hevi] schwer, dick WF

Hello. [hə'ləʊ] Hallo. (Guten) Tag.

help [help] **1** helfen; **2** Hilfe U6: 72

helper ['helpə] Helfer/in U5: 64

her [hɜː] **1** ihr, ihre; **2** ihr, sie

here [hɪə] hier; hierher; **Here you are.** Hier, bitte. U1: 19

hero ['hɪərəʊ] Held, Heldin WF

Hi. [haɪ] Hallo.

hide [haɪd] verstecken WF

hill [hɪl] Hügel, (kleiner) Berg U5: 60

him [hɪm] ihm, ihn

hire ['haɪə] mieten; vermieten U4: 47

his [hɪz] sein, seine

history ['hɪstri] Geschichte U1: 12

hockey ['hɒki] Hockey U1: 13

holiday(s) ['hɒlədeɪ, -z] Ferien, Urlaub; **go on holiday** in den Urlaub fahren; **she's on holiday** sie macht/sie ist im Urlaub

home [həʊm] Heim, Zuhause; **at home** zu Hause, daheim; **go home** nach Hause gehen

home-made [həʊm'meɪd] selbst gemacht U6: 78

homework ['həʊmwɜːk] Hausaufgaben, Schularbeiten; **I do my homework.** Ich mache (meine) Hausaufgaben.

homework diary [həʊmwɜːk'daɪəri] Hausaufgabenheft; Schülerkalender U1: 11

honey ['hʌni] Honig WF

hope [həʊp] hoffen U5: 65

horrible ['hɒrəbl] scheußlich WF

horse [hɔːs] Pferd

horse riding ['hɔːsraɪdɪŋ] Reiten U5: 58

hospital ['hɒspɪtl] Krankenhaus U3: 35

hot dog ['hɒtdɒg] Hot Dog (*heißes Würstchen im Brötchen*) WF

hotel [həʊ'tel] Hotel U6: 72

hound [haʊnd] Jagdhund WF

hour ['aʊə] Stunde U2: 24

house [haʊs] Haus; **at Tim's house** bei Tim (zu Hause) U1: 18; **Let's go to my house.** Gehen wir zu mir (nach Hause). U1: 18

how [haʊ] wie

hungry ['hʌŋgri] hungrig; **I'm hungry.** Ich habe Hunger.

hurry ['hʌri]: **Hurry up!** Beeil dich! U1: 18

hurt [hɜːt] (I hurt, I've hurt) verletzen, wehtun U3: 43; **I hurt my hand** ich verletzte mir die Hand, ich habe mir die Hand verletzt U3: 43

I

I [aɪ] ich; **I'd like ...** Ich möchte .../Ich hätte gern ... U2: 26; **I'd like to go/...** Ich möchte gehen/... U4: 47; **I'm (= I am)** ich bin; **I'll give you your invitations in the break.** Ich gebe euch eure Einladungen in der Pause. U6: 72

ice cream [aɪs'kriːm] (Speise-)Eis

ice skate ['aɪskeɪt] Schlittschuh WF

ice skating ['aɪskeɪtɪŋ] Schlittschuhlaufen WF

idea [aɪ'dɪə] Idee, Einfall

if [ɪf] **1** wenn, falls U3: 37; **2** ob WF

important [ɪm'pɔːtnt] wichtig U2: 24

in [ɪn] in; **in 1596** (im Jahre) 1596 WF; **in April** im April; **in Fairfield Road** in der Fairfield Road; **in German** auf Deutsch; **in the country** auf dem Land; **in the day** tagsüber WF; **in the morning/afternoon/evening** am Morgen/Nachmittag/Abend U1: 15; **in the picture** auf dem Bild; **in the playground** auf dem Schulhof U1: 14; **in the street** auf der Straße U3: 39; **in the world** auf der (ganzen) Welt U2: 26; **come in** hereinkommen U3: 38; **go/crawl in** hineingehen/-kriechen U2: 26

in fact [ɪn'fækt]: **In fact, it was better.** Es war sogar besser. U2: 24

information [ɪnfə'meɪʃn] Informationen, Informations- U5: 60

in-line skate [ɪnlaɪn'skeɪt] Inlineskate, Inliner WF

in-line skating [ɪnlaɪn'skeɪtɪŋ] Inlineskating WF

instead of [ɪn'stedəv] statt U2: 31

interested (in) ['ɪntrəstɪd] interessiert (an) U4: 54

interesting ['ɪntrəstɪŋ] interessant U2: 30

Internet ['ɪntənet] Internet U5: 61

interpreting [ɪn'tɜːprɪtɪŋ] Dolmetschen U2: 29

into ['ɪntu, 'ɪntə] in (... hinein/herein) U4: 50; **into the street** auf die Straße (hinaus) U3: 41

invitation [ɪnvɪ'teɪʃn] Einladung U6: 72

invite [ɪn'vaɪt] einladen

Ireland ['aɪələnd] Irland U6: 70

is [ɪz] ist; **isn't (= is not)** ist nicht; **It's my birthday.** Ich habe Geburtstag. **What colour is your room?** Welche Farbe hat dein Zimmer?

it [ɪt] **1** es (*nicht bei Personen: er, sie*); **2** ihm, es (*nicht bei Personen: ihm, ihn; ihr, sie*); **it's (= it is)** es ist; **It's Sarah.** Hier spricht Sarah. U3: 43

its [ɪts] sein, seine; ihr, ihre U6: 71

J

jacket ['dʒækət] Jacke U5: 60

jam [dʒæm] Marmelade WF

January ['dʒænjuəri] Januar

jeans [dʒiːnz] Jeans U4: 49

job [dʒɒb] **1** Aufgabe, Arbeit; **2** Arbeitsstelle; Beruf

jogger ['dʒɒgə] Jogger, Joggerin

jogging ['dʒɒgɪŋ] Jogging U5: 58

judo ['dʒuːdəʊ] Judo U1: 13

juice [dʒuːs] Saft

July [dʒu'laɪ] Juli

June [dʒuːn] Juni

just [dʒʌst] gerade, soeben U6: 78; **just before** kurz (be)vor U6: 75; **just for fun** nur zum Spaß WF

K

keep [ki:p]: **keep left** auf der linken Seite bleiben WF
kill [kɪl] umbringen WF
killed [kɪld]: **he has killed him** er hat ihn umgebracht WF
kilometre ['kɪləmi:tə] Kilometer U2: 23
kitchen ['kɪtʃɪn] Küche
knew [nju:] (→ know): **I knew** ich wusste, ich habe gewusst U3: 44
know [nəʊ] (I knew, I've known) wissen, kennen

L

label ['leɪbl] Schildchen, Etikett U1: 11
labourer ['leɪbərə] Arbeiter/in WF
last [lɑ:st] letzte, letzter, letztes U3: 36
last-minute trip [lɑ:stmɪnɪt'trɪp] Last-Minute-Reise *(kurzfristig anzutreten, dafür verbilligt)* WF
late [leɪt] spät; zu spät, verspätet; **Jamie is late (for school).** Jamie kommt zu spät (zur Schule).
later ['leɪtə] später
laugh [lɑ:f] lachen U1: 12
learn [lɜ:n] lernen U2: 25; **Learn it by heart.** Lerne es auswendig. U2: 25
leave [li:v] (I left, I've left) verlassen, weggehen (von) U3: 38
left [left] links U2: 23; **on the left** auf der linken Seite U2: 23
left [left] (→ leave): **I left** ich verließ, ich habe verlassen U3: 38
lemonade [lemə'neɪd] (Zitronen-)Limonade U6: 73
lesson ['lesn] (Unterrichts-)Stunde
let [let]: **Let's finish.** Lasst uns aufhören./Hören wir auf.
letter ['letə] **1** Brief U5: 65; **2** Buchstabe U6: 73
letterboxing ['letəbɒksɪŋ] „Letterboxing" *(eine Art Schatzsuche)* U5: 63
library ['laɪbrəri] Bücherei WF
life [laɪf] Leben
light [laɪt] Licht, Lampe
light sabre ['laɪtseɪbə] Lichtschwert WF
like [laɪk] **1** mögen, gern haben; **I like it.** Ich mag es./Es gefällt mir. **I (don't) like walking.** Ich laufe (nicht) gern. **I'd like ...** Ich möchte .../Ich hätte gern ... U2: 26; **I'd like to go/...** Ich

möchte gehen/... U4: 47; **2** wie; **What does she look like?** Wie sieht sie aus? U5: 67
line [laɪn] Zeile
lip [lɪp] Lippe U3: 37
list [lɪst] Liste
listen ['lɪsn] zuhören; **listen to** hören, sich anhören
litter ['lɪtə] Abfall U5: 62
live [lɪv] wohnen, leben
living room ['lɪvɪŋru:m] Wohnzimmer
locked [lɒkt]: **she locked her bike** sie schloss ihr Fahrrad ab WF
lonely ['ləʊnli] einsam U5: 60
long [lɒŋ] lang; lange U2: 24
look [lʊk] **1** schauen, sehen; **look at** ansehen, sich ansehen; **2** aussehen U5: 67; **What does she look like?** Wie sieht sie aus? U5: 67; **look after** sich kümmern um WF; **look for** suchen U3: 36
lots [lɒts]: **lots of** viele; viel
lotto ['lɒtəʊ] Lotto U4: 48; **win the lotto** im Lotto gewinnen U4: 48
love [lʌv] lieben, sehr mögen U3: 37; **Lots of love, ...** Viele liebe Grüße ...
lunch [lʌntʃ] Mittagessen U1: 13; **lunch break** Mittagspause U3: 44
Luxembourg ['lʌksəmbɜ:g] Luxemburg U6: 71

M

made [meɪd] (→ make): **I made** ich machte, ich habe gemacht U3: 39; **I've made** ich habe gemacht U6: 72
magazine [mægə'zi:n] Zeitschrift
make [meɪk] (I made, I've made) machen, herstellen; **Make notes.** Mach dir Notizen.
man, men [mæn, men] Mann, Männer U4: 46
many ['meni] viele
map [mæp] (Land-)Karte U5: 60
March [mɑ:tʃ] März
match [mætʃ] **1** Spiel, Wettkampf; **2 Match the words with the pictures.** Ordne den Wörtern die Bilder zu.
maths [mæθs] Mathe(matik) U1: 12
May [meɪ] Mai
me [mi:] mir, mich
mechanic [mə'kænɪk] Mechaniker, Mechanikerin WF

meet [mi:t] (I met, I've met) **1** (sich) treffen (mit) U1: 18; **2** kennen lernen U2: 30; **Nice to meet you.** Schön, dich/Sie kennen zu lernen. U2: 30
men [men] Männer (→ man) U4: 46
met [met] (→ meet): **I met** ich traf, ich habe getroffen U3: 44
mile [maɪl] Meile U2: 23
milk [mɪlk] Milch
minute ['mɪnɪt] Minute U5: 63
miss [mɪs] vermissen U2: 31
missing ['mɪsɪŋ]: **the missing words** die fehlenden Wörter
mist [mɪst] Nebel WF
mobile (phone) ['məʊbaɪl, məʊbaɪl'fəʊn] Handy, Mobiltelefon U2: 24
modern ['mɒdn] modern
Monday ['mʌndeɪ, 'mʌndi] Montag
money ['mʌni] Geld
month [mʌnθ] Monat
moon [mu:n] Mond WF
moor [mɔ:] (Hoch-)Moor U5: 60
more [mɔ:] mehr, weitere; **more expensive** teurer U2: 24
morning ['mɔ:nɪŋ] Morgen; **in the morning** am Morgen, morgens U1: 15; **Monday morning** Montagmorgen
mosque [mɒsk] Moschee WF
most [məʊst] der/die/das meiste, die meisten U4: 47; **most expensive** teuerste/teuerster/teuerstes, am teuersten U2: 24
mother ['mʌðə] Mutter
motorbike ['məʊtəbaɪk] Motorrad
mountain bike ['maʊntənbaɪk] Mountainbike
mountain biking ['maʊntənbaɪkɪŋ] Mountainbikefahren
move [mu:v] umziehen U3: 36
moved [mu:vd]: **he/we moved** er ist/wir sind umgezogen U1: 14
Mr ['mɪstə]: **Mr Dunn** Herr Dunn
Mrs ['mɪsɪz]: **Mrs Jones** Frau Jones
Ms [mɪz, məz]: **Ms Brown** Frau Brown
much [mʌtʃ] viel
mug [mʌg] Becher, große Tasse WF
mum [mʌm] Mama, Mutti
museum [mju'zi:əm] Museum
music ['mju:zɪk] Musik
Muslim ['mʊzlɪm] Muslim, Muslima WF
my [maɪ] mein, meine

N

name [neɪm] Name; **What's your name?** Wie heißt du?

narrow ['nærəʊ] schmal, eng U6: 74

national park ['næʃnəl'pɑːk] Nationalpark U5: 60

near [nɪə] in der Nähe (von); nah

nearest ['nɪərɪst]: **the nearest airport** der nächste Flughafen U2: 24

need [niːd] brauchen U3: 38

neighbour ['neɪbə] Nachbar, Nachbarin U6: 70

nephew ['nefjuː] Neffe WF

nervous ['nɜːvəs] ängstlich WF

Netherlands ['neðələndz] Niederlande U6: 71

network ['netwɜːk] Netz; Wortnetz, Wörternetz

never ['nevə] (noch) nie, niemals U6: 71

new [njuː] neu

news [njuːz] Neuigkeit, -keiten WF

newspaper ['njuːzpeɪpə] Zeitung U4: 49

New Year's Eve [njuːjɪəz'iːv] Silvester WF

next [nekst] nächste, nächster, nächstes

next to ['nekstu, 'nekstə] neben

nice [naɪs] nett; schön

night [naɪt] Nacht WF; **at night** nachts, in der Nacht WF

no [nəʊ] **1** nein; **2** kein, keine; **There's no such thing.** So etwas gibt es nicht.

nobody ['nəʊbədi] niemand U3: 39

nonsense ['nɒnsns] Unsinn, Blödsinn U1: 16

not [nɒt] nicht

note [nəʊt] Notiz

nothing ['nʌθɪŋ] (gar) nichts

November [nəʊ'vembə] November

now [naʊ] nun, jetzt

nurse [nɜːs] Krankenpfleger, Krankenschwester WF

O

o'clock [ə'klɒk]: **at eight o'clock** um acht/zwanzig Uhr

October [ɒk'təʊbə] Oktober

of [ɒv, əv] von; **a picture of my dog** ein Bild meines Hundes U1: 17; **a cup of tea** eine Tasse Tee U2: 26; **think of** denken an

of course [əv'kɔːs] natürlich, selbstverständlich U2: 31

off [ɒf] von U3: 43

office ['ɒfɪs] Büro WF

officer ['ɒfɪsə]: **police officer** Polizist/Polizistin, Polizeibeamter/-beamtin U3: 34

office worker ['ɒfɪswɜːkə] Angestellte, Angestellter WF

off-road ['ɒfrəʊd] abseits der Straße, im Gelände

often ['ɒfn] oft

OK [əʊ'keɪ] okay, (schon) gut, in Ordnung; **Are you OK?** Ist alles in Ordnung bei dir? U2: 27; **That's OK.** Schon gut./Bitte. U1: 15

old [əʊld] alt

on [ɒn] auf; **on August 5th** am 5. August U3: 44; **on Dartmoor** in Dartmoor U5: 60; **on foot** zu Fuß; **on holiday** in/im Urlaub; **on Saturdays** samstags; **on school days** an Schultagen; **on the bus** im Bus; **on the phone** am Telefon U1: 15; **on the road** unterwegs; **on TV** im Fernsehen

one [wʌn] ein, eine, einer, eines

only ['əʊnli] nur, bloß; erst U2: 24

onto ['ɒntʊ, 'ɒntə] auf (... hinauf/herauf) U6: 74

open ['əʊpən] **1** öffnen, aufmachen; **2** sich öffnen, aufgehen U3: 38; **3** offen, geöffnet U4: 46

or [ɔː] oder

orange ['ɒrɪndʒ] Orange

order ['ɔːdə] Reihenfolge

orienteering [ɔːriən'tɪərɪŋ] Orientierungslaufen WF

other ['ʌðə] andere, weitere

our ['aʊə] unser, unsere

out [aʊt]: **out of** ['aʊtəv] aus (... hinaus/heraus) U4: 50; **I have to get out of this place.** Ich muss hier raus. **out there** da draußen WF; **find out** herausfinden

outdoor activity ['aʊtdɔːræk'tɪvəti] Beschäftigung im Freien U5: 58

over ['əʊvə] vorbei, zu Ende, aus U1: 12

own [əʊn]: **your own room** dein eigenes Zimmer

owner ['əʊnə] Eigentümer, Eigentümerin WF

P

pack [pæk] packen, einpacken U6: 79

page [peɪdʒ] Seite

paid [peɪd] (→ pay): **I paid** ich zahlte, ich habe gezahlt U4: 50

pain [peɪn] Schmerzen U4: 49

painter ['peɪntə] Maler, Malerin WF

pants [pænts]: **baggy pants** Baggy Pants (modisch weite Hose) WF

parent, parents ['peərənt, 'peərənts] Elternteil, Eltern

park [pɑːk] Park

part [pɑːt] Teil

partner ['pɑːtnə] Partner, Partnerin

party ['pɑːti] Party

passage ['pæsɪdʒ] Gang, Korridor U2: 25

past [pɑːst] Vergangenheit U3: 44

past [pɑːst]: **past the house** am Haus vorbei U4: 51; **five past ten** fünf nach zehn; **half past nine** halb zehn

pastries ['peɪstriz] Gebäckstücke WF

pavement ['peɪvmənt] Bürgersteig, Gehsteig

pay [peɪ] (I paid, I've paid) zahlen, bezahlen U4: 50

PE [piː'iː] (= Physical Education) Sport(unterricht) WF

pen [pen] Füller

pence (p) [pens] Pence (britische Währung) U4: 52

pencil ['pensl] Bleistift

pencil case ['penslkeɪs] Federmäppchen, Schreibetui

people ['piːpl] Leute, Menschen

perfume ['pɜːfjuːm] Parfüm WF

pet [pet] Haustier, zahmes Tier

pet shop ['petʃɒp] Zoohandlung, Tierhandlung

phone [fəʊn] **1** anrufen, telefonieren U6: 78; **2** Telefon U1: 15; **on the phone** am Telefon U1: 15

pick [pɪk] aussuchen, wählen

pick up [pɪk'ʌp] aufheben, hochheben U6: 75

picnic ['pɪknɪk] Picknick

picture ['pɪktʃə] Bild, Foto

pig [pɪg] Schwein

pinboard ['pɪnbɔːd] Notizbrett WF

pink [pɪŋk] rosa, pink

pirate ['paɪrət] Pirat, Piratin WF

pizza ['piːtsə] Pizza U3: 37

place [pleɪs] Ort, Stelle, Platz

plan [plæn] **1** planen, vorhaben U5: 60; **2** Plan; Grundriss WF

plane [pleɪn] Flugzeug

planner ['plænə] Planer, Planerin U5: 64

plant [plɑːnt] Pflanze WF

play [pleɪ] spielen; **play sports** Sport treiben; **play the guitar** Gitarre spielen

player ['pleɪə] Spieler/in U5: 64

playground ['pleɪgraʊnd] Schulhof U1: 14; **in the playground** auf dem Schulhof U1: 14

please [pliːz] bitte

plumber ['plʌmə] Klempner/in WF

poem ['pəʊɪm] Gedicht

point [pɔɪnt] Punkt

Poland ['pəʊlənd] Polen U6: 71

police officer [pə'liːsɒfɪsə] Polizist/Polizistin, Polizeibeamter/Polizeibeamtin U3: 34

pony ['pəʊni] Pony U5: 60

poor [pʊə]: **Poor you!** Du Arme!/Du Armer! U3: 42

popular ['pɒpjələ] beliebt U5: 59

postcard ['pəʊstkɑːd] Postkarte, Ansichtskarte

poster ['pəʊstə] Poster

post office ['pəʊstɒfɪs] Post(amt) U4: 46

pound (£) [paʊnd] Pfund (britische Währung) U4: 47

practise ['præktɪs] üben

present ['preznt] Geschenk

pretzel ['pretsl] Bretzel WF

prison ['prɪzn] Gefängnis WF

prize [praɪz] Preis, Gewinn U6: 73

problem ['prɒbləm] Problem WF

programme ['prəʊgræm] (Radio-, Fernseh-)Sendung

project ['prɒdʒekt] Projekt, Projektarbeit U3: 38

pudding ['pʊdɪŋ]: **Christmas pudding** Plumpudding (heiß servierte Nachspeise) WF

pupil ['pjuːpl] Schüler, Schülerin

push [pʊʃ] drücken U4: 50

put [pʊt] (I put, I've put) stellen; legen; (an einen Platz) tun; **put in the right order** in die richtige Reihenfolge bringen U1: 10; **I put** ich tat, ich habe getan U4: 50

put in [pʊt'ɪn] ein-, hinzufügen

Q

quad (bike) [kwɒd, 'kwɒdbaɪk] Quad (eine Art vierrädriges Gelände-Motorrad)

quarter ['kwɔːtə]: **quarter to/past one** Viertel vor/nach eins

queen [kwiːn] Königin WF

question ['kwestʃən] Frage

questionnaire [kwestʃə'neə] Fragebogen

quiet ['kwaɪət] ruhig

quiz, quizzes [kwɪz, 'kwɪzɪz] Quiz

R

rafting ['rɑːftɪŋ] Rafting (das Wildwasserfahren einer Gruppe im Schlauchboot) WF

railway line ['reɪlweɪlaɪn] Eisenbahnstrecke, Gleis U6: 74

rain [reɪn] regnen U5: 62

Ramadan ['ræmədæn] Ramadan (muslimischer Fastenmonat) WF

ran [ræn] (→ run): **I ran** ich rannte, ich bin gerannt U4: 50

ranger ['reɪndʒə] Ranger (Aufseher/in in Nationalparks) U5: 60

rap [ræp] Rap(musik)

rat [ræt] Ratte

RE [ɑː'riː] **(= Religious Education)** Religionslehre WF

read [riːd] (I read, I've read) lesen, vorlesen

reader ['riːdə] Leser, Leserin U5: 64

ready ['redi] fertig, bereit U3: 39

receptionist [rɪ'sepʃənɪst] Empfangschef, Empfangsdame WF

red [red] rot

remember [rɪ'membə] sich erinnern (an) U3: 44

rent [rent] mieten U3: 39

repeat [rɪ'piːt] nachsprechen

report [rɪ'pɔːt] Bericht U4: 51

restaurant ['restrɒnt] Restaurant U3: 35

Rhine [raɪn] Rhein U2: 26

rhyme (with) [raɪm] (sich) reimen (auf) U6: 73

ridden ['rɪdn] (→ ride): **I've ridden** ich bin gefahren U6: 79

ride [raɪd] (I rode, I've ridden): **ride a bike** Rad fahren; **ride a quad bike** (mit einem) Quad fahren

riding ['raɪdɪŋ]: **horse riding** Reiten U5: 58; **quad/Trikke/... riding** Quadfahren/Trikkefahren/... U5: 59

right [raɪt] **1** richtig; **You're right.** Du hast Recht. U2: 26; **2** rechts U2: 23; **on the right** auf der rechten Seite U2: 23

river ['rɪvə] Fluss; **the River Exe** der Exe

road [rəʊd] Straße; **in Fairfield Road** in der Fairfield Road; **on the road** unterwegs

road safety ['rəʊdseɪfti] Verkehrssicherheit

road worker ['rəʊdwɜːkə] Straßenbauarbeiter, -arbeiterin WF

rock [rɒk] Fels, großer Stein U5: 63

rock climber ['rɒkklaɪmə] Kletterer, Kletterin U5: 64

rock climbing ['rɒkklaɪmɪŋ] Klettern U5: 59

roll [rəʊl] Brötchen U3: 39

Rome [rəʊm] Rom U6: 71

room [ruːm] Raum, Zimmer

rubber ['rʌbə] Radiergummi

rugby ['rʌgbi] Rugby U1: 13

rule [ruːl] Regel, Vorschrift U5: 62

ruler ['ruːlə] Lineal

run [rʌn] (I ran, I've run) rennen, laufen U1: 20

runner ['rʌnə] Läufer/in U5: 64

S

safe [seɪf] sicher, in Sicherheit WF; **as safe as houses** vollkommen sicher WF

safety ['seɪfti]: **road safety** Verkehrssicherheit

said [sed] (→ say): **I said** ich sagte, ich habe gesagt U3: 38; **I've said** ich habe gesagt U6: 79

salad ['sæləd] Salat U3: 37

same [seɪm]: **the same** derselbe, dieselbe, dasselbe; der/die/das gleiche U3: 42

sandal ['sændl] Sandale WF

sandwich ['sænwɪtʃ] Sandwich (belegtes Brot) WF

sat [sæt] (→ sit): **I sat** ich saß, ich habe gesessen U2: 25

Saturday ['sætədeɪ, 'sætədi] Samstag, Sonnabend

sausage ['sɒsɪdʒ] Wurst, Würstchen WF; **sausage with curry sauce** ['kʌrisɔːs] Currywurst WF

saw [sɔː] (→ see): **I saw** ich sah, ich habe gesehen U3: 41

say [seɪ] (I said, I've said) sagen; **Say hi to Dawn, please.** Grüße Dawn, bitte. U4: 56; **say sorry** sich entschuldigen U4: 51

scarf [skɑːf] Schal WF

school [skuːl] Schule; **she's at school** sie ist in der Schule; sie geht zur Schule

school day ['skuːldeɪ] Schultag

science ['saɪəns] Naturwissenschaft U1: 12

Scotland ['skɒtlənd] Schottland U6: 70

sea [siː] Meer

secretary ['sekrətri] Sekretär, Sekretärin WF

security guard [sɪ'kjʊərətɪgɑːd] Wachfrau, Wachmann U3: 34

see [siː] (I saw, I've seen) sehen; **See you.** Bis dann. **See you tomorrow/...** Bis morgen/...; **..., you see.** ..., verstehst du? U2: 30

seen [siːn] (→ see): **I've seen** ich habe gesehen U6: 79

sell [sel] (I sold, I've sold) verkaufen

sentence ['sentəns] Satz

September [sep'tembə] September

servant ['sɜːvənt] Diener/in WF

share [ʃeə]: **share a room** sich ein Zimmer teilen

she [ʃiː] sie; **she's (= she is)** sie ist

sheep [ʃiːp] Schaf, Schafe

shelf, shelves [ʃelf, ʃelvz] Regal, Regale U1: 11

ship [ʃɪp] Schiff U2: 22

shirt [ʃɜːt] Hemd WF

shoe [ʃuː] Schuh U5: 60

shop [ʃɒp] Laden, Geschäft

shop assistant ['ʃɒpəsɪstənt] Verkäufer, Verkäuferin U3: 34

shoplifter ['ʃɒplɪftə] Ladendieb, Ladendiebin U4: 51

shopper ['ʃɒpə] Käufer/in U4: 51

shopping ['ʃɒpɪŋ]: **go shopping** einkaufen gehen U4: 47

short [ʃɔːt] kurz WF

shout [ʃaʊt] laut rufen, schreien U1: 15

shouted ['ʃaʊtɪd]: **he shouted** er rief

show [ʃəʊ] **1** zeigen WF; **2** Show

Shut up! [ʃʌt'ʌp] Halt den Mund! U3: 44

side [saɪd] Seite U6: 75

sign [saɪn] Schild; Zeichen

signal ['sɪgnəl] Zeichen, Signal

simple past [sɪmpl'pɑːst] einfache Vergangenheit U3: 44

sing [sɪŋ] (I sang, I've sung) singen

singer ['sɪŋə] Sänger/in U2: 30

Sir [sɜː, sə] Sir (brit. Adelstitel) WF

sister ['sɪstə] Schwester; **brothers and sisters** Geschwister

sit [sɪt] (I sat, I've sat) sitzen; sich setzen U1: 11

skateboarding ['skeɪtbɔːdɪŋ] Skateboardfahren WF

skater ['skeɪtə] Skater, Skaterin

skiing ['skiːɪŋ] Skifahren U5: 58

skirt [skɜːt] Rock WF

slave [sleɪv] Sklave WF

sleep [sliːp] (I slept, I've slept) schlafen

slogan ['sləʊgən] Slogan, Schlagwort WF

small [smɔːl] klein

so [səʊ] so U4: 56; also; daher U1: 15

soldier ['səʊldʒə] Soldat/in WF

Somalia [sə'mɑːlɪə] Somalia U1: 14

some [sʌm] **1** einige, ein paar; **2** etwas U1: 20

something ['sʌmθɪŋ] etwas U2: 26; **something different** etwas anderes U2: 26

sometimes ['sʌmtaɪmz] manchmal U4: 47

song [sɒŋ] Lied

soon [suːn] bald

sorry ['sɒri]: **Sorry./I'm sorry.** Tut mir leid. **I'm sorry I ...** Tut mir leid, dass ich ... U4: 50

sound [saʊnd] Geräusch WF

Spain [speɪn] Spanien

Spanish ['spænɪʃ] spanisch; Spanisch; Spanier/Spanierin WF

speak [spiːk] (I spoke, I've spoken) sprechen; **speak to** sprechen mit U3: 42

special ['speʃl] besondere, besonderer, besonderes WF

spell [spel] buchstabieren

spend [spend] (I spent, I've spent) ausgeben U4: 49

spent [spent] (→ spend): **I spent** ich gab aus, ich habe ausgegeben U4: 49

spider ['spaɪdə] Spinne

sponge [spʌndʒ] Schwamm WF

sport [spɔːt] Sport, Sportart; **play sports** Sport treiben

sports centre ['spɔːtssentə] Sportzentrum

sporty ['spɔːti] sportlich

spring [sprɪŋ] Frühling

squash [skwɒʃ] Squash

stamp [stæmp] Stempel U5: 63

stand [stænd] (I stood, I've stood) stehen

star [stɑː] Stern WF

Star Wars ['stɑːwɔːz] Krieg der Sterne WF

start [stɑːt] **1** anfangen, beginnen U4: 49; **I started to run** ich begann zu rennen U5: 62; **2** Start, Anfang

station ['steɪʃn] Bahnhof; **at Exeter Station** im Bahnhof Exeter

stay [steɪ] bleiben; übernachten

step [step] Stufe U4: 51

stocking ['stɒkɪŋ] Strumpf WF

stole [stəʊl]: **I stole** ich stahl, ich habe gestohlen WF

stolen ['stəʊlən]: **bikes are stolen** Fahrräder werden gestohlen WF

stop [stɒp] anhalten, stoppen

stopped [stɒpt]: **she stopped** sie blieb stehen U2: 27

story ['stɔːri] Geschichte

strange [streɪndʒ] merkwürdig, seltsam WF

street [striːt] Straße

stupid ['stjuːpɪd] dumm, blöd U4: 50

subject ['sʌbdʒɪkt] (Schul-)Fach U1: 12

such [sʌtʃ]: **There's no such thing.** So etwas gibt es nicht.

suddenly ['sʌdnli] plötzlich U4: 51

summer ['sʌmə] Sommer

sun [sʌn] Sonne

Sunday ['sʌndeɪ, 'sʌndi] Sonntag

sunny ['sʌni] sonnig U5: 62

super ['suːpə] super, toll U4: 49

supermarket ['suːpəmɑːkɪt] Supermarkt

sure [ʃʊə] sicher

surfing ['sɜːfɪŋ] Surfing WF

surgery ['sɜːdʒəri] Arztpraxis WF

surprise [sə'praɪz] Überraschung

survey ['sɜːveɪ] Umfrage, Untersuchung U5: 59

swam [swæm] (→ swim): **I swam** ich schwamm, ich bin geschwommen U4: 49

sweatshirt ['swetʃɜːt] Sweatshirt WF

sweet [swiːt] Süßigkeit, Bonbon WF

swim [swɪm] (I swam, I've swum) schwimmen U4: 49

swimmer ['swɪmə] Schwimmer, Schwimmerin U5: 64

swimming ['swɪmɪŋ] Schwimmen U5: 58; **go swimming** schwimmen gehen

swimming pool ['swɪmɪŋpuːl] Schwimmbad

Switzerland ['swɪtsələnd] Schweiz U6: 71

sword [sɔːd] Schwert WF

T

table ['teɪbl] Tisch; **table tennis** Tischtennis U5: 59

take [teɪk] (I took, I've taken) nehmen; bringen U4: 49; **Take a jacket.** Nimm/Bring eine Jacke mit. U5: 60

DICTIONARY

taken ['teɪkən] (→ take): **I've taken** ich habe genommen U6: 78

talk [tɔ:k]: **talk (to)** reden (mit), sprechen (mit), sich unterhalten (mit)

talked [tɔ:kt]: **I/he talked** ich/er sprach WF

tall [tɔ:l] groß (bei Personen) U5: 67

tea [ti:] Tee

teacher ['ti:tʃə] Lehrer, Lehrerin

teachers' room ['ti:tʃəzru:m] Lehrerzimmer WF

team [ti:m] Team, Mannschaft

technology [tek'nɒlədʒi] Technik, technisches Werken WF

tell [tel] (I told, I've told) erzählen; sagen U4: 46

tennis ['tenɪs] Tennis

terrible ['terəbl] schrecklich, furchtbar

test [test] Test, Klassenarbeit U1: 18

text [tekst] Text

text message ['tekstmesɪdʒ] SMS (Textnachricht)

than [ðæn, ðən]: **faster than** schneller als

thank [θæŋk]: **Thank you.** Danke (schön).

Thanks. [θæŋks] Danke. **Thanks for calling.** Danke für den Anruf. U3: 42

that [ðæt] **1** das; der, die, das (da); **2** dass U4: 56; **that night/that evening** in dieser Nacht/an diesem Abend WF; **That's two pounds, please.** Das macht zwei Pfund, bitte. U4: 52; **That's England for you!** So ist England eben! WF; **That's OK.** Schon gut./Bitte. U1: 15; **that's why** deshalb WF

the [ðə, ði] der, die, das; **the next day** am nächsten Tag WF

theatre ['θɪətə] Theater WF

their [ðeə] ihr, ihre

them [ðem] ihnen, sie

then [ðen] dann

there [ðeə] da, dort; dahin, dorthin; **there's (= there is)** da ist, es gibt, es ist; **there are** da sind, es gibt, es sind; **there was** da war, es gab, es war U3: 38; **there were** da waren, es gab, es waren

these [ði:z] die (hier); diese

they [ðeɪ] sie; **they're (= they are)** sie sind

thin [θɪn] dünn WF

thing [θɪŋ] Ding, Sache; **the right/best/... thing** das Richtige/Beste/... U6: 75; **There's no such thing.** So etwas gibt es nicht.

think [θɪŋk] (I thought, I've thought) denken, nachdenken; finden; **think of** denken an; **What do you think of ...?** Was hältst du von ...? U2: 30

this [ðɪs] dies (hier), das (hier); diese, dieser, dieses; **this evening/...** heute Abend/...

thought [θɔ:t] (→ think): **I thought** ich dachte, ich habe gedacht U6: 75

through [θru:] durch, hindurch U2: 22

Thursday ['θɜ:zdeɪ, 'θɜ:zdi] Donnerstag

ticket ['tɪkɪt] Eintrittskarte; Fahrkarte, Flugschein U1: 15

tie [taɪ] Schlips, Krawatte WF

tied up [taɪd'ʌp]: **she was tied up** sie war gefesselt WF

tiler ['taɪlə] Fliesenleger, Fliesenlegerin WF

time [taɪm] Zeit; Uhrzeit; **What time is it?** Wie spät ist es?

timetable ['taɪmteɪbl] Stundenplan U1: 12

tired ['taɪəd] müde

to [tu:, tu, tə] **1** zu, nach; an; **fall to the ground** auf den Boden fallen U4: 51; **go to bed** ins Bett gehen; **I've been to France.** Ich bin (schon einmal) in Frankreich gewesen. U6: 70; **Jamie says goodbye to Tess.** Jamie sagt Tess auf Wiedersehen. **Welcome to London.** Willkommen in London. **things to do** Sachen, die man machen kann; **time to go** Zeit zu gehen WF; **2** bis U2: 23; **It's five to ten.** Es ist fünf vor zehn.

today [tə'deɪ] heute U3: 43

together [tə'geðə] zusammen U4: 48

toilet ['tɔɪlət] Toilette WF

told [təʊld] (→ tell): **I told** ich erzählte, ich habe erzählt U4: 46; **I've told** ich habe erzählt U6: 72

tomorrow [tə'mɒrəʊ] morgen

too [tu:] **1** auch; **2 too old** zu alt

took [tʊk] (→ take): **I took** ich nahm, ich habe genommen U4: 49; **she took things** sie hat Sachen gestohlen WF

tough [tʌf] hart, zäh, stark U6: 74

tour [tʊə] Tour

towards [tə'wɔ:dz] auf ... zu, in Richtung U4: 50

town [taʊn] Stadt

town centre ['taʊnsentə] Stadtzentrum, Stadtmitte

toy [tɔɪ] Spielzeug

track [træk] Weg, Pfad

traffic light ['træfɪklaɪt] (Verkehrs-)Ampel

train [treɪn] Zug, Eisenbahn

trainer ['treɪnə] **1** Trainer; **2** Sportschuh U5: 60

tram [træm] Straßenbahn

treasure hunt ['treʒəhʌnt] Schatzsuche U5: 63

tree [tri:] Baum WF

trip [trɪp] Ausflug, Reise

try [traɪ] versuchen, (aus)probieren U5: 58

T-shirt ['ti:ʃɜ:t] T-Shirt

Tuesday ['tju:zdeɪ, 'tju:zdi] Dienstag

tunnel ['tʌnl] Tunnel U2: 22

turn [tɜ:n]: **turn left/right (into Market Street)** nach links/rechts (in die Market Street) abbiegen U4: 51

TV ['ti:'vi:] Fernsehen; Fernsehgerät

type [taɪp] Typ WF

U

umbrella [ʌm'brelə] Regenschirm WF

underground ['ʌndəgraʊnd] unterirdisch U2: 25

understand [ʌndə'stænd] (I understood, I've understood) verstehen U4: 48

understood [ʌndə'stʊd] (→ understand): **I understood** ich verstand, ich habe verstanden U4: 48

uniform ['ju:nɪfɔ:m] (Schul-)Uniform U1: 10

unit ['ju:nɪt] Lektion U1: 28

up [ʌp]: **What's up?** Was gibt's? U3: 42

us [ʌs] uns

use [ju:z] benutzen, verwenden

usually ['ju:ʒuəli] meistens, normalerweise, gewöhnlich

V

vegetable ['vedʒtəbl] (ein) Gemüse U3: 37

verb [vɜ:b] Verb, Zeitwort

156

one hundred and fifty-six

verse [vɜːs] Strophe
very ['veri] sehr
video ['vɪdiəʊ] Videofilm, Video
village ['vɪlɪdʒ] Dorf
visit ['vɪzɪt] besuchen
visitor ['vɪzɪtə] Besucher, Besucherin, Gast U2: 30
volleyball ['vɒlibɔːl] Volleyball

W

waffle ['wɒfl] Waffel WF
wait [weɪt]: **wait (for)** warten (auf); **I can't wait for it.** Ich kann es kaum erwarten. U3: 44; **Let's wait and see.** Warten wir's ab. U3: 39
waited ['weɪtɪd]: **I waited** ich wartete U2: 25
Wales [weɪlz] Wales U6: 70
walk [wɔːk] gehen, laufen
walker ['wɔːkə] Spaziergänger/in, Wanderer, Wanderin U5: 62
walking ['wɔːkɪŋ] Spazierengehen, Wandern U5: 59
walking shoe ['wɔːkɪŋʃuː] Wanderschuh U5: 60
want [wɒnt] wollen; **want to go** gehen wollen
wanted ['wɒntɪd]: **she wanted** sie wollte
war [wɔː] Krieg WF
warm [wɔːm] warm U5: 62
was [wɒz, wəz] war; **wasn't (= was not)** war nicht; **they thought it was a good idea** sie dachten, es wäre eine gute Idee U2: 24; **he was hanging** er hing (gerade) U6: 74; **he was running** er rannte (gerade) U6: 75; **it was raining** es regnete (gerade) WF
waste-paper basket [weɪst'peɪpəbɑːskɪt] Papierkorb WF
watch [wɒtʃ] beobachten, sich anschauen; **watch TV** fernsehen
water ['wɔːtə] Wasser U2: 25
way [weɪ] Weg
we [wiː] wir; **we're (= we are)** wir sind
wear [weə] (I wore, I've worn) tragen, anziehen U4: 49
weather ['weðə] Wetter
webcode ['webkəʊd] Webcode U5: 61
Wednesday ['wenzdeɪ, 'wenzdi] Mittwoch
week [wiːk] Woche
weekend ['wiːk'end] Wochenende

welcome ['welkəm]: **Welcome to London.** Willkommen in London.
well [wel] **1** gut U1: 20; **2 Well, ...** Nun/Tja, ... U1: 14
went [went] (→ go): **I went** ich ging, ich bin gegangen U3: 36
were [wɜː] waren; warst; wart; **weren't (= were not)** waren/warst/wart nicht; **they were looking for ...** sie suchten (gerade) ... WF
what [wɒt] **1** was; **What a ...!** Was für eine ...! U4: 56; **What about you?** Und du?/Was ist mit dir? **What are they in German?** Wie heißen sie auf Deutsch? **What time is it?** Wie spät ist es? **What's that?** Was ist das? **What's your name?** Wie heißt du? **What's up?** Was gibt's? U3: 42; **2** welche, welcher, welches
wheelchair ['wiːltʃeə] Rollstuhl; **he's in a wheelchair** er sitzt im Rollstuhl
when [wen] **1** wann; **2** wenn U2: 23; **3** als WF
where [weə] wo; wohin; **Where are you from?** Woher kommst du? U1: 14
which [wɪtʃ] welche, welcher, welches
whisper ['wɪspə] flüstern WF
white [waɪt] weiß
who [huː] wer
why [waɪ] warum, weshalb; **that's why** deshalb WF
wide [waɪd] breit U6: 74
wild [waɪld] wild; wild lebend
win [wɪn] (I won, I've won) gewinnen U4: 48
window ['wɪndəʊ] Fenster
windsurfing ['wɪndsɜːfɪŋ] Windsurfing WF
winner ['wɪnə] Gewinner/Gewinnerin, Sieger/Siegerin U5: 64
wishes ['wɪʃɪz]: **Best wishes, ...** Viele Grüße ... U5: 65
with [wɪð] mit; bei
woman, women ['wʊmən, 'wɪmɪn] Frau, Frauen U4: 46
won [wʌn] (→ win): **I won** ich gewann, ich habe gewonnen U4: 48
wood [wʊd] Wald U5: 60
woodwork ['wʊdwɜːk] Werken mit Holz WF
word [wɜːd] Wort
wore [wɔː] (→ wear): **I wore** ich trug, ich habe getragen U4: 49
work [wɜːk] **1** arbeiten; **2** Arbeit

worker ['wɜːkə] Arbeiter, Arbeiterin U5: 64
world [wɜːld] Welt U2: 26; **in the world** auf der (ganzen) Welt U2: 26
worse [wɜːs] schlechter; schlimmer U2: 32
worst [wɜːst] schlechteste, schlechtester, schlechtestes; schlimmste, schlimmster, schlimmstes U2: 26
would [wʊd]: **I'd (= I would) like to go/...** Ich möchte gehen/... U4: 47; **I wouldn't (= would not) like to go/...** Ich möchte nicht gehen/... U4: 47
write [raɪt] (I wrote, I've written) schreiben
writing ['raɪtɪŋ]: **Writing a story/...** Eine Geschichte/... schreiben U3: 41
written ['rɪtn] (→ write): **I've written** ich habe geschrieben U6: 78
wrong [rɒŋ] falsch; **I was wrong** ich hatte Unrecht WF
wrote [rəʊt] (→ write): **I wrote** ich schrieb, ich habe geschrieben U4: 55

Y

year [jɪə] Jahr; Jahrgangsstufe; **What year are you in? – I'm in year 7.** In welcher Jahrgangsstufe bist du? – Ich bin in der 7. Stufe.
yellow ['jeləʊ] gelb
yes [jes] ja
yesterday ['jestədeɪ, 'jestədi] gestern U3: 42
you [juː] **1** du; ihr; Sie; **2** dir, euch, Ihnen; dich, euch, Sie; **you're (= you are)** du bist; ihr seid; Sie sind; **I said you'd be in the shop tomorrow.** Ich habe gesagt, du wärst morgen im Laden. U4: 51
young [jʌŋ] jung
your [jɔː] dein, deine; euer, eure; Ihr, Ihre
yourself [jɔː'self]: **a picture of yourself** ein Bild von dir U5: 67
youth club ['juːθklʌb] Jugendklub

Z

zebra crossing [zebrə'krɒsɪŋ] Zebrastreifen WF

Alphabetische Liste der Wörter aus Band 1 und 2 (Deutsch – Englisch)

* = unregelmäßiges Verb; siehe auch *List of irregular verbs*, S. 169

A

abbiegen: nach links/rechts (in die Market Street) abbiegen turn left/right (into Market Street)
Abend evening
abends in the evening
aber but
Abfall litter
abseits der Straße off-road
Abzeichen badge
Actionfilm action film
Aktivität activity
alle all (the); *(jeder)* everybody
allein alone
alles everything
Alphabet alphabet
alphabetisch alphabetical
als when; **schneller als** faster than
also so
alt old
am: am 5. August on August 5th; **am Abend** in the evening; **am nächsten Tag** the next day; **am Telefon** on the phone; **24 Stunden am Tag** 24 hours a day
Amerika America
Ampel traffic light
an 1 *(bei)* at; **2** *(nach)* to; **an den Armen** by his arms; **an Schultagen** on school days; **denken an** *think of
andere other; **andere/r/s, anders (als)** different (from)
ändern, sich ändern change
Anfang start
anfangen start
Angeln fishing
Angestellte/r *(Büro)* office worker
Angst: ich habe Angst I'm frightened
ängstlich nervous
anhalten stop
Anhänger/in fan
anhören: sich die CD anhören listen to the CD
ankommen arrive
Anruf: Danke für den Anruf. Thanks for calling.
anrufen phone
anschauen: sich den Film anschauen watch the film
ansehen: (sich) das Bild ansehen look at the picture
Ansichtskarte postcard

Antwort answer
antworten answer
Anzeige advert
anziehen *(tragen)* *wear
Apfel apple
April April
Arbeit work; job
arbeiten work
Arbeiter/in worker; labourer
Arbeitsgemeinschaft *(Klub)* club
Arbeitsstelle job
arm: Du Arme/r! Poor you!
Arm arm
Arzthelfer/in doctor's assistant
Arztpraxis surgery
auch too
auf on; *(auf … hinauf/herauf)* onto; **auf das Haus zu** towards the house; **auf dem Bild** in the picture; **auf dem Land** in the country; **auf dem Schulhof** in the playground; **auf den Boden fallen** *fall to the ground; **auf der (ganzen) Welt** in the world; **auf der Straße** in the street; **auf Deutsch** in German; **auf die Straße (hinaus)** into the street; **Auf Wiedersehen.** Goodbye.
Aufgabe job
aufgehen *(sich öffnen)* open
aufheben pick up
aufhören (mit) finish
aufmachen open
aufregend exciting
aufstehen *get up
August August; **20. August** August 20th
Aula hall
aus from; *(aus … hinaus/heraus)* out of; *(zu Ende)* over; **aus der Schule zurück** back from school
ausbrechen escape
Ausflug trip
ausgeben *spend
ausprobieren *try
aussehen look; **Wie sieht sie aus?** What does she look like?
ausstehen: nicht ausstehen können hate
aussuchen pick
auswendig: Lerne es auswendig. Learn it by heart.
Auto car
Autofahrer/in driver
Autogramm autograph
Autowerkstatt garage

B

Bäcker/in baker
Bäckerei bakery
Bad, Badezimmer bathroom
Badminton badminton
Bagel bagel
Baggy Pants baggy pants
Bahnhof station; **im Bahnhof Exeter** at Exeter Station
bald soon
Ball ball
Banane banana
Band *(Musikgruppe)* band
Bank *(Sparkasse)* bank
Basketball basketball
Bauarbeiter/in builder
Bauer/Bäuerin farmer
Bauernhof farm
Baum tree
Baustelle building site
beantworten answer
Becher *(große Tasse)* mug
beeilen: Beeil dich! Hurry up!
beenden finish
beginnen start; **ich begann zu rennen** I started to run
bei 1 *(an)* at; **2** *(mit)* with; **bei Tim (zu Hause)** at Tim's house
Beispiel example
bekommen *get
Belgien Belgium
beliebt popular
benutzen use
beobachten watch
bereit ready
Bericht report
Beruf job
berühmt famous
Beschäftigung activity; *(im Freien)* outdoor activity
Beschreibung description
(sich) beschweren complain
besondere/r/s special
besser better
beste/r/s best
besuchen visit
Besucher/in visitor
Bett bed
bevor before
bewölkt cloudy
bezahlen *pay
Bild picture
billig cheap
bin: ich bin I'm (= I am)
bis to; **Bis dann.** See you. **Bis morgen/…** See you tomorrow/…

bist: du bist you're (= you are);
  Bist du schon einmal ...?
  – Ja./Nein. Have you ever ...?
  – Yes, I have./No, I haven't.
bitte please; **Hier, bitte.** Here
  you are. **Bitte.** *(Schon gut.)*
  That's OK.
blau blue
bleiben stay; **auf der linken Seite**
  bleiben *keep left
Bleistift pencil
blieb: sie blieb stehen she
  stopped
blöd stupid
Blödsinn nonsense
blond blonde
bloß only
Blut blood
Boden ground
Bonbon sweet
Boot boat
Bote/Botin courier
Bowls bowls
Brauch custom
brauchen need
braun brown
breit wide
Bretzel pretzel
Brief letter
bringen *bring; *take; **in die**
  richtige Reihenfolge bringen
  *put in the right order
Broschüre brochure
Brot bread; *(belegt)* sandwich
Brötchen roll
Brücke bridge
Bruder brother
Buch book
Bücherei library
Buchhandlung, -laden bookshop
Buchstabe letter
buchstabieren spell
Bürgersteig pavement
Büro office
Bus bus
Busfahrer/in bus driver
Butter butter
Button badge

Café cafe
Cafeteria cafeteria
Camping camping
CD CD
Cheeseburger cheeseburger
Chicken Nuggets chicken
  nuggets
Cola cola
Computer computer

cool cool
Cornflakes cornflakes
Cousin/Cousine cousin
Currywurst sausage with curry
  sauce

da: da(hin) there; **da ist** there's;
  da sind there are; **da war/**
  waren there was/were;
  Ich bin wieder da! I'm back!
daheim at home
daher so
Dänemark Denmark
Danke (schön). Thank you./
  Thanks. **Danke für den Anruf.**
  Thanks for calling.
dann then
das the; *das (da)* that; *das (hier)*
  this; **Das ist ...** That's ...
dass that; **Tut mir Leid, dass**
  ich ... I'm sorry I ...
dasselbe the same
Datum date
dein/e your
Dekoration decoration
denken (an) *think (of)
der the; *der (da)* that
derselbe the same
deshalb that's why
Detektiv/in detective
deutsch; Deutsch; Deutsche/r
  German
Deutschland Germany
Dezember December
Dialog dialogue
dich you
dick heavy
die the; *(die da;* Einzahl) that;
  (die hier; Mehrzahl) these
Diener/in servant
Dienstag Tuesday
dies (hier) this
diese *(Mehrzahl)* these
diese/r/s this; **in dieser Nacht/**
  an diesem Abend that night/
  evening
dieselbe the same
Ding thing
dir you; **ein Bild von dir**
  a picture of yourself
DJ (= Discjockey) DJ
Dolmetschen interpreting
Dönerkebab doner kebab
Donnerstag Thursday
Donut doughnut
Dorf village
dort(hin) there
draußen: da draußen out there

drücken push
du you
dumm stupid
dünn thin
durch *(hindurch)* through
dürfen can
DVD DVD

eben: So ist England eben! That's
  England for you!
Ei egg
Eid *(Fest)* Eid
eigen: mein eigenes Zimmer my
  own room
Eigentümer/in owner
ein/e a; an; *(Zahl)* one
eine/r/s one
einfach easy; **einfache Vergan-**
  genheit simple past
Einfall idea
einfügen *put in
einige some
einkaufen gehen *go shopping
einladen invite
Einladung invitation
einpacken pack
einsam lonely
Eintrittskarte ticket
Eis *(Speiseeis)* ice cream
Eisenbahn train
Eisenbahnstrecke railway line
Elektriker/in electrician
elektronisch electronic
Eltern, Elternteil parents, parent
E-Mail e-mail
Empfangschef/-dame receptionist
Ende end; **zu Ende** over
eng narrow
England England
Engländer/in(nen): er ist Englän-
  der he's English
englisch; Englisch English
Englischlehrer/in English teacher
entfliehen escape
entlang along; **die Straße ent-**
  lang along the street
entschuldigen: (sich) entschuldi-
  gen *say sorry
er he; *(nicht bei Personen)* it
Erdgeschoss ground floor
Erdkunde geography
erinnern: sich erinnern (an)
  remember
erklären explain
erraten guess
erst only
erste/r/s first

erwarten: Ich kann es kaum erwarten. I can't wait for it.
erzählen *tell
es it; **es ist/gibt** there's; **es sind/gibt** there are; **es war/gab** there was; **es waren/gab** there were
essen *eat; **ein Eis essen** *have an ice cream; **zu essen geben** *feed
Essen food
Etikett label
etwas something; **etwas anderes** something different; **etwas Schokolade** some chocolate
euch you
euer/eure your
Euro euro (€)

F

Fabrik factory
Fach (Schulfach) subject
fahren *go; (ein Auto/einen Bus) *drive; **Quad/Rad fahren** *ride a quad/bike
Fahren: Quadfahren/Trikkefahren/... quad/Trikke/... riding
Fahrer/in driver
Fahrkarte ticket
Fahrrad bike; **Fahrrad fahren** *ride a bike
fair fair
fallen *fall; **auf den Boden fallen** *fall to the ground
falls if
falsch wrong
Familie family
Fan fan
Farbe colour
Fastfood fast food
Februar February
Federball(spiel) badminton
Federmäppchen pencil case
fehlend: die fehlenden Wörter the missing words
feiern celebrate
Feld field
Fels rock
Fenster window
Ferien holiday/s
fernsehen watch TV
Fernsehen, Fernsehgerät TV
fertig ready
Festessen dinner
Feuerwehrfrau/-mann firefighter
Feuerwerk fireworks
Film film
finden *find; *think
Fisch, Fische fish

Fischen fishing
fliegen (Flugzeug) *go
fliehen escape
Fliesenleger/in tiler
Florist/in florist
Flughafen airport; **am Flughafen Exeter** at Exeter Airport
Flugschein (plane) ticket
Flugzeug plane
Flur hall
Fluss river
flüstern whisper
folgen follow
Form form
Foto picture
Frage question; **eine Frage stellen** ask a question
Fragebogen questionnaire
fragen ask
fragte: sie fragte she asked
Frankreich France
Franzose(n)/Französin(nen); französisch; Französisch French
Frau, Frauen woman, women; (Anrede allgemein) Ms; (Anrede für verheiratete Frauen) Mrs
Freitag Friday
fressen *eat
Freund/in friend; (feste Freundin) girlfriend
freundlich friendly
Friseur/in hairdresser
froh happy; **Frohe Ostern!** Happy Easter!
Früchte fruit
früh early
Frühling spring
Frühstück breakfast
frühstücken *have breakfast
fühlen: sich fühlen *feel
führen (Weg) *go
Führer/in (für Sehenswürdigkeiten) guide
Füller pen
für for; **für immer** forever
furchtbar terrible
Fuß, Füße foot, feet
Fußball football
Fußboden floor
füttern *feed

G

gab: ich gab I gave
Gang (Korridor) passage
ganz: das ganze Wochenende all weekend; **die ganze Familie** all the family
gar: gar nichts nothing

Garderobe cloakroom
Gardine curtain
Garten garden
Gärtner/in gardener
Gast visitor
Gebäckstücke pastries
geben *give; **Gib Tim das Buch.** *Give the book to Tim. **eine Party geben** *have a party; **Was gibt's?** What's up?
Geburtstag birthday
Gedicht poem
gefährlich dangerous
gefallen: Es gefällt mir. I like it.
Gefängnis prison
gefesselt: sie war gefesselt she was tied up
Gegend area
gehen *go; walk; **sie geht zur Schule** she's at school; **Wie geht's?** How are you?
Gehsteig pavement
Gelände: im Gelände off-road
gelangen *get
gelb yellow
Geld money
Gemüse vegetable/s
geöffnet open
Geografie geography
Gepäckabfertiger/in baggage handler
gerade just
Geräusch sound
gerecht fair
gern: gern haben like; **Ich laufe (nicht) gern.** I (don't) like walking.
Geschäft shop
geschehen happen
Geschenk present
Geschichte 1 (Erzählung) story; 2 (Schulfach) history
geschlossen closed
Geschwister brothers and sisters
gesehen: du hast ihn nicht gesehen you didn't see him
Gespräch dialogue
gestern yesterday
gestohlen: sie hat Sachen gestohlen she took things; **Fahrräder werden gestohlen** bikes are stolen
gesund healthy
Getränk drink
Gewinn prize
gewinnen *win; **im Lotto gewinnen** *win the lotto
Gewinner/in winner
gewöhnlich usually
Gitarre guitar; **Gitarre spielen** play the guitar

Glas glass

Glatze: Er hat eine Glatze. He's bald.

glauben believe

gleich: der/die/das gleiche the same

Gleis railway line

glücklich happy

Glückwunsch: Herzlichen Glück-wunsch zum Geburtstag! Happy birthday!

Gold gold

grau grey

Grill; Grillfest barbecue

groß big; *(bei Personen)* tall

großartig great

Großmutter grandma

Großvater grandfather; *(Opa)* grandad

grün green

Grundriss plan

Gruppe group

Grüße: Viele Grüße ... Best wishes, ...; **Viele liebe Grüße ...** Lots of love, ...

grüßen: Grüße Dawn, bitte. Say hi to Dawn, please.

gut good; fine; *(schon gut)* OK; **gut kennen/sprechen/...** *know/*speak/... well; **Gute(n) Abend/Morgen/Nacht.** Good evening/morning/night. **Guten Tag.** Hello. **Wie geht's? - Danke, gut.** How are you? - I'm fine, thanks.

H

Haar, Haare hair

haben *have; **Ich habe Geburts-tag.** It's my birthday. **Welche Farbe hat dein Zimmer?** What colour is your room?

Hähnchen *(Brathähnchen)* chicken

halb: halb zwei/... half past one/...

Hallo. Hello./Hi.

Halloween Halloween

halten: Was hältst du von ...? What do you think of ...? **Halt den Mund!** Shut up!

Hamburger hamburger

Hamster hamster

Hand hand

handeln: Der Text handelt von ... The text is about ...

Handy mobile (phone)

Handzeichen hand signal

hart hard; *(zäh)* tough

Hase rabbit

hassen hate

hast: Hast du schon einmal ...? - Ja./Nein. Have you ever ...? - Yes, I have./No, I haven't.

hätte: Ich hätte gern ... I'd like ...

Haus house; **nach Hause gehen** *go home; **zu Hause** at home; **bei Tim zu Hause** at Tim's house; **Gehen wir zu mir nach Hause.** Let's go to my house.

Hausaufgaben homework

Hausaufgabenheft homework diary

Hausmeister/in caretaker

Hausmeisterbüro caretaker's room

Haustier pet

Heft book

Heiligabend Christmas Eve

Heim home

heißen: Ich heiße Sarah. I'm Sarah. **Wie heißt du?** What's your name? **Wie heißen sie auf Deutsch?** What are they in German?

Held/in hero

helfen help

Helfer/in helper

Hemd shirt

herausfinden *find out

herauskommen *come out

hereinkommen *come in

Herr *(Anrede)* Mr

herstellen *make

herüber across

Herzlichen Glückwunsch zum Geburtstag! Happy birthday!

heute today; **heute Morgen/...** this morning/...

hier(her) here; **Hier, bitte.** Here you are. **Hier spricht Sarah.** It's Sarah.

Hilfe help

hinein in; **hineingehen** *go in; **hineinkriechen** crawl in

hing: er hing (gerade) he was hanging

hinter behind; **hinter einem Ball her** after a ball

hinüber across

hinzufügen *put in

hochheben pick up

Hockey hockey

Hof *(Bauernhof)* farm

hoffen hope

holen *get

Honig honey

hören *(sich anhören)* listen to

hörte: ich hörte I heard

Hot Dog hot dog

Hotel hotel

Hügel hill

Huhn chicken

Hund dog

Hunger: Ich habe Hunger. I'm hungry.

hungrig hungry

Hut hat

I

ich I

Idee idea

ihm, ihn him; *(nicht bei Personen)* it

ihnen them

Ihnen you

ihr **1** *(Wer?)* you; **2** *(Wem?)* her; *(nicht bei Personen)* it

ihr/e **1** *(Einzahl)* her; *(nicht bei Personen)* its; **2** *(Mehrzahl)* their

Ihr/e your

im: im April in April; **im Bahnhof Exeter** at Exeter Station; **im Bus** on the bus; **im Fernsehen** on TV; **im Jahre 1596** in 1596; **im Urlaub** on holiday

immer always

in in; at; *(in ... hinein/herein)* into; **in Dartmoor** on Dartmoor; **in den Urlaub fahren** *go on holiday; **in der Fairfield Road** in Fairfield Road; **in der Nacht** at night; **in der Schule** at school; **In welcher Jahrgangs-stufe bist du? - Ich bin in der 7. Stufe.** What year are you in? - I'm in year 7. **ins Bett gehen** *go to bed; **Willkommen in London.** Welcome to London. **Ich bin (schon einmal) in Frankreich gewesen.** I've been to France.

Informationen, Informations- information

Inliner, Inlineskate in-line skate

Inlineskating in-line skating

interessant interesting

interessiert (an) interested (in)

Internet Internet

Irland Ireland

ist is

J

ja yes

Jacke jacket

Jagdhund hound

Jahr year

Jahrgangsstufe year; **In welcher Jahrgangsstufe bist du?** What year are you in?
Jalousie blind
Januar January
Jeans jeans
jede/r/s every
jeder (alle) everybody
jemals ever
jetzt now
Jogger/in jogger
Jogging jogging
Judo judo
Jugendklub youth club
Juli July
jung young
Junge boy
Juni June

K

Kaffee coffee
Kakao cocoa
Kalender calendar
kalt cold
kam: er/sie/es kam an it arrived
Kanal canal
Kantine cafeteria
Kanu canoe; **Kanu fahren** canoeing
Kappe cap
Karfreitag Good Friday
Karte card; (Landkarte) map
Kartoffelchips crisps
Käse cheese
Kasten box
Katze cat
kaufen *buy
Käufer/in shopper
Kaufhaus department store
kein/e no
kennen *know; **kennen lernen** *meet; **Schön, dich/Sie kennen zu lernen.** Nice to meet you.
Kilometer kilometre
Kind, Kinder child, children
Kino cinema
Kirche church
Kiste box
Klasse class
Klassenarbeit test
Klassenlehrer/in class teacher
Klassenzimmer classroom
Kleid dress
Kleider, Kleidung clothes
klein small
Klempner/in plumber
Kletterer/Kletterin rock climber
klettern: auf einen Hügel klettern climb a hill

Klettern rock climbing
Klub club
Koch/Köchin cook
komisch funny
kommen *come; (gelangen) *get; **Ich komme aus London.** I'm from London. **Jamie kommt zu spät.** Jamie is late.
Königin queen
können can
konnte: ich konnte I could
kontrollieren check
Kopf head
Kopftuch headscarf
Korridor passage
Kosmetika cosmetics
Kosmetiker/in beautician
Kosmetikstudio beauty salon
Krankenhaus hospital
Krankenpfleger/-schwester nurse
Krawatte tie
Kreide chalk
kriechen crawl
Krieg war; **Krieg der Sterne** Star Wars
Kriminelle/r criminal
Küche kitchen
Kuchen cake
Kuh cow
kümmern: sich kümmern um look after; **sich um Taschen kümmern** deal with bags
Kumpel buddy
Kunst art
Kurier/in courier
kurz short; **kurz (be)vor** just before

L

lachen laugh
Laden shop
Ladendieb/in shoplifter
Lampe light
Land country; **auf dem Land** in the country
Landkarte map
lang/e long
langweilig boring
Lasst uns aufhören. Let's finish.
Last-Minute-Reise last-minute trip
laufen *run; walk
Läufer/in runner
leben live
Leben life
Lebensmittel food
legen *put
Lehrer/in teacher

Lehrerzimmer teachers' room
leicht easy
leid: Tut mir leid. (I'm) Sorry.
leihen: sich einen Füller (aus)leihen borrow a pen
Lektion unit
lernen learn; **Lerne es auswendig.** Learn it by heart.
lesen *read
Leser/in reader
„Letterboxing" letterboxing
letzte/r/s last
Leute people
Licht light
Lichtschwert light sabre
Lidschatten eyeshadow
lieb: Liebe/r ... Dear ...; **mein lieber Watson** my dear Watson; **Viele liebe Grüße ...** Lots of love, ...
lieben love
Liebling; Lieblings- favourite
Lied song
Limonade lemonade
Lineal ruler
links left; **auf der linken Seite** on the left
Lippe lip
Liste list
Lotto lotto
lustig funny
Luxemburg Luxembourg

M

machen *do; *make; **ein Picknick machen** *have a picnic; **Das macht zwei Pfund, bitte.** That's two pounds, please. **Es macht Spaß.** It's fun. **Ich mache Hausaufgaben.** I *do my homework. **Mach dir Notizen.** *Make notes. **sie macht Urlaub** she's on holiday; **Was machst du (da)?** What are you doing?
Mädchen girl
Mai May
Maler/in painter
Mama mum
manchmal sometimes
Mann, Männer man, men
Mannschaft team
Marmelade jam
März March
Mathe(matik) maths
Mechaniker/in mechanic
Meer sea
mehr more
Meile mile
mein/e my

meiste/n: der/die/das meiste, die meisten most
meistens usually
Menschen people
merkwürdig strange
mich me
mieten rent; *(Fahrrad/Kanu)* hire
Milch milk
Minute minute
mir me
mit with; **mit dem Rad/Bus/ Auto/...** by bike/bus/car/...
mitbringen, mitnehmen *take
Mittagessen lunch
Mittagspause lunch break
Mittwoch Wednesday
Mobiltelefon mobile (phone)
modern modern
mögen like; **sehr mögen** love; **Ich möchte (gehen/...)** I'd like (to go/...); **Ich möchte nicht gehen/...** I wouldn't like to go/...
Monat month
Mond moon
Montag Monday
Moor *(Hochmoor)* moor
morgen tomorrow
Morgen morning; **Montag-morgen** Monday morning
morgens in the morning
Moschee mosque
Motorrad motorbike
Mountainbike mountain bike
Mountainbikefahren mountain biking
müde tired
Mund: Halt den Mund! Shut up!
Museum museum
Musik music
Muslim/a Muslim
müssen *have to
Mutter mother; **Mutti** mum

N

nach 1 *(Wann?)* after; **nach der Schule** after school; **fünf nach zehn** five past ten; **Viertel nach elf** quarter past eleven; **2** *(zu)* to; **nach Hause gehen** *go home
Nachbar/in neighbour
nachdenken *think
Nachmittag afternoon
nachmittags in the afternoon
nachsprechen repeat
nächste/r/s: der nächste Flug-hafen the nearest airport; **nächste Woche** next week
Nacht night

nachts at night
Nähe: in der Nähe von near
Name name
Nationalpark national park
natürlich of course
Naturwissenschaft science
Nebel mist
neben next to
Neffe nephew
nehmen *take
nein no
nett nice
Netz network
neu new
Neuigkeit/en news
nicht not; **nicht können** can't; **Iss nicht.** Don't eat.
nichts nothing
nie, niemals never
Niederlande Netherlands
niemand nobody
nirgendwo(-hin/-her) not ... anywhere
noch: noch ein/e/er/s another; **noch einmal** again; **noch nie** never
normalerweise usually
Notiz note
Notizbrett pinboard
November November
nun now; **Nun, ...** Well, ...
nur only; **nur zum Spaß** just for fun

O

ob if
Obst fruit
oder or
offen open
öffnen, sich öffnen open
oft often
okay OK
Oktober October
Oma grandma
Opa grandad
Orange orange
Ordnung: in Ordnung OK; **Ist alles in Ordnung bei dir?** Are you OK?
Orientierungslaufen orienteering
Ort place
Oster-; Ostern Easter
Österreich Austria

P

paar: ein paar some
packen pack

Paddeln canoeing
Papa dad
Papierkorb waste-paper basket
Parfüm perfume
Park park
Parkplatz car park
Parterre ground floor
Partie: eine Partie Bowls a game of bowls
Partner/in partner
Party party
passieren happen
Pause break
Pence pence (p)
Pfad track
Pferd horse
Pflanze plant
Pfund pound (£)
Picknick picnic
pink pink
Pirat/in pirate
Pistole gun
Pizza pizza
Plan plan
planen plan
Planer/in planner
Platz place
plötzlich suddenly
Plumpudding Christmas pudding
Polen Poland
Polizeibeamter/-beamtin, Poli-zist/in police officer
Pommes frites chips
Pony pony
Post(amt) post office
Poster poster
Postkarte postcard
Preis *(Gewinn)* prize
preiswert cheap
pro: 24 Stunden pro Tag 24 hours a day
probieren *try
Problem problem
Projekt(arbeit) project
Punkt point

Q

Quad quad (bike)
Quiz quiz

R

Rad *(Fahrrad)* bike; **Rad fahren** *ride a bike
Radfahren cycling
Radiergummi rubber
Rafting rafting
Ramadan Ramadan

Ranger ranger
rannte: er rannte (gerade) he was running
Rap(musik) rap
raten guess
Ratte rat
Raum room
Raumpfleger/in cleaner
raus: Ich muss hier raus. I have to get out of this place.
Rechner computer
Recht: Du hast Recht. You're right.
rechts right; **auf der rechten Seite** on the right
reden (mit) talk (to)
Regal, Regale shelf, shelves
Regel rule
Regenschirm umbrella
regnen rain
regnete: es regnete (gerade) it was raining
Reihenfolge order
reimen, sich reimen (auf) rhyme (with)
Reise trip
Reiten horse riding
Religionslehre RE (= Religious Education)
rennen *run
Restaurant restaurant
Rhein Rhine
richtig right; **das Richtige** the right thing
Richtung: in Richtung Haus towards the house
rief: er rief he shouted
riesengroß enormous
Rock skirt
Rolladen blind
Rollstuhl wheelchair; **er sitzt im Rollstuhl** he's in a wheelchair
Rom Rome
rosa pink
rot red
rufen: laut rufen shout
Rugby rugby
ruhig quiet

S

Sache thing; **Sachen, die man machen kann** things to do
Saft juice
sagen *say; *tell; **Jamie sagt Tess auf Wiedersehen.** Jamie says goodbye to Tess.
sagte: ich/er sagte I/he said
Salat salad
sammeln collect

Samstag Saturday
samstags on Saturdays
Sandale sandal
Sandwich sandwich
Sänger/in singer
Satz sentence
Schaf, Schafe sheep
schaffen *do
Schal scarf
Schatzsuche treasure hunt
schauen look
Schauspieler/in actor
scheußlich horrible
schießen: mit einer Pistole schießen fire a gun
Schiff ship; boat
Schild sign
Schildchen label
Schinken ham
schlafen *sleep
Schlafzimmer bedroom
Schlagwort slogan
schlecht bad
schlechter worse
schlechteste/r/s worst
schließen close
schlimm bad
schlimmer worse
schlimmste/r/s worst
Schlips tie
Schlittschuh ice skate
Schlittschuhlaufen ice skating
schloss: sie schloss ihr Fahrrad ab she locked her bike
schlug: ich schlug I beat
schmal narrow
Schmerzen pain
Schmuck (*Dekoration*) decoration
schmutzig dirty
schnell fast
Schnellimbiss (*Fisch und Pommes frites*) fish and chip shop
Schokolade chocolate
Schokoladenriegel chocolate bar
schon: schon einmal ever; **Schon gut.** (*Bitte.*) That's OK. **schon wieder** again
schön nice; fine
Schottland Scotland
Schrank cupboard
schrecklich terrible
schreiben *write; **Eine Geschichte/... schreiben** Writing a story/...
Schreibetui pencil case
schreien shout
Schuh shoe
Schularbeiten homework
Schule school
Schüler/in pupil
Schülerkalender homework diary

Schulheft exercise book
Schulhof playground; **auf dem Schulhof** in the playground
Schulleiter/in head teacher
Schultag school day
Schultasche bag
Schwamm sponge
schwarz black
Schwein pig
Schweiz Switzerland
schwer hard; (*dick*) heavy
Schwert sword
Schwester sister
Schwimmbad swimming pool
schwimmen *swim; **schwimmen gehen** *go swimming
Schwimmen swimming
Schwimmer/in swimmer
sehen look; *see
sehr very
seid: ihr seid you're (= you are)
sein *be; **„Kumpel" zu sein ist okay.** Being a buddy is OK.
sein/e his; (*nicht bei Personen*) its
Seite side; (*Buch/Heft*) page
Sekretär/in secretary
selbst gemacht home-made
selbstverständlich of course
seltsam strange
Sendung (*Radio/Fernsehen*) programme
September September
Sessel chair
setzen: sich setzen *sit
Show show
sicher sure; (*in Sicherheit*) safe; **vollkommen sicher** as safe as houses
Sicherheit: in Sicherheit safe
sie **1** (*Wer?*) she; (*nicht bei Personen*) it; (*Mehrzahl*) they; **2** (*Wen?*) her; (*nicht bei Personen*) it; (*Mehrzahl*) them
Sie you
Sieger/in winner
Signal signal
Silvester New Year's Eve
sind are
singen *sing
Sir Sir
sitzen *sit; **er sitzt im Rollstuhl** he's in a wheelchair
Skateboardfahren skateboarding
Skater/in skater
Skifahren skiing
Sklave slave
Slogan slogan
SMS text message
so so; **So etwas gibt es nicht.** There's no such thing. **So ist**

England eben! That's England for you!

soeben just

sogar: Es war sogar besser. In fact, it was better.

Soldat/in soldier

Somalia Somalia

Sommer summer

Sonnabend Saturday

Sonne sun

sonnig sunny

Sonntag Sunday

Spanien Spain

spanisch; Spanisch; Spanier/in(nen) Spanish

spannend exciting

Spaß fun; **Es macht Spaß.** It's fun.

spät, zu spät late; **Jamie kommt zu spät.** Jamie is late. **Wie spät ist es?** What time is it?

später later

Spazierengehen walking

Spaziergänger/in walker

Speiseeis ice cream

Spiel game; (Wettkampf) match

spielen play; **Gitarre spielen** play the guitar; **Spielt das Gespräch nach.** Act the dialogue.

Spieler/in player

Spielzeug toy

Spinne spider

Sport, Sportart sport; **Sport treiben** play sports

Sportunterricht PE (= Physical Education)

sportlich sporty

Sportschuh trainer

Sportzentrum sports centre

sprach: ich/er sprach I/he talked

sprechen (mit) *speak (to); talk (to); **Hier spricht Sarah.** It's Sarah.

Springen (vom Sprungbrett) diving

Squash squash

Stadt town

Stadtmitte town centre

stahl: ich stahl I stole

stark tough

Start start

statt instead of

stehen *stand

Stein (Fels) rock

Stelle place

stellen *put; **Fragen stellen** ask questions

Stempel stamp

sterben die

Stern star

Stiefel boot

Stockwerk floor; **im ersten Stock(werk)** on the first floor

stoppen stop

Strand beach

Straße road; street

Straßenbahn tram

Straßenbauarbeiter/in road worker

Strophe verse

Strumpf stocking

Stufe step; (Jahrgangsstufe) year; **Ich bin in der 7. Stufe.** I'm in year 7.

Stuhl chair

Stunde hour; (Unterricht) lesson

Stundenplan timetable

suchen look for

suchten: sie suchten (gerade) ... they were looking for ...

super super

Supermarkt supermarket

Surfing surfing

Süßigkeit sweet

Sweatshirt sweatshirt

T

Tafel board

Tag day

tagsüber in the day

tanzen gehen *go dancing

Tasche bag

Tasse cup; (große Tasse, Becher) mug; **eine Tasse Tee** a cup of tea

Team team

Technik, technisches Werken technology

Tee tea

Teil part

teilen: sich ein Zimmer teilen share a room

Telefon phone; **am Telefon** on the phone

telefonieren phone

Tennis tennis

Test test

teuer expensive

Text text

Theater theatre

Tier animal; (Haustier) pet

Tierhandlung pet shop

Tisch table

Tischtennis table tennis

Tja, ... Well, ...

Tochter daughter

Toilette toilet

toll cool; great; super

Tor gate

tot dead

Tour tour

tragen (anziehen) *wear

Trainer trainer

Traum dream

träumen dream

treffen, sich treffen (mit) *meet

trinken *drink; **eine Cola trinken** *have a cola

Tschechische Republik Czech Republic

Tschüs. Bye.

T-Shirt T-shirt

tun *do; (an einen Platz tun) *put

Tunnel tunnel

Tür door

Turnhalle gym

Tut mir Leid. I'm sorry./Sorry.

Tüte bag

Typ type

U

üben practise

über about; (über die Straße) across

überall everywhere

übernachten stay

überprüfen check

Überraschung surprise

Übung exercise

Uhr clock; **um acht/zwanzig Uhr** at eight o'clock

Uhrzeit time

um: um acht/zwanzig Uhr at eight o'clock

umbringen kill

Umfrage survey

umgebracht: er hat ihn umgebracht he has killed him

umgezogen: er ist/wir sind umgezogen he/we moved

umziehen move

und and; **Und du?** What about you?

Unfall accident

ungefähr about

Uniform uniform

Unrecht: ich hatte Unrecht I was wrong

uns us

unser/e our

Unsinn nonsense

unterhalten: sich unterhalten (mit) talk (to)

unterirdisch underground

Unterrichtsstunde lesson

Untersuchung (Umfrage) survey

unterwegs on the road

Urlaub holiday/s; **in den Urlaub fahren** *go on holiday; **sie**

macht Urlaub, sie ist im Urlaub she's on holiday

V

Vater father; **Vati** dad
(sich) verändern change
Verb verb
verfolgen follow
Vergangenheit past
vergessen *forget
verkaufen *sell
Verkäufer/in shop assistant
Verkehrssicherheit road safety
verlassen *leave
verletzen *hurt
verletzt: ich habe mir die Hand verletzt I hurt my hand
verließ: ich verließ I left
vermieten hire
vermissen miss
verschenken: Geld an Menschen verschenken *give money to people
verschieden different
verschwunden: er war verschwunden he was gone
verspätet late
verstecken hide
verstehen *understand; **..., verstehst du?** ..., you see.
versuchen *try
verwenden use
Video(film) video
viel lots of; much
viele lots of; many; **Viele Grüße ...** Best wishes, ...
Viertel vor/nach eins quarter to/past one
Vogel bird
Volleyball volleyball
vollkommen sicher as safe as houses
von from; of; *(durch)* by; off; **fünf vor zehn** five to ten
vorbei *(zu Ende)* over; **am Haus vorbei** past the house
vorhaben plan
Vorhang curtain
vorlesen *read
Vormittag morning
Vorschrift rule
Vorsicht! Careful!
Vorsitzende/r chairperson

W

Wachfrau/-mann security guard
Waffel waffle
wählen pick

Wald wood
Wales Wales
Wanderer, Wanderin walker
Wandern walking
Wanderschuh walking shoe
wann when
war was
wäre: sie dachten, es wäre eine gute Idee they thought it was a good idea
waren, warst, wart were
warm warm
wärst: Ich habe gesagt, du wärst morgen im Laden. I said you'd be in the shop tomorrow.
warten (auf) wait (for); **Warten wir's ab.** Let's wait and see.
wartete: ich wartete I waited
warum why
was what; **Was für ein/e ...!** What a ...! **Was gibt's?** What's up? **Was ist das?** What's that? **Was ist mit dir?** What about you?
Wasser water
Webcode webcode
Weg way; *(Pfad)* track
weggehen (von) *leave
wehtun *hurt
Weihnachten; Weihnachts- Christmas; **Erster Weihnachtsfeiertag** Christmas Eve
weil because
weiß white
weitere **1** *(andere)* other; **2** *(mehr)* more
welche/r/s what; which; **Welche Farbe hat dein Zimmer?** What colour is your room?
Welt world; **auf der (ganzen) Welt** in the world
wenn when; if
wer who
werden: ich werde gewinnen, ich gewinne I'm going to win; **Ich werde Ranger.** I'm going to be a ranger. **Es wird gut werden.** It's going to be OK.
Werken mit Holz woodwork
weshalb why
Wetter weather
Wettkampf match
wichtig important
wie **1** how; **Wie geht's?** How are you? **Wie heißen sie auf Deutsch?** What are they in German? **Wie heißt du?** What's your name? **Wie spät ist es?** What time is it? **2** *(so wie)* like; **Wie sieht sie aus?** What does she look like?

wieder again; **Ich bin wieder da!** I'm back!
Wiedersehen. Bye.
Wiese field
wild wild
Willkommen in London. Welcome to London.
Windsurfing windsurfing
wir we
wissen *know
wo(hin) where
Woche week
Wochenende weekend
woher: Woher kommst du? Where are you from?
wohnen live
Wohnung flat
Wohnzimmer living room
Wolke cloud
wollen want; **gehen wollen** want to go
wollte: sie wollte she wanted (to)
Wort word
Wörterbuch, -verzeichnis dictionary
Wortnetz, Wörternetz network
Wurst, Würstchen sausage

Z

zäh tough
zahlen *pay
zahmes Tier pet
Zahnarzthelfer/in dentist's assistant
Zebrastreifen zebra crossing
Zeichen sign; signal
zeichnen *draw
zeigen show
Zeile line
Zeit time
Zeitschrift magazine
Zeitung newspaper
Zeitwort verb
Zentrum centre
Zimmer room
Zoohandlung pet shop
zu **1** to; **zu Fuß** on foot; **zu Hause** at home; **Zeit zu gehen** time to go; **sie geht zur Schule** she's at school; **Jamie kommt zu spät zur Schule.** Jamie is late for school. **2 zu alt** too old; **3** *(geschlossen)* closed
zuerst first
Zug train
Zuhause home
zuhören listen
zum: zum Frühstück for breakfast; **nur zum Spaß** just for fun

ENGLISH NUMBERS

1	one [wʌn]		1st	first [fɜːst]	
2	two [tuː]		2nd	second ['sekənd]	
3	three [θriː]		3rd	third [θɜːd]	
4	four [fɔː]		4th	fourth [fɔːθ]	
5	five [faɪv]		5th	fifth [fɪfθ]	
6	six [sɪks]		6th	sixth [sɪksθ]	
7	seven ['sevn]		7th	seventh ['sevnθ]	
8	eight [eɪt]		8th	eighth [eɪtθ]	
9	nine [naɪn]		9th	ninth [naɪnθ]	
10	ten [ten]		10th	tenth [tenθ]	

11	eleven [ɪ'levn]		11th	eleventh [ɪ'levnθ]	
12	twelve [twelv]		12th	twelfth [twelfθ]	
13	thirteen ['θɜː'tiːn]		13th	thirteenth ['θɜː'tiːnθ]	
14	fourteen ['fɔː'tiːn]		14th	fourteenth ['fɔː'tiːnθ]	
15	fifteen ['fɪf'tiːn]		15th	fifteenth ['fɪf'tiːnθ]	
16	sixteen ['sɪks'tiːn]		16th	sixteenth ['sɪks'tiːnθ]	
17	seventeen ['sevn'tiːn]		17th	seventeenth ['sevn'tiːnθ]	
18	eighteen ['eɪ'tiːn]		18th	eighteenth ['eɪ'tiːnθ]	
19	nineteen ['naɪn'tiːn]		19th	nineteenth ['naɪn'tiːnθ]	
20	twenty ['twenti]		20th	twentieth ['twentiəθ]	

21	twenty-one ['twenti'wʌn]		21st	twenty-first ['twenti'fɜːst]	
...			...		
30	thirty ['θɜːti]		30th	thirtieth ['θɜːtiəθ]	
40	forty ['fɔːti]		40th	fortieth ['fɔːtiəθ]	
50	fifty ['fɪfti]		50th	fiftieth ['fɪftiəθ]	
60	sixty ['sɪksti]		60th	sixtieth ['sɪkstiəθ]	
70	seventy ['sevnti]		70th	seventieth ['sevntiəθ]	
80	eighty ['eɪti]		80th	eightieth ['eɪtiəθ]	
90	ninety ['naɪnti]		90th	ninetieth ['naɪntiəθ]	
100	a hundred [ə'hʌndrəd]		100th	hundredth ['hʌndrədθ]	
	one hundred ['wʌn'hʌndrəd]				

101	one hundred and one		101st	one hundred and first	
	[wʌnhʌndrədn'wʌn]			[wʌnhʌndrədn'fɜːst]	
...			...		
1000	a thousand [ə'θaʊznd]		1000th	thousandth ['θaʊznθ]	
	one thousand ['wʌn'θaʊznd]				

THE ENGLISH ALPHABET

a	[eɪ]	n	[en]
b	[biː]	o	[əʊ]
c	[siː]	p	[piː]
d	[diː]	q	[kjuː]
e	[iː]	r	[ɑː]
f	[ef]	s	[es]
g	[dʒiː]	t	[tiː]
h	[eɪtʃ]	u	[juː]
i	[aɪ]	v	[viː]
j	[dʒeɪ]	w	['dʌbljuː]
k	[keɪ]	x	[eks]
l	[el]	y	[waɪ]
m	[em]	z	[zed]

ENGLISH SOUNDS

[iː]	eat, see, he
[ɑː]	ask, class, car
[ɔː]	or, ball, door, four
[uː]	ruler, blue, too, two, you
[ɜː]	early, her, girl, work
[ɪ]	in, big, expensive
[e]	yes, bed, again, breakfast
[æ]	animal, cat, black
[ʌ]	bus, colour
[ɒ]	on, dog, what
[ʊ]	put, good
[ə]	again, sister, tomorrow
[i]	video, happy
[u]	July, museum, usually

[eɪ]	eight, name, play, great
[aɪ]	I, time, right, my
[ɔɪ]	boy, toy
[əʊ]	old, no, road, yellow
[aʊ]	house, now
[ɪə]	near, here, we're
[eə]	airport, share, there, their
[ʊə]	you're, sure

[b]	bike, table, verb
[p]	pen, pupil, shop
[d]	day, window, good
[t]	ten, matter, at
[k]	kitchen, car, back, book
[g]	go, again, bag
[ŋ]	wrong, morning, bank
[l]	like, old, small
[r]	ruler, friend, sorry
[v]	very, seven, have
[w]	we, where, quarter
[s]	six, poster, yes
[z]	present, quiz, his, please
[ʃ]	she, station, English
[tʃ]	child, teacher, match
[dʒ]	job, German, orange
[ʒ]	usually
[j]	yes, you, young
[θ]	thing, bathroom
[ð]	the, father, with

[iː] [ɑː] [ɔː]

Girls/Women

Amy ['eɪmi]
Anna ['ænə]
Bina ['biːnə]
Dawn [dɔːn]
Emma ['emə]
Emily ['emɪli]
Jane [dʒeɪn]
Jenny ['dʒeni]
Kylie ['kaɪli]
Lilly ['lɪli]
Lisa ['liːsə]
Lucy ['luːsi]
Lynn [lɪn]
Sally ['sæli]
Sandra ['sændrə]
Sarah ['seərə]
Serina [sə'riːnə]
Sophie ['səʊfi]
Stacey ['steɪsi]
Sue [suː]

Other names

Armada [ɑː'mɑːdə]
Barry Stone ['bæri'stəʊn]
BBC TV [biːbiːsiː'tiː'vi]
Bionic Bunny [baɪ'ɒnɪk'bʌni]
Dave's Disco ['deɪvz'dɪskəʊ]
Debenhams ['debənəmz]
Eurostar ['jʊərəʊstɑː]
Exeter City ['eksɪtə'sɪti]
Francis Drake ['frɑːntsɪs'dreɪk]
Harry Klone ['hæri'kləʊn]
Heathrow [hiː'θrəʊ]
James Bond ['dʒeɪmz'bɒnd]
Manchester United
   ['mæntʃɪstəju'naɪtɪd]
Mark Marlowe ['mɑːk'mɑːləʊ]
Max Miller ['mæks'mɪlə]
Mr Bean [mɪstə'biːn]
Odeon Cinema ['əʊdiən'sɪnəmə]
Quinn's Quads ['kwɪnz'kwɒdz]
Queen Elizabeth [kwiːnɪ'lɪzəbəθ]
Saddles and Paddles
   ['sædlzən'pædlz]
Sammy ['sæmi]
Securex [sə'kjʊəreks]
Shakespeare ['ʃeɪkspɪə]
Spendex ['spendeks]
Spider Academy ['spaɪdərə'kedəmi]
Supermacs ['suːpəmæks]
Teen Scene ['tiːnsiːn]
Terry Lee ['teri'liː]
Tesco ['teskəʊ]
The Gang Girls [ðə'gæŋgɜːlz]
The Pink Panther [ðə'pɪŋk'pænθə]
Trikke [traɪk]
Turf Cafe [tɜːf'kæfeɪ]

Boys/Men

Ahmad ['ɑːmed]
Alex ['ælɪks]
Andy ['ændi]
Bob [bɒb]
David ['deɪvɪd]
Jake [dʒeɪk]
Jamie ['dʒeɪmi]
John [dʒɒn]
Josh [dʒɒʃ]
Justin ['dʒʌstɪn]
Kevin ['kevɪn]
Mike [maɪk]
Mohamed [mə'hæmɪd]
Pete [piːt]
Peter ['piːtə]
Philip ['fɪlɪp]
Ralph [rælf]
Robert ['rɒbət]
Ryan ['raɪən]
Sam [sæm]
Tariq ['tærɪk]
Thomas ['tɒməs]
Tom [tɒm]

Places

Alphington ['ælfɪŋtən]
Church Road ['tʃɜːtʃ'rəʊd]
Dartmoor ['dɑːtmɔː]
Dawlish ['dɔːlɪʃ]
Devon ['devən]
Drake School ['dreɪk'skuːl]
Exe [eks]
Exeter ['eksɪtə]
Exmouth ['eksməθ]
Fairfield Road ['feəfiːld'rəʊd]
Florida ['flɒrɪdə]
Fore Street ['fɔː'striːt]
Green Hill Farm ['griːnhɪl'fɑːm]
Hartland Tor ['hɑːtlənd'tɔː]
High Street ['haɪstriːt]
Kenton ['kentən]
Lille [liːl]
London ['lʌndən]
Manchester ['mæntʃɪstə]
Market Street ['mɑːkɪtstriːt]
Newcastle ['njuːkɑːsl]
Oban ['əʊbən]
Plymouth ['plɪməθ]
Postbridge ['pəʊstbrɪdʒ]
Princetown ['prɪnstaʊn]
Sidwell Street ['sɪdwelstriːt]

Families

Baker ['beɪkə]
Brown [braʊn]
Fraser ['freɪzə]
Hassan [hə'sɑːn]
Hill [hɪl]
Holt [həʊlt]
Johnson ['dʒɒnsn]
Lee [liː]
Price [praɪs]
Rooney ['ruːni]
Ryan ['raɪən]
Trevor ['trevə]

The hound of the Baskervilles

Barrymore ['bærɪmɔː]
Baskerville ['bæskəvɪl]
Baskerville Hall ['bæskəvɪl'hɔːl]
Beryl ['berəl]
Black Tor ['blæk'tɔː]
Charles [tʃɑːlz]
Doctor Watson ['dɒktə'wɒtsən]
Grimpen ['grɪmpən]
Henry ['henri]
Holmes [həʊmz]
Hugo ['hjuːgəʊ]
Seldon ['seldən]
Sherlock ['ʃɜːlɒk]
Stapleton ['steɪpltən]
Watson ['wɒtsən]

IRREGULAR VERBS

Infinitive form (Grundform)	Simple past form (Einfache Vergangenheit)	Present perfect form (Vollendete Gegenwart)	
be	I was, you were, she was	I've been	sein
have	I had	I've had	haben
do	I did	I've done [dʌn]	tun, machen
bring	I brought	I've brought	bringen
buy	I bought	I've bought	kaufen
come	I came	I've come	kommen
deal	I dealt [delt]	I've dealt [delt]	sich kümmern
draw	I drew	I've drawn	zeichnen
drink	I drank	I've drunk	trinken
drive	I drove	I've driven ['drɪvn]	fahren
eat	I ate [et]	I've eaten	essen
fall	I fell	I've fallen	fallen
feed	I fed	I've fed	füttern
feel	I felt	I've felt	sich fühlen
find	I found	I've found	finden
forget	I forgot	I've forgotten	vergessen
get	I got	I've got	bekommen; holen
give	I gave	I've given	geben
go	I went	I've gone [gɒn]	gehen; fahren
hurt	I hurt	I've hurt	verletzen
know	I knew	I've known	wissen; kennen
leave	I left	I've left	verlassen
make	I made	I've made	machen
meet	I met	I've met	treffen; kennen lernen
pay	I paid	I've paid	zahlen, bezahlen
put	I put	I've put	stellen, legen, tun
read	I read [red]	I've read [red]	lesen, vorlesen
ride	I rode	I've ridden	(Rad/Quad) fahren
run	I ran	I've run	rennen
say	I said [sed]	I've said [sed]	sagen
see	I saw	I've seen	sehen
sell	I sold	I've sold	verkaufen
sing	I sang	I've sung	singen
sit	I sat	I've sat	sitzen; sich setzen
sleep	I slept	I've slept	schlafen
speak	I spoke	I've spoken	sprechen
spend	I spent	I've spent	ausgeben
stand	I stood	I've stood	stehen
swim	I swam	I've swum	schwimmen
take	I took	I've taken	nehmen; bringen
tell	I told	I've told	erzählen; sagen
think	I thought	I've thought	(nach)denken; finden
understand	I understood	I've understood	verstehen
wear	I wore	I've worn	tragen, anziehen
win	I won	I've won	gewinnen
write	I wrote	I've written	schreiben

Lösungen S. 131–146

S. 131: a) collect, find out, help, listen, make, play, read, talk, work, write; b) ball, fan, football match, team; c) class, classroom, holidays, homework, lesson, pupil, teacher, year

S. 133: **1:** 1 maths; 2 geography; 3 science; 4 art; **2:** 1 brochure; 2 buddy; 3 ticket; **3:** 1 over; 2 from; 3 Hurry; 4 Here, are; 5 well 4 nonsense!

S. 134: a) bike, bus, car, motorbike, plane, train; b) eight o'clock, five to nine, half past seven, quarter past two, quarter to ten, ten past eleven; c) arrived, had, said, thought, was, went; d) apple, banana, cake, chicken, chocolate, fish, hamburger, ice cream, orange

S. 136: **1:** a) cousin, guide, visitor, singer; b) tunnel, ship, water, Rhine; c) mile, kilometre, hour; **2:** i, n, s, t, e, a, d = instead; **3:** fastest, through, drive, right, interesting, Rhine, bad, miss, right, worst

S. 137: a) buy, go, have, know, make, say, see, visit, work; b) chair, cupboard, table; c) baggage handler, bus driver, farmer, teacher; d) airport, bank, bookshop, café, farm, museum, park, school, shop, sports centre, supermarket, youth club

S. 139 (oben): **1:** a) hard, healthy, funny; b) love – hate; arrive – leave; everybody – nobody; tomorrow – yesterday; forget – remember; c) vegetable, chips, salad, crisps, fruit, roll; **2:** had, got, went, came in, said, leave, bought, made, saw, tall, hurt, knew, met

S. 139 (unten): a) bag, buy, money, shop, supermarket, town centre; b) go canoeing, go to the river, meet friends, ride a quad bike, visit people; c) at the weekend, in the afternoon, next week, on Sundays, this Saturday, tomorrow

S. 141/142: **1:** 1 stupid; 2 canoe; 3 pain; 4 report; **2:** 1 from; 2 in; 3 to; **3:** told, won, understood, swam, wear, drink, take, paid, put, ran

S. 142 (Mitte): Dictionary: **1** a) 12; b) 11; c) 16; **2** a) 7; c) 9; **2** a) 10; b) 3; c) 6; Seitenzahlen: a) S. 147: a; b) S. 150: field; c) S. 163: meiste/n

S. 142 (unten): a) big, boring, exciting, interesting, nice, quiet, small, wild; b) football, go canoeing, go swimming, mountain biking, tennis, volleyball; c) animals, cows, rivers, sheep, tracks, villages

S. 144: **1:** a) sunny, warm, cold, rain, cloudy; b) popular, lonely, tall, blonde, friendly; **2:** ou - oo, oo, oo, oe, ou, ou; **3:** jogging; fishing; walking/walker; sunny, cloudy, friendly; **4:** 1 Because; 2 going; 3 information; 4 a; 5 like

S. 145: a) England, Exeter, Germany, Kenn, London, Somalia, Spain; b) climbed, fell, ran, shouted, stayed, went; c) finish at 11 o'clock, have a picnic, have a quiz, invite, play football, start at 6 o'clock

S. 146: **1:** been, made, found, bought, done, wrote, told, taken, said, had, seen, ridden; **2:** 1 been, haven't; 2 rhymes; 3 pack; 4 never

QUELLEN

Bildquellen

www.a340.net (S. 86 Bild C); Alamy, Oxon (S. 7 Bild C / Fotosonline, Bild F / Robert Slade; S. 22 Bild B / Jon Arnold Images, Bild E / Big Cheese Photo LLC, Bild F / Iain Davidson Photographic; S. 23 Big Ben / The Photolibrary Wales, clock collage o-li / Alex Segre, u-li / Rob Casey; S. 32 Rhein / JupiterMedia; S. 34 Bild B / Design Pics Inc, D / Holt Studios International, I / Ace Stock Ltd; S. 35 li / Jeff Morgan, Mitte / Janine Wiedel Photolibrary; re / Brand X Pictures; S. 37 crisps / Cheapshots, salad / Brand X Pictures, ice cream / Purple Marbles, chicken / Ingram Publishing, vegetables / D. Hurst; S. 46 Tesco / Mark Dyball; S. 47 Bild C / Peter Titmuss, Bild F / Thinkstock; S. 50 zweites bild / Ron Buskirk, S. 61 Bild 1 / David Stares; S. 66 Bild B / Marc Hill; S. 70 sign / Jeff Morgan, background / Ace Stock Ltd; S. 86 Bild 6 / Jack Sullivan; S. 88 girl / Stockbyte Platinum; S. 98 bus driver / Janine Wiedel Photolibrary; S. 104 & 105 / Image 100; S. 110 Bild 1 / Steve Allen, Bild 7 / foodfolio; S. 125 pinboard / Jeff Greenberg, chalk / Stockbyte Gold, sponge / Photodesign Elisabeth Coelfen / Stills and Concepts, waste-paper basket / Ingram Publishing, plant / Stockbyte Silver, blinds / Image 100, curtains / IML Image Group Ltd, map / Sally and Richard Greenhill, PE / Photofusion Picture Library, RE / Design Pics Inc, technology / Janine Wiedel Photolibrary; S. 126 roll / plainpicture, butter / imagebroker, jam / Stockbyte Platinum, egg / Eye Candy Images, ham / Image Source, cornflakes / Up the Resolution, honey / D.Hurst, cocoa / foodfolio, roadworker / image 100, mechanic / Photofusion Picture Library, painter / Image Source, doctor's assistant / Thinkstock, office worker / imageshop - zefa visual media uk ltd, beautician / Medioimages, firefighter / John Powell Photographer; S. 127 pastries / Lightworks Media, hotdog / Image Source, sausage with curry sauce / Westend61, doner kebab / Ingram Publishing, sandwich / Richard Nuade, sausage / foodcollection.com, pretzel / Stockdisc Classic, chocolate bar / bildagentur-online.com/th-foto, chicken nuggets / foodcollection.com, cosmetics / S.T.Yiap, sweets / Ingram Publishing, theatre / Photolibrary Wales, waffles / Medioimages Fresca Collection, boat / Comstock Images, ice skates / Comstock Images, in-line skates / Comstock Images; S. 128 scarf / Image 100, mug / Eddie Gerald, skirt / Design Pics Inc., DVD / Pixoi Ltd, sweatshirt / Hemera Technologies, eyeshadow / Dynamics Graphics Group / IT Stock Free, perfume / S.T.Yiap, surfing / Nicholas Stubbs, badminton / Shotfile, in-line skating / Superstock, diving / plainpicture, rafting / Ingram Publishing, ice skating / Swerve, canoeing / Stockshot, skateboarding / picturesbyrob, orienteering / Tetra Images, windsurfing / Dynamic Graphics Group / Creatas; S. 129 thin / Design Pics Inc, heavy / Image Source, long hair / Bananastock, grey hair / Tim Graham, bald / Ingram Publishing, friendly / Big Cheese Photo LLC, stupid / Chris Warren, baggy pants / RubberBall, dress / Image 100, sandals / Iain Davidson Photographic, boots / Comstock Images, shirt and tie, presents, games / Image 100, dance / RubberBall, cake & waffle / Stockbyte Silver, barbeque / Imagebroker, kebab / Goodshoot); Avenue Images, Hamburg (S. 58 Bild A / Index Stock / HIRB; S. 59 Bild I / Image Stock / Greg Epperson); BAA Plc (S. 32 Heathrow / In-Press / Steve Bates); www.JohnBirdsall.co.uk (S. 6, S. 34 Bild A, S. 94 oben, S. 95); www.Britainonview.com (S. 32 Exe / Howard Mo; S. 60; S. 70 Loch Ness); Bubbles Photo Library (S. 125 woodwork / JW); Corbis (S. 7 Bild B / Hubert Stadler, Bild H / Tim Pannell; S. 23 clock collage u-re / Colin Garratt / Milepost 921/2; S. 34 Bild F / RF; S. 58 Bild B / A.Inden / zefa, Bild E / Pete Saloutos / zefa; S. 61 Bild 2 / Catherine Karnow; S. 77 Bild 2 / RF; S. 98 ranger / Catherine Karnow; S. 121 Bettmann); Corel (S. 23 clock collage o-re; S.110 Bilder 3 & 5); Cornelsen Archive (S. 23 A,B,C; S. 94 unten; S. 110 Bild 4); Cornish Picture Library (S. 50 links / Julia Seaton; S. 66 Bild A / Sonja Claydon; S. 88 Hintergrund / Gordon Hill); David Cornforth, Exeter (S. 47 Bild D; S. 50 rechts); Creatas, Starnberg (S. 110 Bild 6 / Stockbyte); Ken & Clare Cromb, Ealing (S.67 unten); Natasha Doerrie, Berlin (S.70 Welsh Village); Education Photos, Surrey (S. 10 Bild C / John Walmsley); Exeter Underground Passages (S. 25 unten); Exeterviews.co.uk (S. 46 oben / Barry Bolt); Fabfoodpix.com, London (S. 110 Bild 2); Bob Forder, Gosport (S. 10 Bilder A & D); Fotosearch.de (S. 58 Bild D / TongRo; S. 98 farmer / Digital Vision, hairdresser / Stock Connection, cook / Comstock, teacher / Comstock; S. 110 großes Bild / Digital Vision); Freefoto.com (S. 22 Bild C / Ian Britton); Getty Images (S. 7 Bild C / Digital Vision / Chris Robbins; S. 34 Bild C / Digital Vision; S. 59 Bild H / Digital Vision / Chris Robbins; S. 77 fish and chips / Brand X Pictures / Burke / Triolo Productions; S. 111 / Ami Vitale / Stringer; S. 129 headscarf / Tom Le Goff); Globetrotter Ausrüstung (S. 61 Bild 8); S&R Greenhill, London (S. 10 Bild B); Images.de (S. 7 Bild D / John Birdsall); Ingram Publishing (S. 37 hamburgers; S. 77 5 & 6; S. 125 clock; S. 126 bread, cheese; S. 127 bagel, cheeseburger, doughnut, coffee); Irish Image Collection (S. 70 o-re); Valery Joncheray, France (S. 7, Bild A); Keystone Pressedienst, Hamburg (S. 34 Bild E, Bild G; S. 47 Bild E; S. 50 drittes bild; S. 61 Bild 5 (alle Topham Picturepoint)); Lokomotiv, Stadtlohn (S. 23 o-re / Thomas Willemsen); Matthias Lüdecke, Berlin (S. 7 Bild E); Matton Images, Karlsruhe (S. 34 Bild H / Bananastock; S. 59 Bild 2 / Corbis); Christine Maxwell (S. 32 CDs; S.46 Bank; S. 61 Bild 3,4,6; S. 77 Bild 3,8; S. 86 Bild 4); Mauritius Images, Mittenwald (S. 58 Bild C / Photononstop; S. 59 Bild G / Photononstop; S. 86 Bild 1 / Photononstop, Bild 2 / Foodpix; S. 110 Bild 8 / RF / Goodshoot); Jürgen Moers, Dorsten (S. 34 Bild I); Motoring Picture Library, Hants (S. 22 Bild D); Philips (S. 86 Bild 5); Photolibrary Wales (S. 98 courier); Saddles and Paddles, Exeter (S. 47 Bild B); SeaFrance, Paris (S. 22 Bild A); Stills Online, Hamburg (S. 37 pizza, fruit, chips; S. 49; S. 61 Bild 7); Stock Scotland, Tain (S. 70 monster / Iain Sarjeant); Trikke Tech, Inc (S. 59 Bild J); ullstein bild, Berlin (S. 32 Bild 2 / Vision Photos; S. 98 baggage handler / ecopix); Vario Press, Bonn (S. 7 Bild G / Rainer Unkel); Visum, Hamburg (S. 47 Bild A / Wolf Kern); WestCountryViews.co.uk (S. 66 Bild C / Simon Lewis).

Umschlag: www.JohnBirdsall.co.uk

New Highlight
Band 2

Im Auftrage des Verlages herausgegeben und erarbeitet von
Roderick Cox, Aachen · Frank Donoghue, Nenagh, Ireland

Verlagsredaktion
Susanne Döpper (Projektleitung) · Silvia Wiedemann (verantwortliche Redakteurin)
Christine Maxwell · Karin Jung · Jenny Dames · Undine Griebel · Sandhya Gupta

Anhang
Redaktionsbüro Birgit Herrmann, Aachen

Beratende Mitwirkung
Hans Bebermeier, Bielefeld · Dr. Johannes Berning, Münster · Hartmut Bondzio, Bielefeld
Annette Bondzio-Abbit, Bielefeld · Gisela Feldmann, Haltern · Joachim Grötzinger, Stuttgart
Prof. Dr. Liesel Hermes, Karlsruhe · Ingrid-Barbara Hoffmann, Böblingen · Dagmar Höffner, Ingelheim
Barbara Hohkamp, Stuttgart · Petra Klein, Runkel · Gunhild Krekeler, Unna
Martina Kriebel, Brigachtal · Inge Kronisch, Flensburg · Geraldine Lewington-Happe, Paderborn
Christa Lüdemann, Hannover · Hermann Mohr, Sinsheim · Dr. Michaela Sambanis, Karlsruhe
Ellen Wiegard-Kaiser, Bielefeld · Herbert Willms, Herford

Illustration/Grafik
Adrian Barclay, Bristol · Karen Donnelly, Brighton · Klaus Ensikat, Berlin

Umschlaggestaltung
Leonardi.Wollein, Berlin

Layoutkonzept
Christoph Schall

Layout und technische Umsetzung
Klein & Halm Grafikdesign, Berlin

www.cornelsen.de

1. Auflage, 4. Druck 2009 / 06

Alle Drucke dieser Auflage sind inhaltlich unverändert und können im Unterricht
nebeneinander verwendet werden.

© 2006 Cornelsen Verlag, Berlin

Druck: CS-Druck CornelsenStürtz, Berlin

ISBN 978-3-464-34449-1 – broschiert

ISBN 978-3-464-34344-9 – gebunden

 Inhalt gedruckt auf säurefreiem Papier aus nachhaltiger Forstwirtschaft.